medal, silver British Wa...
horseback, skull and crossbones below. Ins...
with orange, white, black and blue watered silk ribbon.
Remembrance", machine-embroidered with violet and yellow flowers and
n the centre Opens with two centre pages which have printed messages
broidered "To my dear wife", in blue, with red flowers Embossed card
lap lifts to reveal a smaller card inscribed "Hope and Love"

with bar and pin at top Stamped on the obverse, 'Presented by the
ow to John W. Black, Special Constable, in acknowledgement of services
rs' on the bar and '1914-1919 Let Glasgow Flourish' with coat of arms
E' and indistinct hallmarks. Contained in a velvet and satin lined case

k jug, transfer decoration, Glasgow Coat of Arms (in colour) on opposite
d rim. Transfer printed side, 'Special Message from the Rt. Hon. D
nister "I have no hesitation in saying that economy in the consumption
ountry is a matter of the greatest possible importance to the Empire an
s inscribed, 'The War Time Milk jug for a family of ten Made by the
g the winter of 1917 when the boys were in the trenches fighting for
nwades. Stoke on Trent'

k, in porcelain. Transfer printed on side, Glasgow Coat of Arms in
onner Blitzen', a model of British tank first used by British Troops
pt. 1916', No.515 on side, also numbered 643 on the base

g mug with gilt rim and bottom and pink and gilt rose on either
tion written in gold, 'James C Yuill, 21 January 1899 (he was
es Yuill, iron moulder of Finnieston and his wife who died in

for a balaclava helmet ...

r a cardigan
e general army issue to troops in the trenches. Used in
I R Paterson and served in the Glasgow Highlanders

Porcelain given by Danish Doctors to Dr John Brownlee
se of bubonic plague or Black death in a sailor in

I say nothing

A WORLD WAR I CENTENARY ART COMMISSION

CHRISTINE BORLAND

WITH CONTRIBUTIONS FROM JO MEACOCK,
ANDREW PATRIZIO, BETTINA BILDHAUER,
CHRIS DORSETT, DAISY LAFARGE,
FRANCIS MCKEE, STEPHANIE DE ROEMER

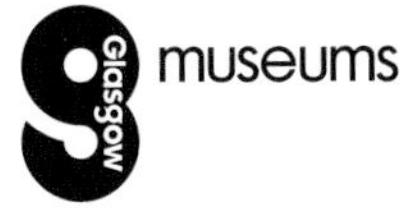

ISBN 978-1-908638-28-1

British Library Cataloguing in Publication Data.

A catalogue record for this book is available from the British Library.

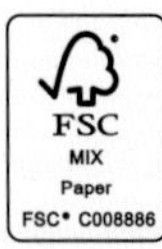

Publication of this book was made possible by Art Fund and 14–18 NOW support.

Contents

14–18 NOW Foreword

I Say Nothing is a new artwork co-commissioned by 14–18 NOW and Glasgow Museums, made possible by Art Fund support.

14–18 NOW is the UK's arts programme for the centenary of the First World War. This five-year-long programme has been one of extraordinary arts experiences connecting people with the First World War. Working with arts and heritage partners all across the UK, we have commissioned new artworks from leading contemporary artists, musicians, designers and performers, inspired by the period 1914–18. Since the start of the First World War centenary in 2014, 14–18 NOW has commissioned over 325 artworks, which have been seen by more than 30 million people.

We firmly believe in the transformative power of the arts to bring the stories of the First World War to life. Perceptions of the war have been shaped by the artists of the time, including poets, painters, photographers and film-makers – many of whom served and who reflected on the war and its effects. One hundred years later, today's artists are opening up new perspectives on the present as well as the past.

It has been a tremendous pleasure to be part of the process of commissioning *I Say Nothing*, particularly as from time to time we were allowed in to hear more about Christine's mining of Glasgow Museums' Collection and outreach resources, and the objects that were emerging for her as important to focus on.

On behalf of 14–18 NOW I'd like to thank and congratulate the artist Christine Borland, whose unique approach to research has led to the creation of an extraordinary new work that will remain as a legacy in Glasgow Museums' contemporary art collection, for a wide range of audiences now and in the future. We also thank our partners, Glasgow Museums and the fantastic, skilled and dedicated team there, and also the historian Simon Jones.

Lastly, a very special thanks to all those whose support has enabled this commission, to Art Fund and to 14–18 NOW's principal funders the National Lottery through the Heritage Lottery Fund and Arts Council England, and the Department for Digital, Culture, Media and Sport.

Tamsin Dillon
Curator, 14–18 NOW: WW1 Centenary Art Commissions

Art Fund Foreword

Over the last five years contemporary artists have activated, provoked and moved us to engage with World War I in ways we could never have imagined. The events and emotions experienced a century ago have been brought vividly back into our lives today by the sensitive commissioning of the 14-18 NOW artistic programme, which we've been proud to play a part in helping becoming a reality.

As we approach the final momentous centenary of Armistice Day, it is the turn of much-admired Scottish artist Christine Borland to stir us with her challenging new work *I Say Nothing*, co-commissioned by Glasgow Museums and 14–18 NOW and made possible with Art Fund support.

Christine Borland was invited to research Glasgow Museums' World War I collection and to produce a new artwork in response to it: her intelligent way of fluidly drawing from and adding to objects she has encountered, bringing new layers of meaning to them for a wider audience, is truly inspiring.

More than ever before at Art Fund are we committed to building collections for everyone, for ever, and responding willingly to the creativity and ambition of museums in commissioning new works of art which impact on people's lives.

We were also delighted to be able to lend support to this thoughtful publication, which will extend the legacy of this eloquent commission by giving readers an insight into the artist's processes and thinking, as well as an introduction to Glasgow Museums' fascinating World War I collection.

Rachael Browning
Head of Programmes, Art Fund

Glasgow Museums Foreword

The World War I centenary period has stimulated astonishing investment in the arts, largely the result of the ambitious commissioning of 14-18 NOW. This ground-breaking cultural programme, all the more extraordinary in a time of cutbacks, has at its heart a desire to encourage reflection on both World War I and more recent and ongoing warfare. Glasgow Museums was keen to be involved in such an inspiring project. When 14-18 NOW invited proposals for co-commissions, we seized the opportunity to put forward the idea of working with internationally renowned Scottish artist Christine Borland on an art commission responding to Glasgow Museums' extensive World War I collection. We were delighted that 14-18 NOW chose this project to support.

This commission is part of a five-year programme of events that has been undertaken by Glasgow Museums across its venues as part of the World War I Centenary Partnership led by Imperial War Museums. This has included exhibitions, talks and workshops relating to the war, such as: *In Honour's Cause: Glasgow World War I Memorials* at St Mungo Museum, a photographic exhibition depicting memorials across the city, dedicated to the more than 18,000 war dead from Glasgow; the installation in Kelvingrove Art Gallery and Museum of the Harry Clarke stained-glass window *The Coronation of the Virgin* (purchased with Art Fund support), which was commissioned as a war memorial; the UK's first dedicated display of wheelchairs, in Riverside Museum, which includes an early wheelchair designed for veterans; a display at St Mungo Museum of charms and talismans carried by soldiers; a display at the People's Palace focusing on Mary Barbour and the 1915 Rent Strike in Glasgow, a response to landlords raising rents when large numbers of people came to the city to work in the shipyards and munitions factories; a collaboration with Poppy Scotland to host in three Glasgow Museums venues a marble sculpture by Simon Burns-Cox representing the last tree remaining on a battlefield; and *Brushes with War*, an exhibition at Kelvingrove Art Gallery and Museum of artwork by soldiers of many different nationalities and with different perspectives.

Glasgow Museums' programme contributes towards a city-wide response to the commemoration of the war being led by Glasgow City Council. The City commissioned artists Ross Ashton and Karen Monid to create *Glasgow's War*, a film and audio projection displayed on the exterior of the prestigious City Chambers building; Heritage Lottery funding has supported Glasgow school pupils in undertaking research into the stories behind the names on community war memorials; and Glasgow City Council is also supporting *Digging In*, an ambitious project which has recreated a section of Allied and German trenches in Pollok Country Park, which runs until November 2018. In August 2014 Glasgow was proud to be a focal point for centenary events marking the start of the war, with the World War I Centenary Commonwealth Service at Glasgow Cathedral attended by Prince Charles, Duke of Rothesay and Commonwealth heads of state.

It is fitting that Glasgow will close its programme in 2018 with the culmination of an art commission of this significance; Glasgow Museums is excited by the opportunity that this centenary art commission affords to exhibit an important new artwork, which will enter its contemporary art collection, and stimulate discussion, debate, creativity and reflection amongst our visitors in relation to conflicts old and new.

Duncan Dornan
Head of Museums and Collections, Glasgow Life

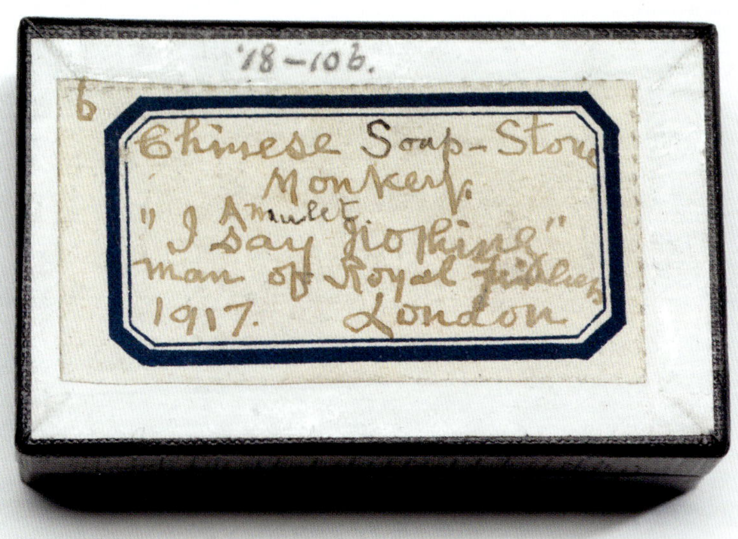
'18 – 106.
6
Chinese Soap-Stone
Monkey.
Amulet
" I say Jioking "
man of Royal fiddlers
1917.   London

Making Connections:

An introduction to *I Say Nothing*, a World War I centenary art commission by Christine Borland

JO MEACOCK

As an artist, Christine Borland often deals with dark and challenging subject matter. Absence and destruction are recurring concepts in her works, which seek to reclaim histories in imaginative ways. Themes relevant to World War I have permeated her practice. *I Say Nothing*, the new artwork Borland has created as part of 14–18 NOW's inspirational World War I centenary arts commissioning programme, is a layered and nuanced response to Glasgow Museums' historic collection. It is the result of an intense period of research, during which Borland made unexpected and thought-provoking connections between apparently unrelated objects, bringing out human stories and surprising object biographies, and sometimes creating object narratives where they did not already exist. The artwork explores and interrogates ideas around materials and meaning, superstition and memorialization, institutional care (museum and other) and absence and loss.

The commission has been a collaborative research-led venture, innately suited to the artistic practice of Borland, who has often worked co-operatively with institutions and their collections. The two-year-long commission included a year's residency at Glasgow Museums Resource Centre (GMRC), a pioneering storage and research facility, where Borland had access to Glasgow Museums' collection and supporting materials, with assistance from curators, conservators and collections management staff. As it developed, the commission continued this participatory approach with the artist organizing a creative symposium, *Doubtful Occasion*, in October 2017, at which fellow artists, academics and museum professionals had the opportunity to respond to Borland's research and feed into the direction the artwork would take. This research was also shared in public tours and talks at GMRC. In April 2018 the artist devised *PhotoScuplture*, an event at Kelvingrove Art Gallery and Museum at which participants were invited to take simultaneous photographs of posed models, the silhouettes from these photographs to be used by Borland in the creation of the sculptural groups for her new work. At each stage of the commission Borland has endeavoured to make her research process and art practice visible and accessible. Originating at GMRC, the sculpture was also brought to completion at GMRC, enabling museum staff to be involved in a practical and meaningful way in the artwork's final production, and giving further unique and privileged access and insight into Borland's working methods and practice. Such a collaborative approach complements Glasgow Museums' ethos of increasing access and of fostering public participation, partnership and dialogue.

It was significant for Glasgow Museums to offer the commission to an artist who had trained in the city and whose practice is still closely associated with the city and its museum collections. The commissioning of a woman artist was also a conscious decision, helping to address the historical bias towards male artists within our collection, and in conscious recognition of the fact that so few women were commissioned as official war artists during World War I – about five per cent. Glasgow commissioned its own war artist during World War I, the only city in Britain to do so; Glasgow artist Fred A Farrell (1882–1935) produced 50 drawings documenting the city's war effort on the frontline and back home in the shipyards, engineering works and munitions factories. At a time when the Government was primarily interested in art as propaganda, Farrell created a unique historical record and memorial to commemorate the sacrifice of local soldiers.

The commissioning of Christine Borland reflects Glasgow one hundred years on, a city that has become a remarkable place for innovative contemporary art practice and collecting. Borland's new artwork for Glasgow Museums is no memorial or record, but rather a multifaceted, reflective rejoinder, intended to stimulate critical debate and creative responses to World War I, museum collecting and art's relation to historical and present conflict. Throughout the commission Borland has challenged convention and pushed boundaries. The final artwork is the result of creative experimentation and exploration of processes and materials, and utilizes new sculptural techniques and technologies, including drone photography, 3D scanning and printing, and photogrammetry, as well as historical methods such as photo-sculpture, invented in nineteenth-century France. During her research at the museum Borland has constantly questioned accepted museum practice and inspired museum staff to think more creatively and boldly about the ways in which our collection is used.

Glasgow Museums' diverse World War I collection of more than 2,000 objects and its support materials have proved a rich and fertile resource for the commission. Crossing disciplines and media, objects in the collection include artworks (paintings, drawings, sculpture and prints), militaria (munitions, medals, coins, identification tags, uniforms, badges, gas masks), commemorative items (memorial plaques, rolls of honour), personal items (presents for the troops, lucky charms, photographs, letters, postcards) and propaganda (leaflets, posters). It also comprises a miscellany of objects relating to the home front, munitions factories, fundraising efforts, hospitals, spies, rent strikes, conscientious objectors and the anti-war movement.

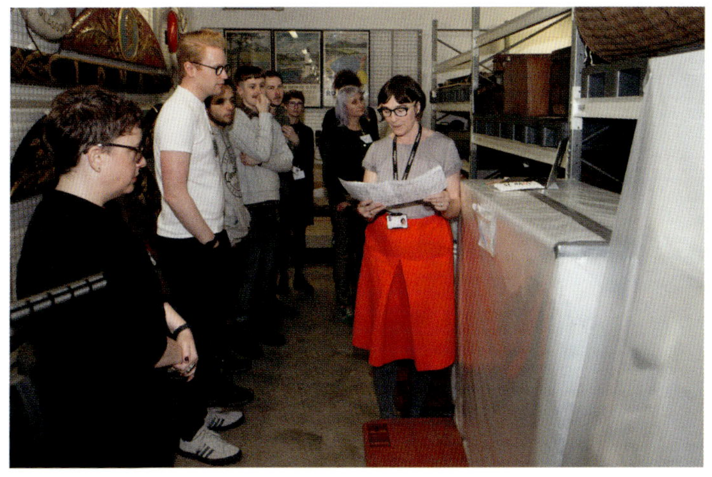

◔ Christine Borland leading a tour as part of the *Doubtful Occasion* symposium at Glasgow Museums Resource Centre.

By the end of her year of research at Glasgow Museums, Christine Borland had narrowed her interest to a small group of, perhaps unlikely, objects in our collection and associated resources – many of which are represented in this publication – including a Berlin iron watch chain, a muslin pillow filled with dried sphagnum moss, a hyoid bone of a sheep – one of a group of lucky charms carried by soldiers to the Front – a roll of honour by artist Frank Brangwyn, a wicker patient carrier, a towel made from paper, a number of mule hooves, two German identification discs and in particular an invalid feeder cup, an item widely used in nursing during World War I, both at home and in field hospitals near the front line. What links many of these objects is absence: the willow stretcher carries the negative shape of the bodies it once carried; the roll of honour is empty of names; the ID tags have been separated from the casualties they were intended to identify; the mule hooves, themselves a form of identification, poignantly highlight missing body parts; and the stained moss pillow, possibly from a field ambulance, suggests injury, pain and loss. The artwork itself takes its title from an

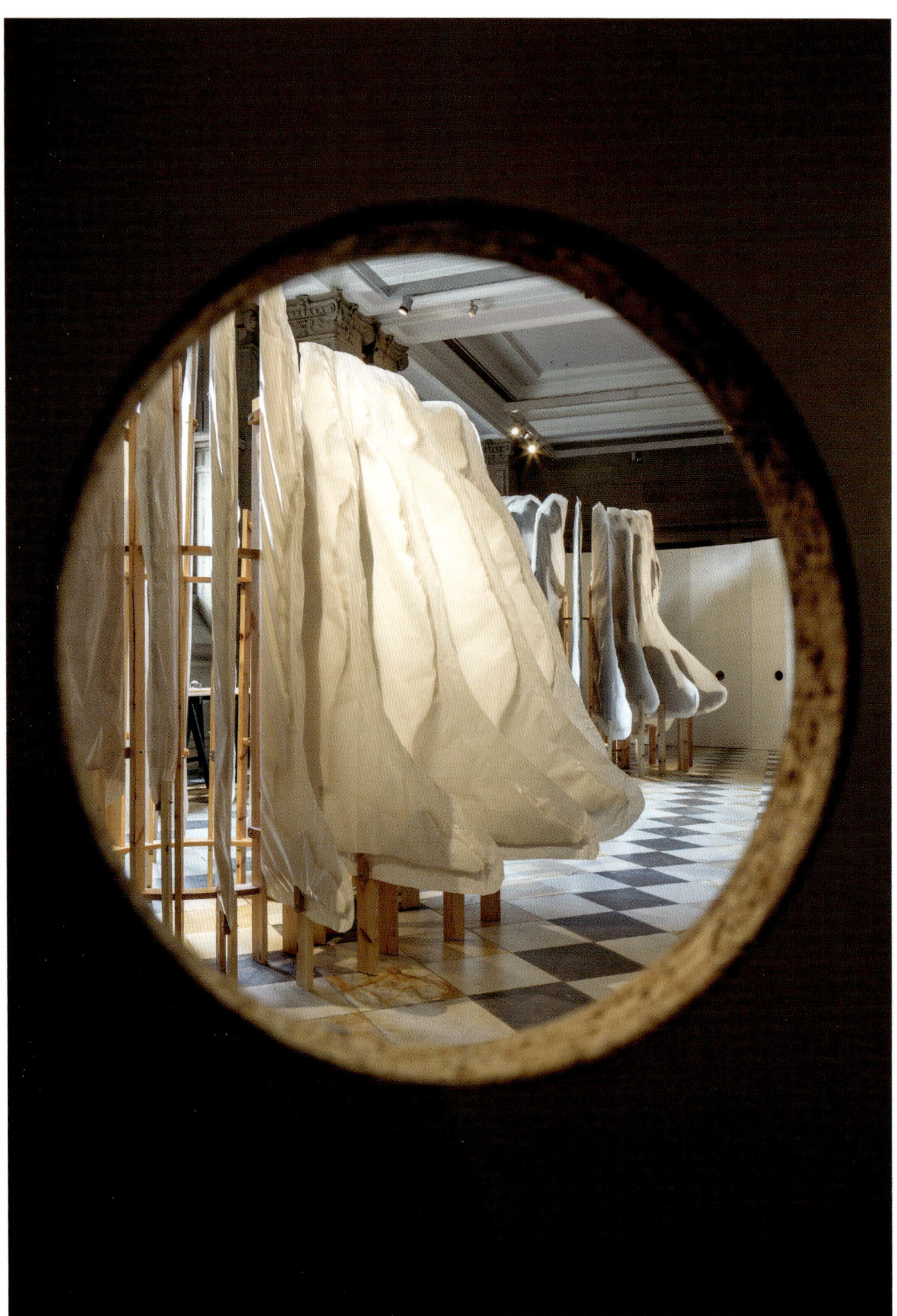

inscription on a box that contained a World War I charm, but which was found to be empty, the Chinese soapstone monkey amulet it once held missing. The box evocatively reads, '*I Say Nothing*'. Borland has been drawn by the very lack of provenance and biographical information for some of these objects, an absence regarded as a challenge and creative opportunity.

Borland's new artwork is all about transformation, releasing new potential and meaning in matter, shape and form. The objects themselves foreground a kind of material alchemy: iron for gold, paper for cotton, moss for down. Borland is fascinated by the almost magical importance and transformative power ascribed to ostensibly unexceptional objects, most apparent in relation to World War I charms and amulets, which tend to be objects of no inherent value in themselves and yet which carry weighty hopes and beliefs, providing strange comfort and emotional security. This transference of meaning and importance to common objects has proved a relevant concept in wider museum discussions around the commission, touching on collecting, interpretation and care. The museum code of ethics requires that even the humblest of objects on entering our collection is stored in carefully controlled environmental conditions with acid-free tissue paper and supports, handled with gloves, cared for by professional conservators and sometimes exhibited behind glass – this can seem like an alchemy of sorts, a new, quasi-sacred status conferred at times on the apparently mundane and ordinary.

The completed artwork on display on the south balcony of Kelvingrove Art Gallery and Museum is far from ordinary. Multifaceted in more ways than one, it is a conscious acknowledgement by the artist of building and history, a careful orchestration of collection and locale. The faces of the central figures within its two sculptural groupings reference the bronze statues of *Peace* and *War* on Kelvin Way Bridge, which crosses the River Kelvin beside Kelvingrove Art Gallery and Museum, and the arrangement of the artwork is carefully conceived around the symmetry of the building's architecture. Central to the conception of the groups is the invalid feeder cup, an apparently innocuous and indeed nurturing object but with a more sinister history; not only used in the care of wounded soldiers, it was also an instrument employed to force-feed hunger-striking suffragettes in the years leading up to 1914. The two figural groups, based on tableaux set up by Borland at the *PhotoSculpture* event at Kelvingrove, pivot on the cup's diametrically opposed functions.

The 24 silhouettes that constitute each sculptural group are powerfully suggestive and enigmatic in form. Care and violent action seem to be played out in unexpected ways. Foreshortening of figures, a result of the photo-sculpture process, makes limbs appear truncated, suggesting amputation and trauma. Each is enveloped in a translucent material called glassine, a water-resistant substance that has a wide range of practical uses, including holding drugs – prescription and illicit – explosives and police evidence. These glassine covers darkly evoke a body bag or shroud, a forensic suggestion in keeping with the drone footage that was taken from above during the *PhotoSculpture* event and the camera peep holes in the *PhotoSculpture* structure, which introduce the idea of surveillance. The veiling also has a poetic aspect, increasing the sense of drama and mystery, a kind of shadow theatre being created. In the museums world glassine was historically used as a protective covering in the storage and preservation of artworks and archival material. Partially concealing what lies beneath, the glassine aptly conveys something of the way in which we view and understand museum objects at a historical remove, taken out of original contexts and obscured by layers of ownership, physical movement and cultural change.

The feeder cup itself is notably absent from the figural arrangements, playing out the theme of loss that has been recurrent throughout the commission. The multiple silhouettes created by the photo-sculpture process have the effect of making the figural groups look blown apart, and appropriately the feeder cup that inspired the work (an unaccessioned object purchased by Glasgow Museums as part of a community handling kit) was taken by the artist to Flanders and exploded by the Belgian bomb disposal unit DOVO-SEDEE, its shards on display as part of the artwork. This is the ultimate transformation of the humble, low-value, mass-produced object into art, its remains carrying a new weight of meaning and signification – a modern relic, imbued with poignant expressive power. The violence of the action seems somehow fitting and the location of the act resonant, as shells, body parts and detritus – including feeder cups – from World War I are still being found in Flanders today.

This extraordinary commission is much more than an end product, but rather has been a journey for both artist and Glasgow Museums. It is a commission that has generously invited the input and involvement of others. The legacy it leaves is a provocation, for the viewer, the participant, the museums service to continue in this creative vein and to look with transformative vision on our historic World War I collections, considering the stories behind lesser-known objects within the nuances and complexities of war. This many-sided artwork surely challenges us to think about the many different faces and perspectives that history presents and to respond in an equally open, enquiring and imaginative way.

◗ Museum objects in storage, wrapped in acid-free tissue paper.

OG·1947·98·mg·3·dup·1

O.1693?
sheep corns

TEMP. 16393
3 mule's hooves

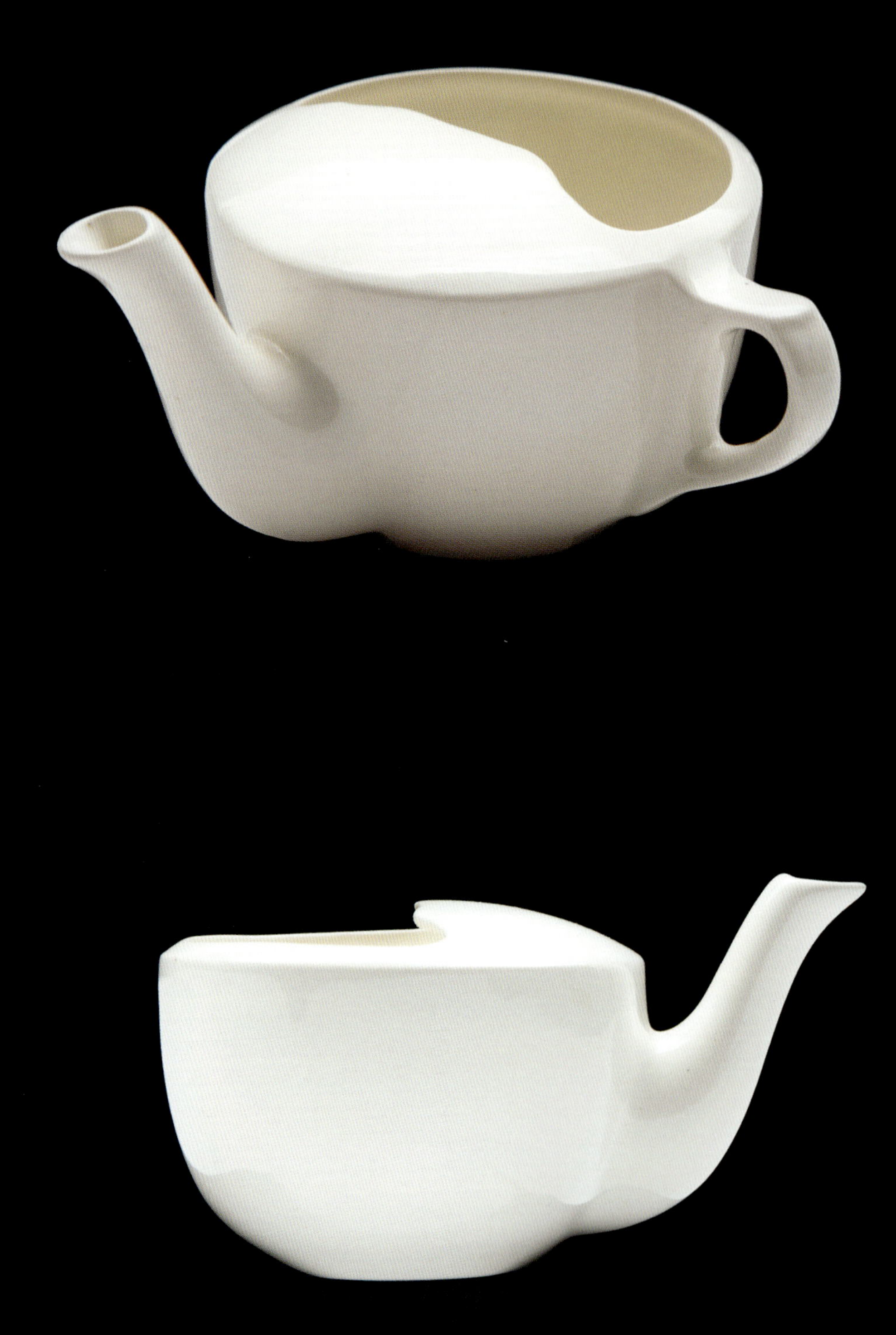

Pre-War, at War, Post-War

ANDREW PATRIZIO

'One day the science of genetics may decode the secrets of this custodianship, but meanwhile we may rest assured that there exists an allegiance between the dead and the unborn of which we the living are merely the ligature.'

Robert Pogue Harrison, *The Dominion of the Dead* [1]

When Christine Borland and I started to discuss ideas for this essay, and which themes were uppermost in her mind for her new artwork, she mentioned how one small object at Glasgow Museums had particularly caught her attention. She described it and I followed up, coming to the conclusion that this artefact might be a gateway to thinking about her work as a whole and certainly in relation to *I Say Nothing*. The object is an invalid feeder cup, dating from World War I.

It is a modest ceramic hybrid, part teacup, part teapot, used by nursing staff to feed patients who could not feed themselves. The forms and patterns of these cups vary and they can still be tracked down today for a modest price. Yet it is not as collectibles that Borland admires them. Rather it is the fact that feeder cups are simple, intimate, intermediary objects used chiefly to nurse the sick and injured back to health. Though that is not the only story that attaches to them. Feeder cups of various designs were used to force-feed people unwilling to eat, including prisoners, slaves and hunger strikers.

The word 'ligature', or binding, used by Robert Harrison in the opening quotation is helpful here in understanding Borland's approach; often we need the backstory, where human agents, objects and high emotions are bound into a complex bundle that Borland seeks to unpick. So the feeder

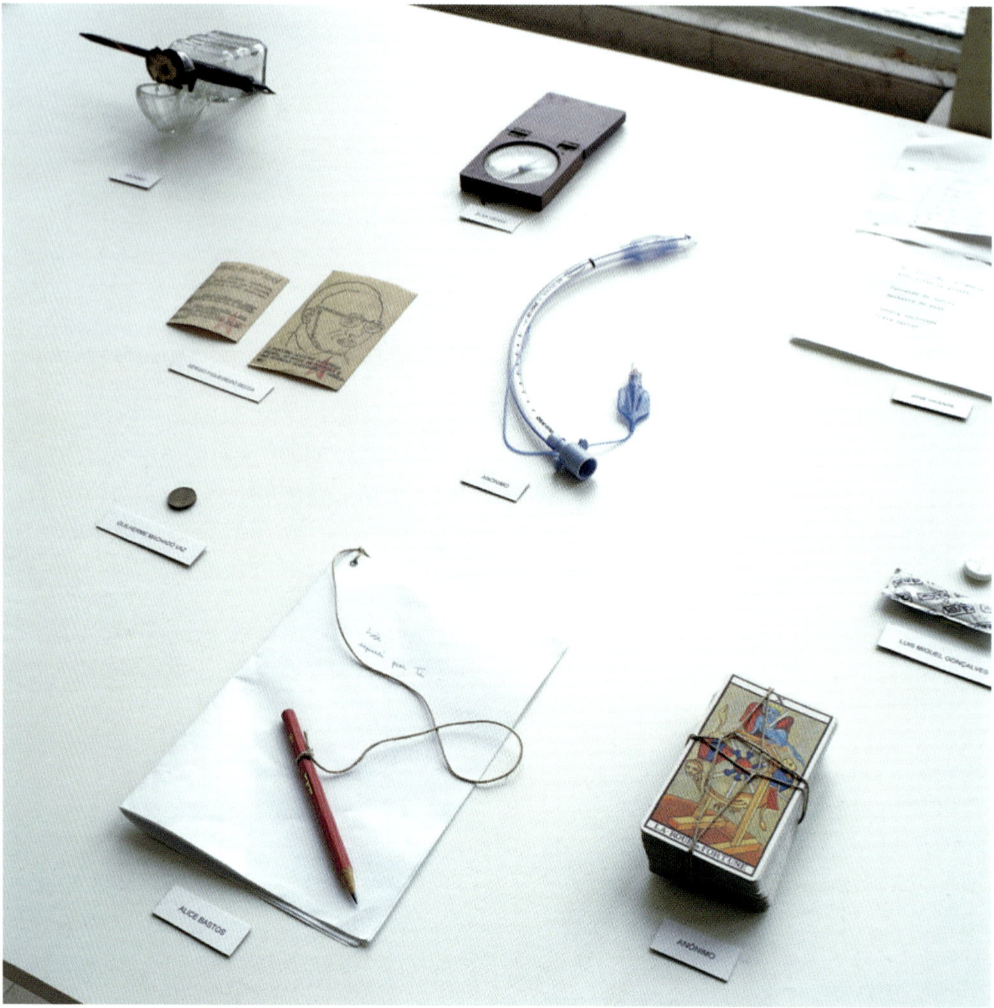

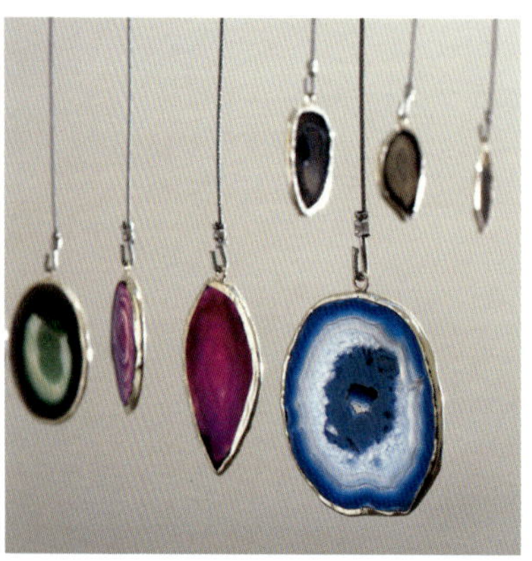

Small Objects
That Save Lives,
1991–present.

A Treasury of Human
Inheritance: Huntington's
Disease, Entre's Case,
2001 (detail). Courtesy
of Collection Mendel
Museum, Brno.

cup is actually more like one element in multi-part portraits that include
a nurse or another administering agent, a patient or coerced victim and,
held between them, the cup itself. And this kind of portrait sits within the
wider context of Borland's interest in ideas of war and violence; illness,
death and health; intimacy and care; and small objects that, when held
in the hand, save or threaten lives. It is not insignificant that an important
early work of Borland's is called *Small Objects that Save Lives* (1991–
present). This small cup reflects many of the most central themes that
have featured in Borland's work over the last thirty years.

I propose, then, that the feeder cup is really an expanded human portrait.
And indeed it is obvious from looking over Borland's career that the
genre of portraiture – single, group and family – is a central preoccupation.
Her portraits are a little different, though. For a start, she widens the
normal approach of capturing visible human likenesses to include
referencing aspects of some of humankind's attempts to understand
the deep biological processes of life – genetics and embryology, DNA
research, health scans and cloning, for example. Then she extends the
boundaries of her interest to the other side: the afterlife of living creatures
exemplified in cadavers, body parts, the dust to which we return, and
finally the forgotten, anonymous or unidentified body, as well as the
known and labelled one.

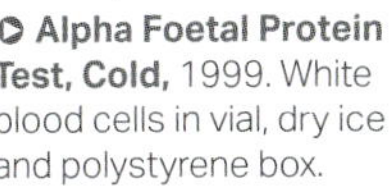

◐ **Alpha Foetal Protein
Test, Cold,** 1999. White
blood cells in vial, dry ice
and polystyrene box.

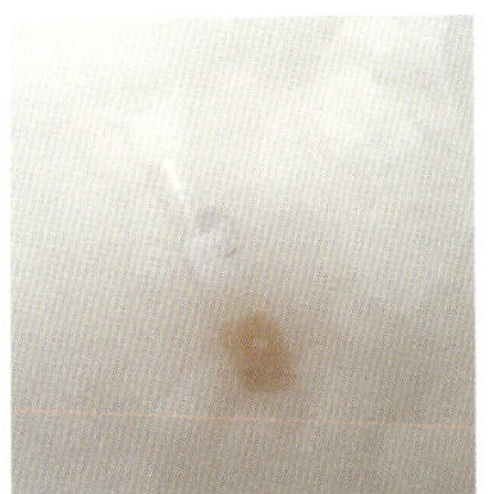

Artworks in the first category include those
with reasonably self-explanatory titles such as
Alpha Foetal Protein Test, Cold (1999) and
*A Treasury of Human Inheritance: Huntington's
Disease, Entre's Case* (2001). Such works
speak of categorization, in-vitro existences in
test tubes and glass flasks, labelled boxes and
hidden shelves – so much so that we cannot
always be sure if Borland has found her inspiration in a research laboratory
or a museum storeroom, and whether the samples are inert or alive.

Works in the second category include *Supported* (1990), *To Dust We Will
Return* (1996) and *HeLa, Hot* (1999). The latter work was based around
the story – better known now than it was in 1999 – of an African-American
woman called Henrietta Lacks, whose cancerous cells, known by the
shorthand 'HeLa' after her death in 1951, have since been shared and
cultivated in numerous cancer research laboratories around the world,
without her or her family's permission ever being obtained. It is one of
many works by Borland that, among other things, seeks to restore named
identity to people who have lost it, unknowingly or unwillingly, to the

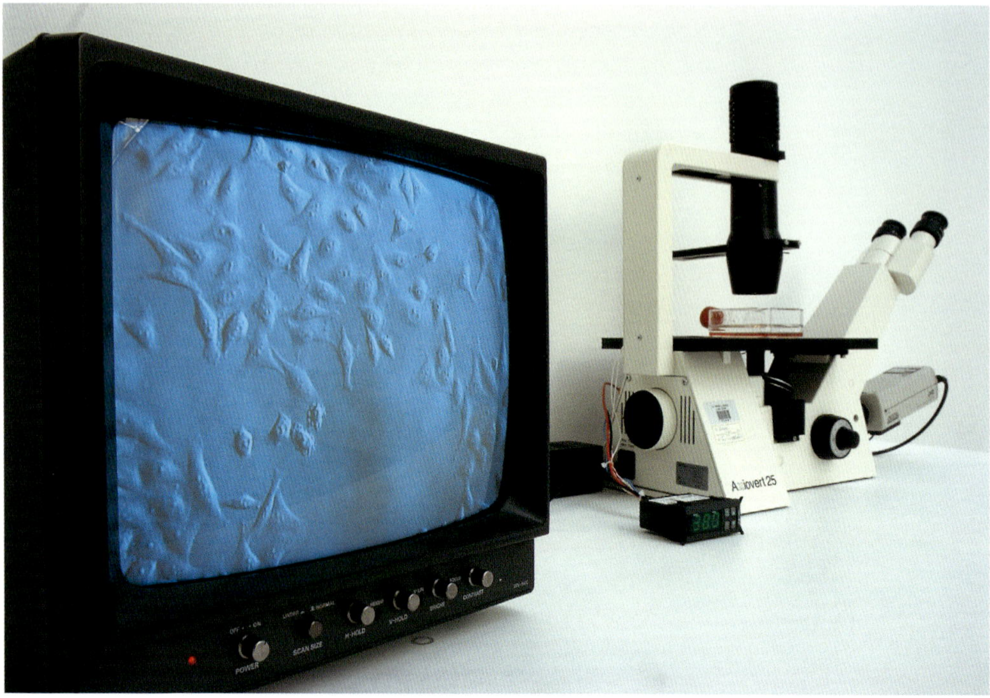

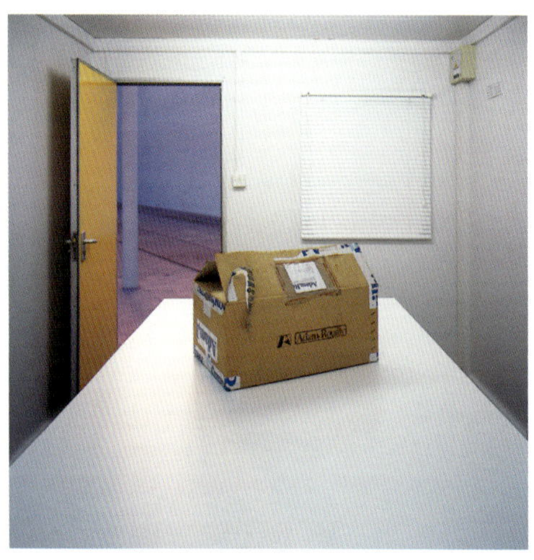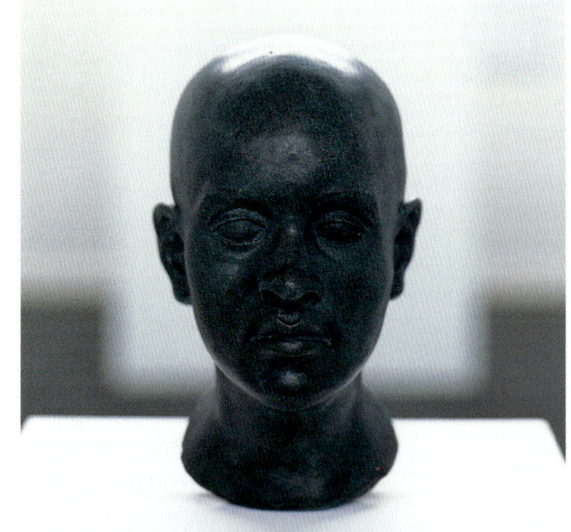

regime of science. In passing, you may notice the conjunction of 'cold' and 'hot' in a number of Borland's titles. At a metaphoric level, she is always taking the temperature of objects and situations, seeking to generate warmth and a beating heart into the contexts of extremes where she finds her inspiration.

The expansiveness I am proposing is fundamental to understanding how Borland approaches any theme in her work: what she does in effect is parse – take apart, lay out for examination, seek to understand the ligatures that knot around any subject she is exploring – so that we too might expand our own perspectives. Wartime remembrance and commemoration is, in this sense, a kind of expanded portraiture too, where communities of named and unnamed dead are remembered by the currently living, through a set of a myriad objects and rituals – such as cenotaphs and memorial services – that as a whole make up a portrait of a remembering globe. We have all kinds of ways of remembering named individuals, from family trees to memorial chapels, but Borland, ever attentive to the shadow side of such phenomena, is probably more interested in those who remain anonymous and unnamed. The plight of those without identity and provenance – in museum terms, the object with an unknown source or that has lost its label – is a common theme.

Borland realized early in her career – for example in her first discoveries among the jars of anatomical specimens at the Hunterian Museum, Glasgow, in the early 1990s – that unknown *objects* could in fact be unidentified *persons* and their histories were far from pleasant. Responding to this in *From Life* (1994), a major early installation, involved in effect a collusion with and parsing of the system of acquiring real human bones through mail order. The installation was set in three Portakabin units at Tramway, a cavernous gallery in a converted Glasgow City Council tram depot. Here we encountered the details of Borland's purchase and perused the information of a forensic assessment that the skeleton and skull were of an unidentified Asian woman of around 25 years old, whose head Borland had reconstructed in clay by a forensic artist. The installation culminated in the final cabin, where a bronze cast of the young woman's clay portrait head was set on a simple plinth. Attempts to restore, however partially, the identity of the unnamed and powerless – particularly unwitting women in these categories – continued to inspire later pieces, such as *Ecbolic Garden* (2001), *To Be Set and Sown in the Garden* (2002) and *The History of Plants, According to Women, Children and Students* (2002).

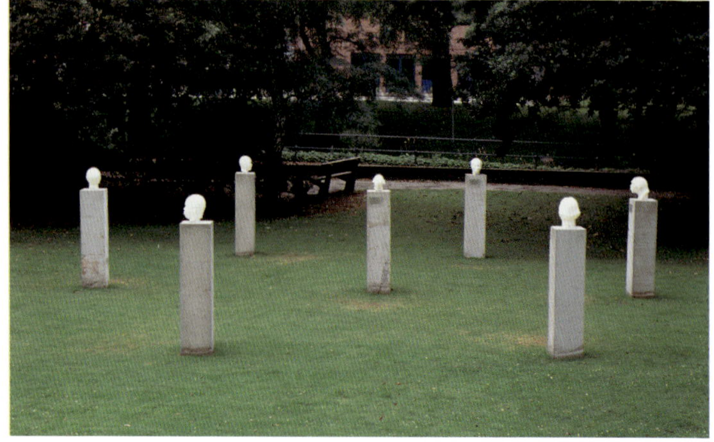

Another major work, *The Dead Teach the Living* (1997), is more aligned to anonymous wartime histories that have also preoccupied Borland. It takes the form, too, of 'expanded portraits' of exploited and marginalized people at the mercy of Nazi science. The title is a phrase coined by the famous Renaissance anatomist Vesalius, extolling the importance of cadavers to the medical profession – whether the bodies were bequeathed willingly or otherwise – and which Borland saw inscribed on the walls of the dissection theatre at Münster in Germany, where this work was first made.

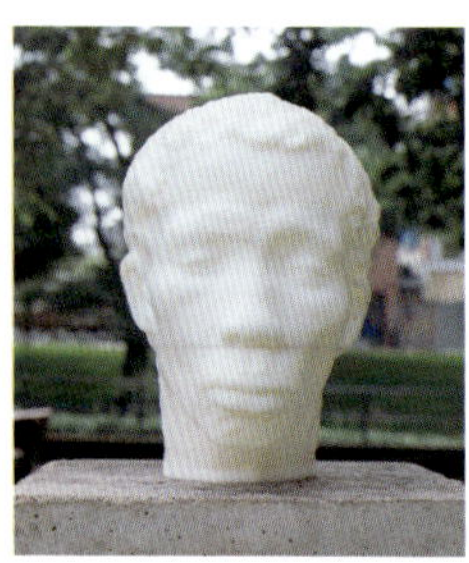

But *The Dead Teach the Living* is a wider injunction and one very relevant to wartime commemoration and remembrance. In this context, the phrase could be seen as an injunction to study history for its lessons for today. For the pacifist, this might be a call to empathize fully with the horror that millions of individuals suffered, once more, in the name of the powerful. On the other hand, the non-pacifist might take the phrase as a prompt for thanks to those whose sacrifice was ultimate. As we will see at the end of this text, Borland allows these and other possible meanings to remain open and available, refusing to become openly ideological on such a delicate point.

The Dead Teach the Living was only one among many of Borland's works made during the 1990s and since that have dealt with war and violence in the abstract, as well as specific wars and moments of conflict that Borland has researched over the years. As she herself notes, 'as well as being linked to slaughter, wars are linked to medical advances. That duality is always there: destruction and healing.'[2] Early works include *Apples*

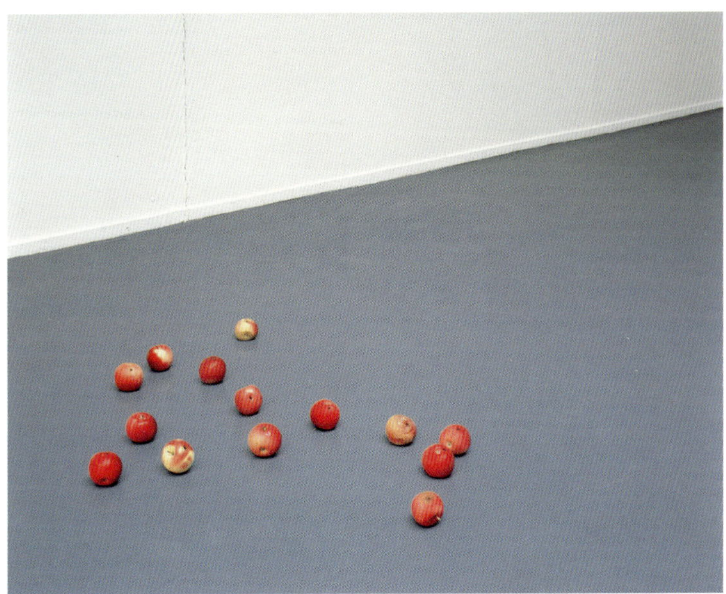

with Holes and *Shot Glass* (both 1991) and *Sturmgewehr* (1994), which involved the simple unmarked burying by Borland of a Kalashnikov AK-47 in the garden of an East German country house. Her numerous visits to Germany over the years have offered many opportunities to get to know the country well and to make ambitious exhibition projects there that reflect, in nuanced and complex ways, on the nature of twentieth-century conflict.

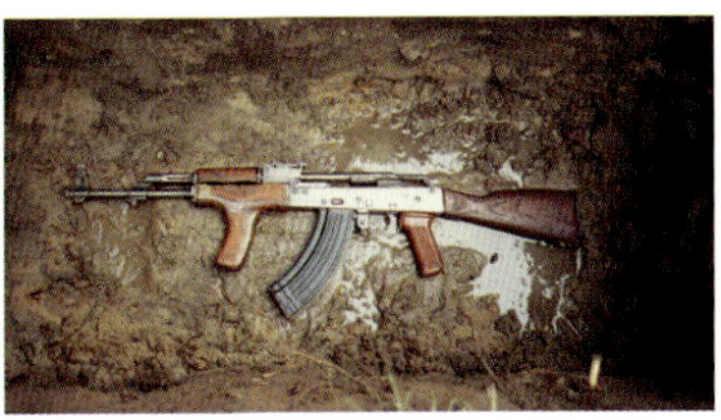

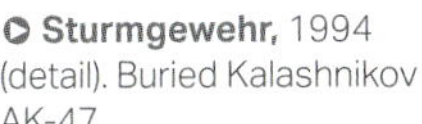

Sturmgewehr, 1994 (detail). Buried Kalashnikov AK-47.

If in the black-and-white simplification of both world wars of the last century, it seemed easy to tell who the victors and villains really were, Borland's own work seems to question such assumptions, as well as alluding to the contemporary conditions of war, where complicity, technology and shifting alliances have made any such assumptions impossible.

I am not sure that Borland is interested in war as such, or any historical war in particular, but rather how wars are imbued with heightened moments of compassion, intimacy, remembrance and sacrifice – moments, though, that are still framed by sheer terror and destruction. By pairing destruction and healing, she not only reminds us that many medical advances have been pushed through under conditions of war, but also that both human conflict and human ill-health lead to their opposites: hence her interest in

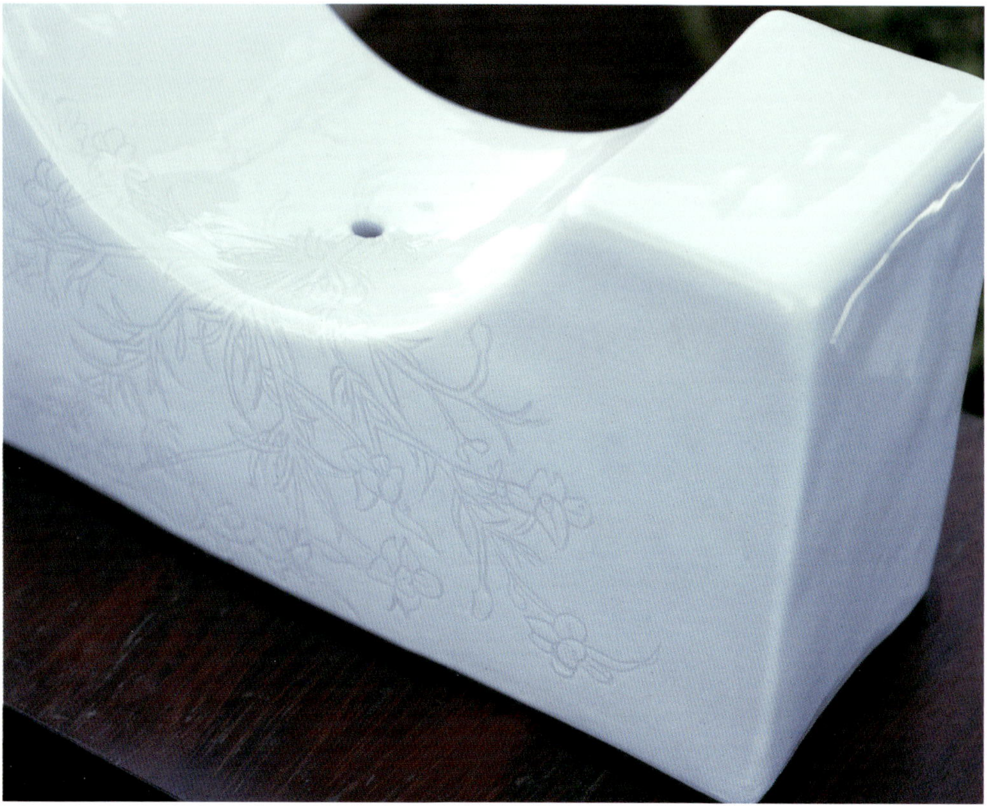

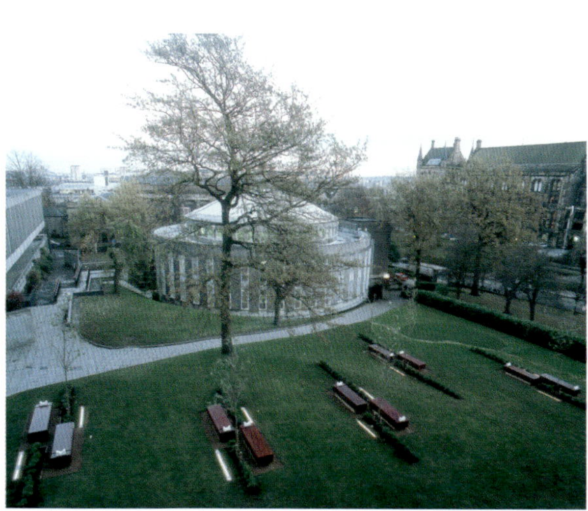

△ **To be Set and Sown in the Garden,** 2002 (detail). Ceramic headrest.

◁ **To be Set and Sown in the Garden,** 2002. Permanent outdoor sculpture, University of Glasgow.

care and healing. We are back to the world of the feeder cup and of other objects in Glasgow Museums' stores that particularly interested Borland, including a patient wicker basket from Gartnavel Hospital and moss-stuffed pillows used in ambulances to absorb blood from the wounds of the travelling injured. They echo works which Borland has made on the theme of support, repair and rest, such as *To be Set and Sown in the Garden* (2002). We have already mentioned this work in connection with honouring anonymous women lost to medical history, but such is the richness of Borland's work that we can also unravel the associations around this work in yet another direction altogether.

I mean by this the clear centrality of the memorial, as a symptom of both war and caring. *I Say Nothing* is far from a conventional memorial sculpture, but, as with so much of her work, memory, the memorial and commemoration are never far away from her thoughts. *Memor* – echoed in so many words in English – is the Latin for 'mindful', and the Greek for 'care', *mermēra*, also feeds into 'memory/memorial'.

Importantly, Borland does not work towards art with a form she knows in advance, but works through a set of ideas that ultimately will seek to prompt an idea of memory and mindfulness in the mind of the viewer. Memorials help to do precisely this. They serve to shape and preserve remembrance. Therefore, again we see Borland looking to extend time, to extrude memory, pulling it out and making it longer, just as her 'expanded portraits' open up what it means to be human. All memorials do this, too, from a solid stone war monument to a moment in time, like a memorial service. In Britain we associate such services with Remembrance Day, a very public and perhaps increasingly abstract and distant kind of media event broadcast on television.

Just as prescient is another kind of memorial service that Borland knows well – the one that many anatomy departments around the world hold for body donors, attended by medical and teaching staff, students and the donors' families. Works that have been inspired directly by these themes are *Circles of Focus* (2015, with Brody Condon) and *Positive Pattern* (2017), commissioned by the Organ Donation Committee of the Newcastle upon Tyne Hospitals NHS Foundation Trust. Despite all the multiple associations that typically surround Borland's work, at the heart is a 'bringing back into mind', or a 'holding in the mind', which ultimately is an act of remembrance, including but extending far beyond the war dead.

I began this essay with the idea of the 'extended portrait' as a way to understand the conceptual breadth of Borland's work. Linked to the idea

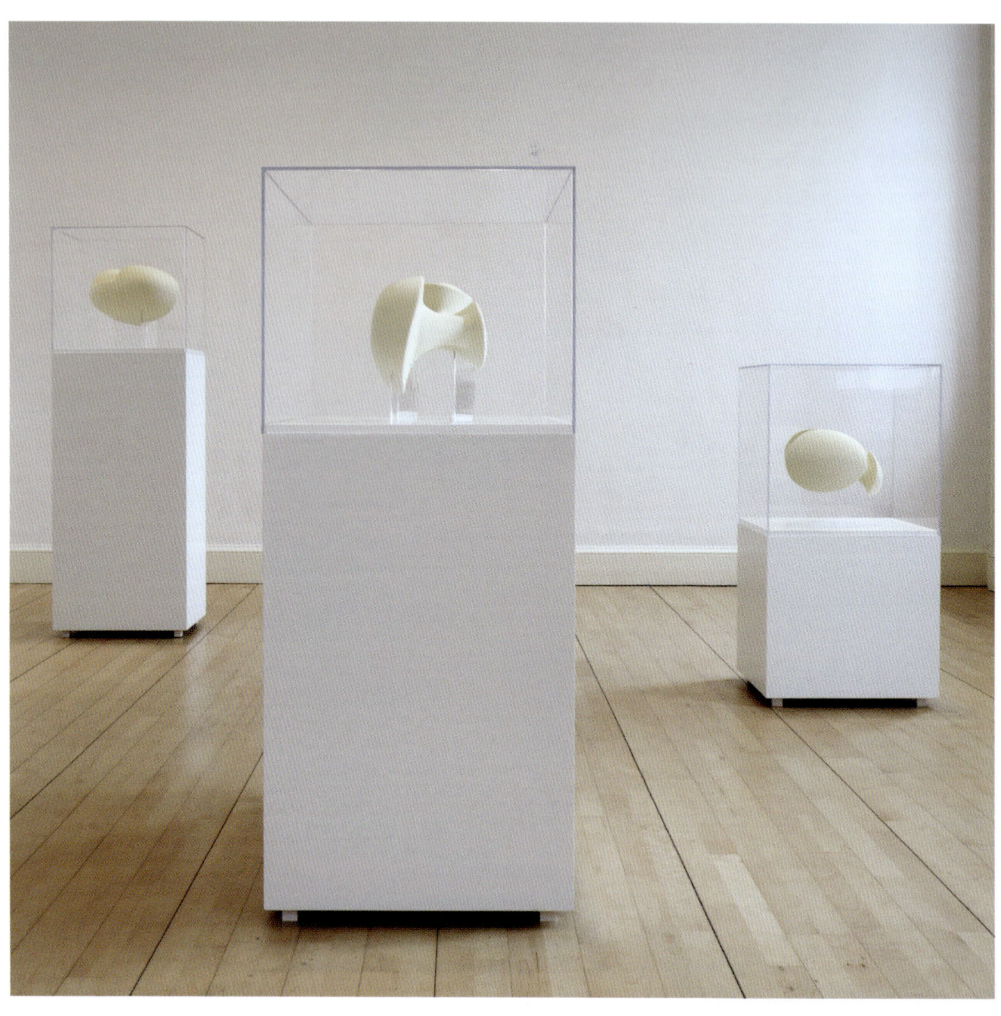

⬥ **Positive Pattern,** 2016 (detail).
Courtesy of National Galleries Scotland.
Purchased with the Iain Paul Fund, 2018.

of the memorial, there is a sense of 'extended time' that accompanies the way she works with human identity. Survival is the key term, in the sense that objects and ideas persist in Borland's work over decades: they return and reappear, they are like artefacts from the past that literally 'survive' – that is to say, they live beyond their first appearance. This is why so many of the commentators on Borland's work highlight terms such as 'trace' and 'memory', 'storage' and 'unearthing'. It takes time to find things in the dark and to intuit the best way to bring them to light. The invariable visual quietness of her work often gives the sense of a trauma that has already happened, and a sense of us living in the afterlife of that trauma, trying to reassemble it from the remaining parts.

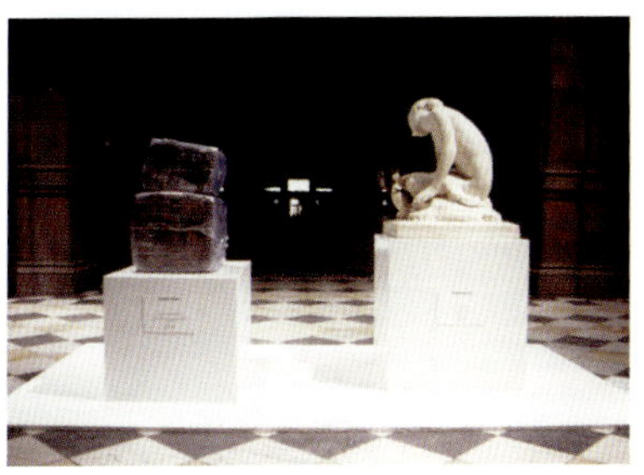

○ Human Being, 1990 (detail from a multi-site installation). Sculpture (*Youth, Time, Eternity* by Charles Rutland, from Glasgow Museums' collection) and compacted, baled and shrink-wrapped refuse.

And this is where working with museums and museum professionals has been so rewarding for Borland over the years, beginning with her first museum installation, which was at Kelvingrove Art Gallery and Museum as part of the *Sites/ Positions* Glasgow-wide project in 1990. At that time, Borland was a recent master's graduate returning to the city from Belfast. She produced, in *Human Being*, a wonderful reflection on the valued and the discarded, in the form of an ambitious group of installations of heavy, densely compressed blocks of refuse material set within the archaeology and sculpture galleries at Kelvingrove. A parallel installation was created at Summerston Landfill, which supplied the rubbish.[3] Behind such museum-based projects, of which *I Say Nothing* is the latest, lies an idea of preservation which has been just as persistent in her work. Her major retrospective in 2006 at the Fruitmarket Gallery in Edinburgh was even called *Preserves*. The term 'preservation' carries with it the idea of keeping from harm or protecting from decay, which resonates too with death, the memorial and the elongation of time. If war memorials entreat us to 'preserve the memory' of the fallen, Borland widens the entreaty on many fronts. As often with terms that run through Borland's art, their meanings are layered and seem deliberately designed to set the mind going, as suggestive supports to the material works themselves. 'Preservation', after all, has Latin origins – *prae-* and *servare* – which mean keeping, guarding and observing. This tells us something about the way that Borland binds together looking and preserving, so suited to the workings of a visual artist and, of course, also as a sign for the function of museums.

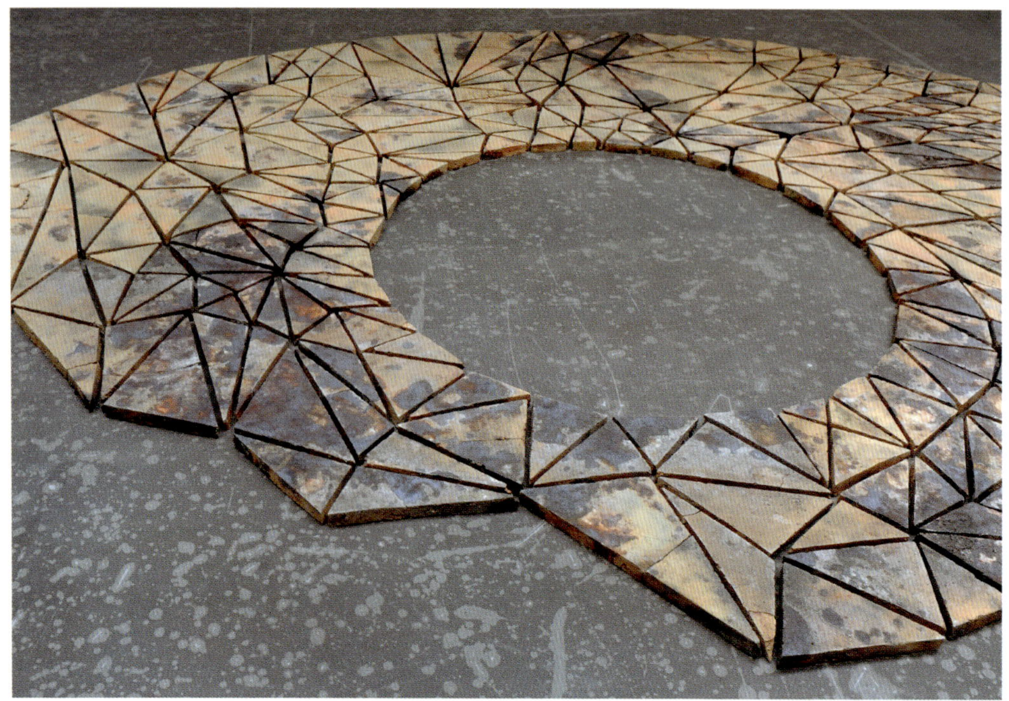

As a way of bringing this reflection on Borland's work to a close, I want to suggest that her approach is described as an artistic version of agnosticism, first coined by the famed Darwinist supporter TH Huxley in 1869 to capture a sense of scepticism or unknowability about ultimate reality.[4] This denoted a method of exploring a topic that is, as far as possible, reasonable, whilst still recognizing that reason may not take you all the way and, therefore, that some things cannot be known. Or in Katrina Brown's elegant phrase, her art 'allows us the presence and protection of doubt.'[5] It is about following a journey with an open mind, genuinely respectful and investigative, without cynicism. What makes Borland's agnosticism so striking and original has much to do with her lack of cynicism, which incidentally is the reason I believe she has been able from the start to engage and recruit non-art experts so willingly to her artistic projects. It is also to do with how agnosticism flips so decisively into intuitive decision-making when she comes to final choices and creating the work. Intuition is a learned yet unlaboured skill, brought to bear on every work Borland has ever made.

With its range of 'hot' topics, from genetics and medicine to war and crime, Borland's art might seem on the face of it very 'issue based', in the sense of belonging to a direction in art, which arose in the 1960s

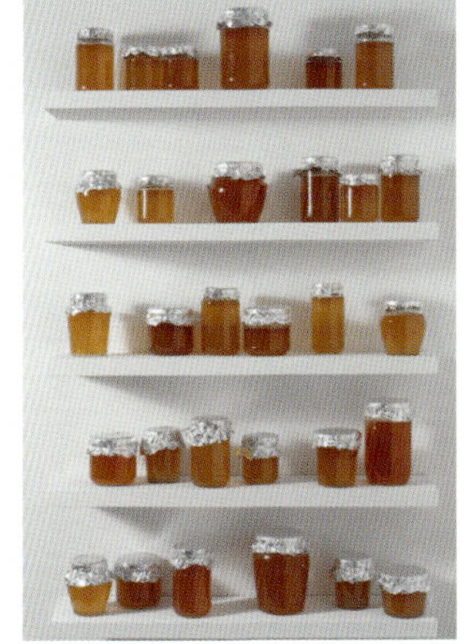

onwards, that treated important issues directly within the art itself. But unlike the art of this genre, made by artists who already know how they would like audiences to understand it, she faces those issues with curiosity, opening her processes up to in-built tensions that shape but do not determine exactly what the message is going to be in advance. This is true agnosticism and why her art matters so deeply. To enact this in art, Borland has developed a nuanced process that is not poetic in a vague sense, nor rationalist in a scientific sense, but involves withholding judgement, listening to experts, following her intuition, forming ideas that keep forensically close to the evidence, yet in the end resolves by falling over that plateau of reason into circumstantial poetics, which is often where her final artwork rests. Borland's art, including this newly created commission, is a bullet-proof example of agnostic poetics. And it is as oblique and intimate as the relationship between the handle and spout of the feeder cup that caught her attention from the start.

1. Robert Pogue Harrison (2003) *The Dominion of the Dead*, University of Chicago Press, p.ix.

2. Christine Borland quoted in Susan Mansfield 'Pushing the parameters', *The Scotsman*, 6 January 2018.

3. The project was one that I had the pleasure to facilitate, alongside fellow curators at Glasgow Museums, Helen Adamson and Hugh Stevenson, and Malcolm Dickson of *Sites/Positions*.

4. TH Huxley, 'The Theological Statute at Oxford', *The Spectator*, 29 May 1869.

5. Katrina Brown (2001) 'What makes for the fullness and perfection of life, for beauty and happiness is good. What makes for death, disease, imperfection, suffering is bad.' *Progressive disorder*, Dundee/London, Dundee Contemporary Arts; Book Works, p.28.

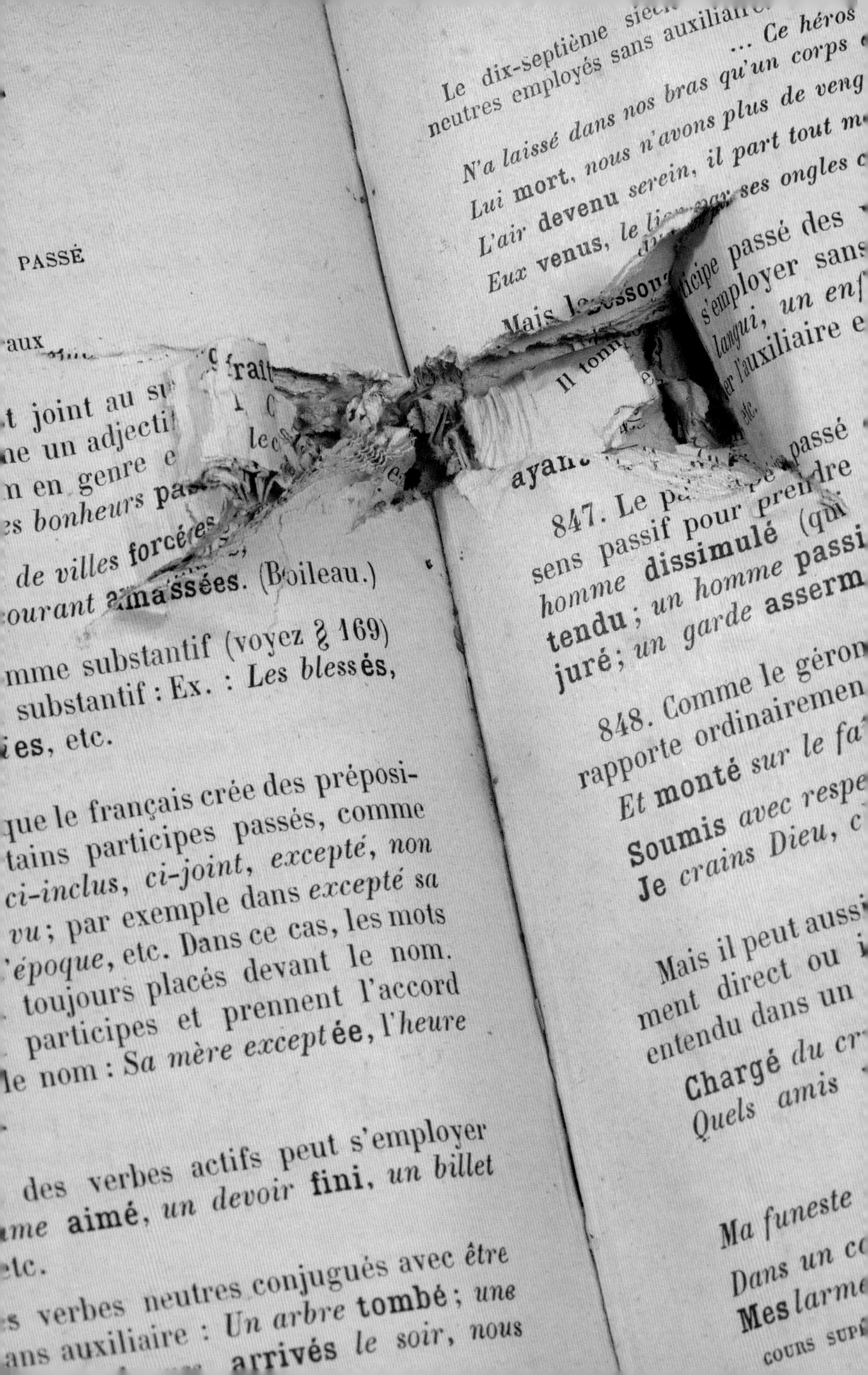

aux

t joint au su...
ne un adjecti...
n en genre e...
es bonheurs pa...
de villes forcé(es...
ourant *amassées*. (Boileau.)

...mme substantif (voyez § 169)
substantif : Ex. : *Les bless**és**,*
...es, etc.

...que le français crée des préposi-
...tains participes passés, comme
*ci-inclus, ci-joint, excepté, non
vu*; par exemple dans *excepté sa
...époque*, etc. Dans ce cas, les mots
toujours placés devant le nom.
participes et prennent l'accord
le nom : *Sa mère except**ée**, l'heure*

...des verbes actifs peut s'employer
...me **aimé**, *un devoir* **fini**, *un billet*
...etc.

...s verbes neutres conjugués avec être
...ans auxiliaire : *Un arbre* **tombé**; *une*
...**arrivés** *le soir, nous*

Le dix-septième siè...
neutres employés sans auxilia...
*N'a laissé dans nos bras qu'un corps...
Lui mort, nous n'avons plus de veng...
L'air devenu serein, il part tout m...
Eux venus, le li... ses ongles...*
Mais le... passé des
Il tonn...

847. Le pa... passé
sens passif pour pren dre
homme **dissimulé** (qu...
tendu; *un homme* passi...
juré; un garde **asserm**...

848. Comme le géron...
rapporte ordinairemen...
Et **monté** *sur le fa...*
Soumis *avec* respe...
Je crains Dieu, c...

Mais il peut aussi...
ment direct ou i...
entendu dans un

Chargé *du cr...*
Quels amis...

Ma funeste...
Dans un co...
Mes larmes...
cours sup...

Doubtful Occasion

**A CREATIVE SYMPOSIUM BASED ON
CHRISTINE BORLAND'S RESEARCH
AT GLASGOW MUSEUMS RESOURCE CENTRE**

5 OCTOBER 2017

CHRISTINE BORLAND, CAT AUBURN,
BETTINA BILDHAUER, TAMSIN DILLON,
CHRIS DORSETT, LYN HAGAN,
BIRTHE JORGENSEN, DAISY LAFARGE,
RACHEL LOWTHER, FRANCIS MCKEE,
JO MEACOCK, STEPHANIE DE ROEMER

◖ Pages of a French grammar book damaged by
gunfire, found in a World War I dugout at Givenchy,
now in Glasgow Museums' World War I collection.

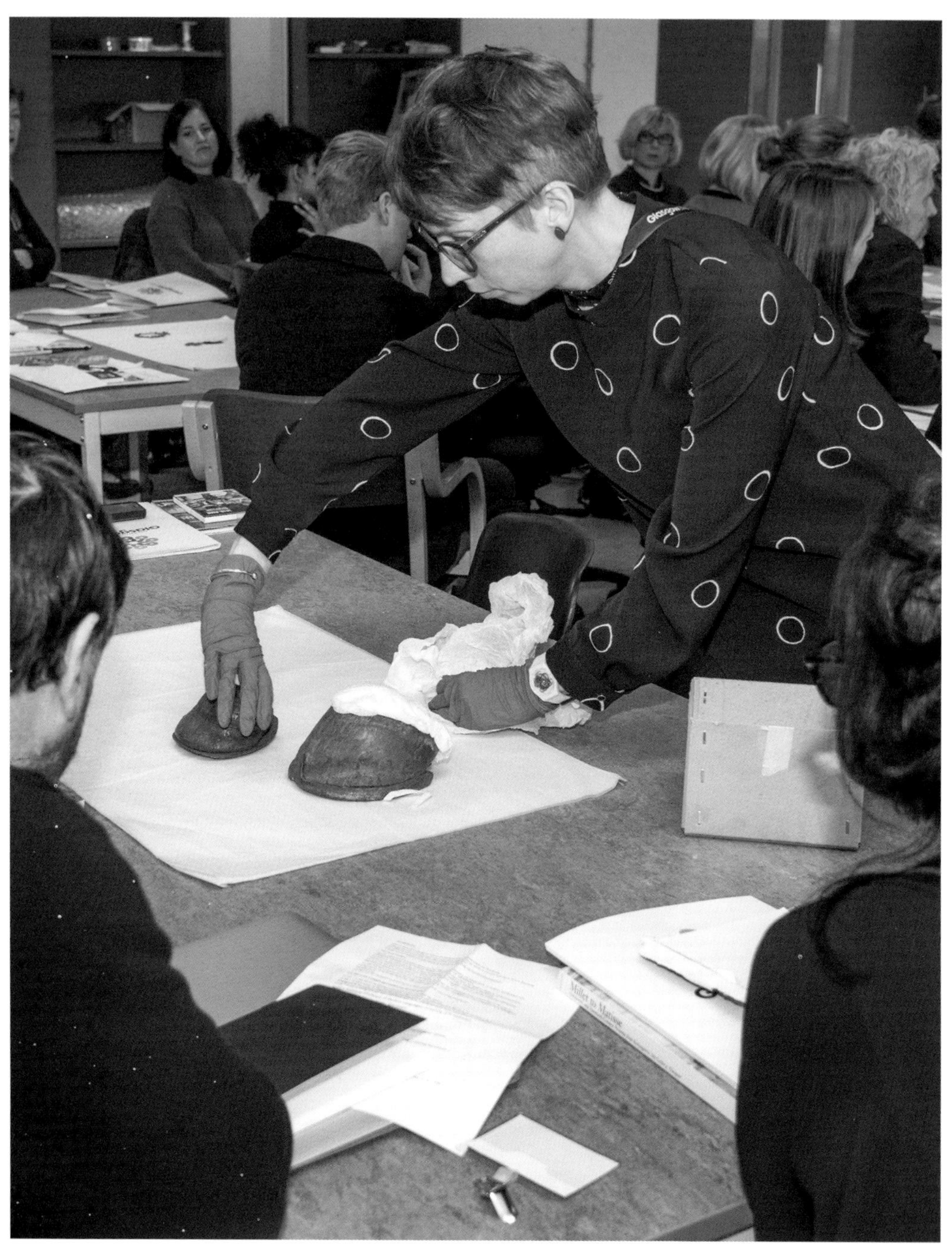

⬥ Jo Meacock unwrapping mule hooves at the *Doubtful Occasion* symposium.

ARTIST'S NOTES:

Doubtful Occasion was a one-day symposium at Glasgow Museums Resource Centre (GMRC), when an invited audience of artists, academics, students and other interested individuals were introduced to its stores and research spaces. Working closely with the Glasgow Museums team, I felt it useful to share – at a moment when my ideas for the artwork were still in development – some of my experiences at GMRC and thoughts about the objects in the stores, especially those which had become most meaningful to me.

During a year spent exploring Glasgow Museums' World War I collection, I referred continuously to a spreadsheet collated from information fields on MIMSY, the collections management system used by the museums service. When I was first given the spreadsheet of more than two thousand objects, I saw something very reduced, with all the emotion removed: lists of numbers and brief, objective descriptions of materials, country of origin, dates and locations. I came to enjoy the imaginative power of responding intuitively to the terse lists of materials or to the merest suggestion of a narrative inherent in the descriptions.

Each time I selected an object or a group of objects to view – either in their location in the stores or brought to the research room – I considered the journey to retrieve them as a small performance, and by extension thought about the performativity of museum storage generally: how objects are carefully recorded, wrapped in tissue, boxed and shelved, unwrapped, moved, relocated and possibly put on public display.

The gradual and careful unboxing, unwrapping and revealing of selected objects with which *Doubtful Occasion* began is only a day-to-day activity for the curators and collections staff who were assisting me, but this everyday performance primed us to connect, to share the transient moment before a piece of work is fixed in concept and form: an important phase in the development of the sculpture for the balcony in Kelvingrove. I spoke about the selected objects presented on the following pages, using extracts from their descriptions on MIMSY together with additional annotations from my own sketchbooks and notebooks which briefly introduced ideas the objects suggested to me. Once unwrapped, these objects lay on our tables to be scrutinized, referred to, and bear witness to our presentations and conversations, before they were wrapped in tissue again and returned to the stores, perhaps for decades or centuries.

In addition to presentations by invited speakers, two 'recorders' were commissioned to respond creatively to the day. Daisy Lafarge's poem written and performed at the symposium later expanded into the 'Doubtful: Glossary' which is included at the end of this section (pp.55–9), with some of artist Birthe Jorgensen's drawings from the day scattered throughout it.

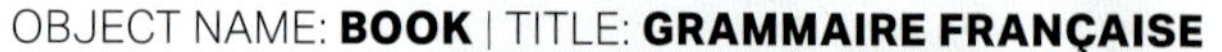

OBJECT NAME: **BOOK** | TITLE: **GRAMMAIRE FRANÇAISE**

Date made: **1895** | Maker: **L. Hachette et Compagnie** | Place Made: **Paris** | Description: **French grammar book damaged by gunfire, found in a dugout at Givenchy** | Materials: **Paper, cloth** | Measurements: **17.8 x 11.8 x 3.5 cm** | Category: History | ID Number: **1.b.1918**

CB: The book has a handwritten inscription of a verse by Victor Hugo, in fountain-pen ink, on the inside cover. It is inscribed throughout with handwritten annotations, all in French.

From the way the holes and rents are compacted together, I felt sure the book hadn't been opened since they were made in the dugout. Much of the book, therefore, must remain closed as it risks serious further damage if the compacted holes are rent apart.

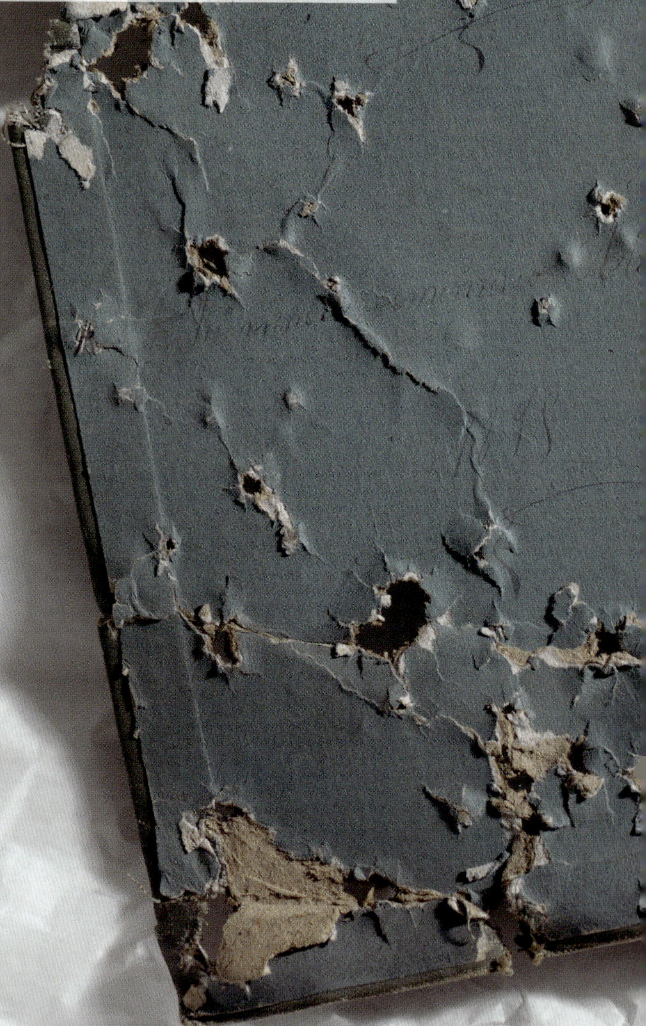

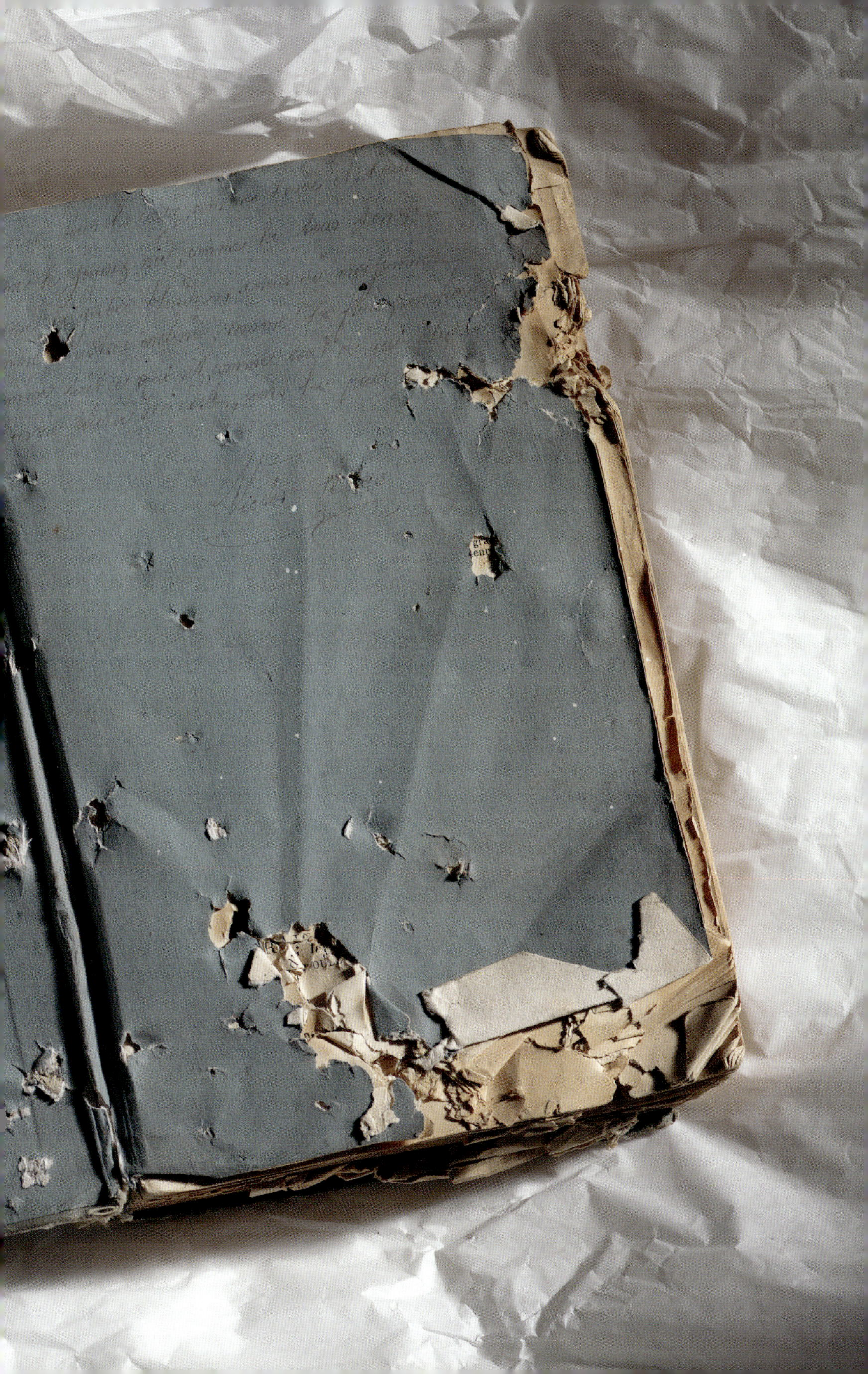

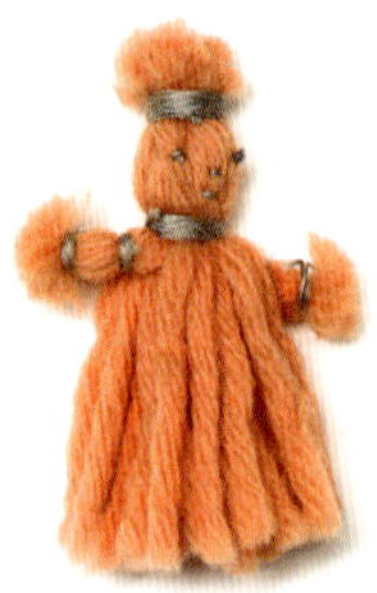

OBJECT NAME: **YARN DOLL CHARM**

Date made: **1917** | Place Made: **England, East London (place associated)** | Description: **Charm in the form of a yarn poppet, of pink wool fashioned into human doll shape, owned by a soldier from East London, 1917, from a collection of mascots or charms carried by soldiers during World War I** | Materials: **Wool, cotton thread** | Measurements: **6 x 4 x 1 cm** | Category: **History** | ID Number: **1918.10.d**

CB: One of a collection of 32 charms and amulets, this yarn doll charm was removed from its original box to be included in an Open Museum handling kit (where it is contained in a bespoke handling box).

The museum register tells us that the objects were purchased in two lots in 1918 and 1919 from folklorist Edward Lovett. Lovett worked at a bank by day, and gathered all manner of amulets, charms and talismans in his free time. His book *Magic in Modern London* (1925) tells us that his methods for collecting centred around quiet, friendly conversations and the giving of small gifts in exchange – often a small succulent planted in a whelk shell, which he carried in his pocket.

When I encountered the collection, twelve of the original charm boxes, labelled in ink on the reverse by Lovett himself, were found to be empty, their contents missing.

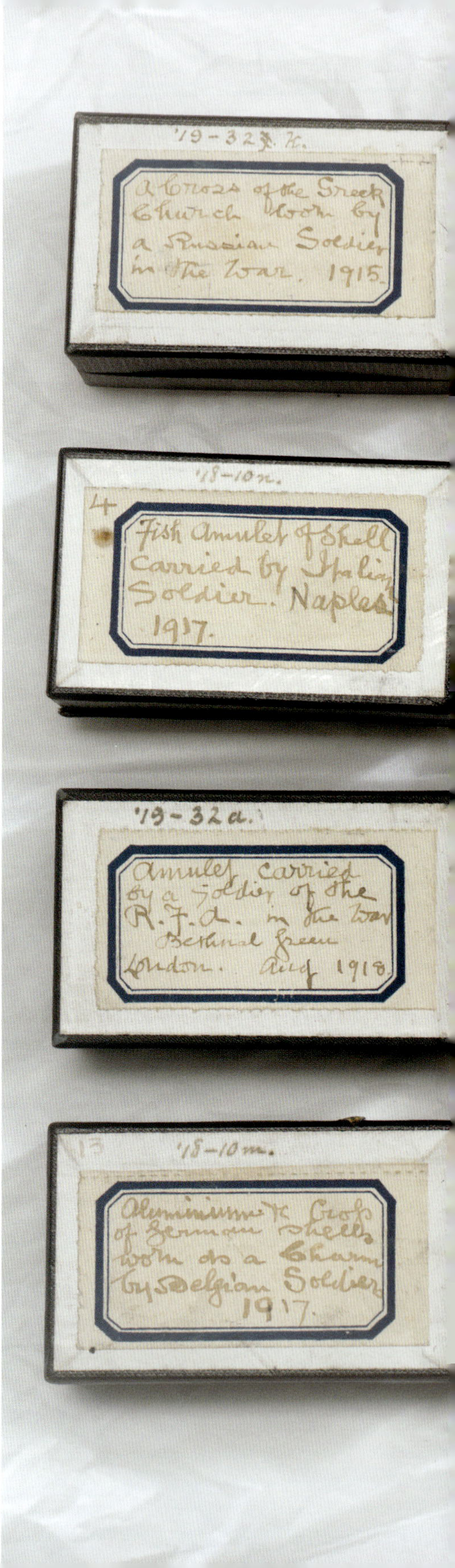

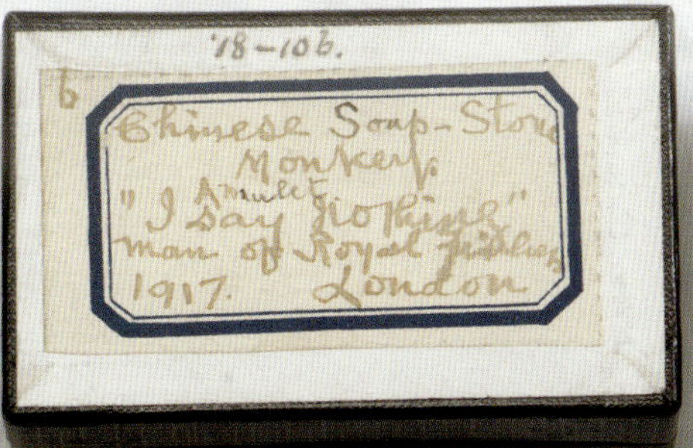

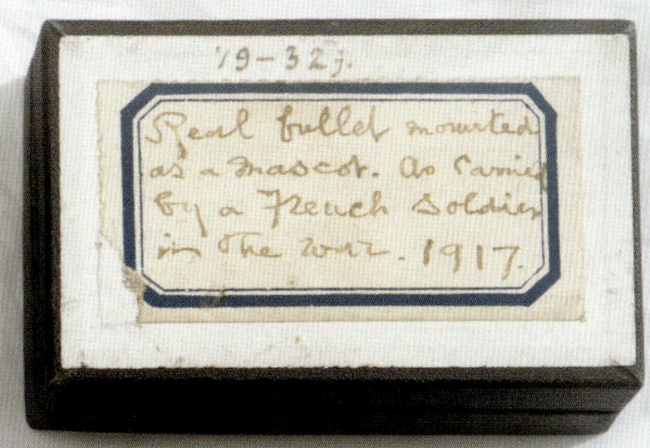

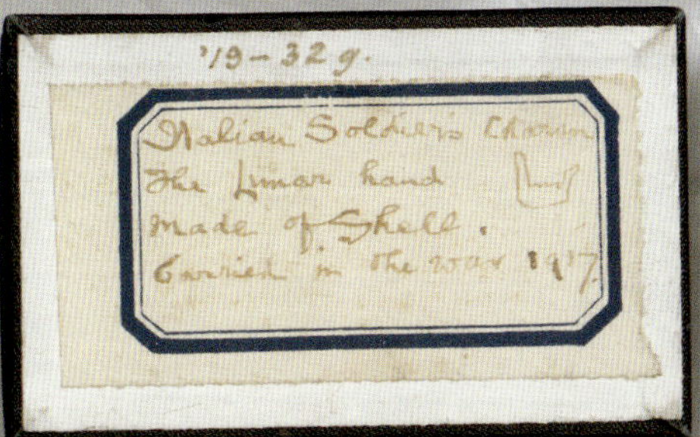

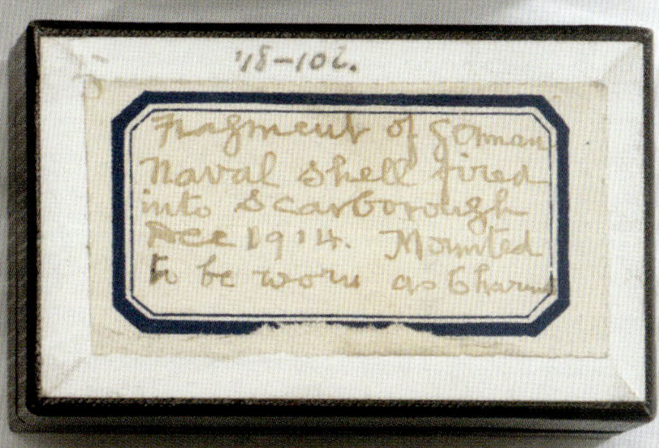

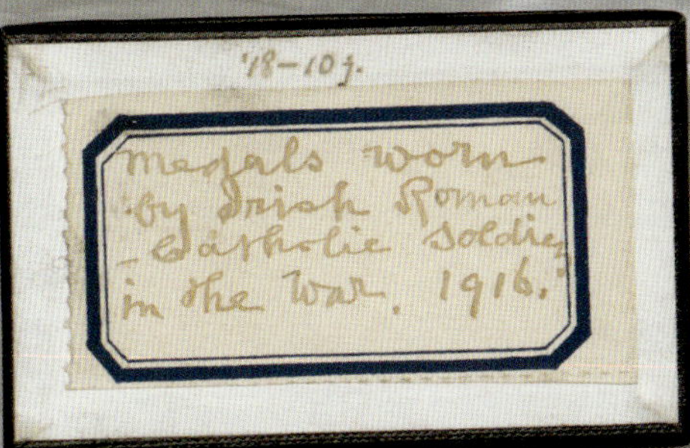

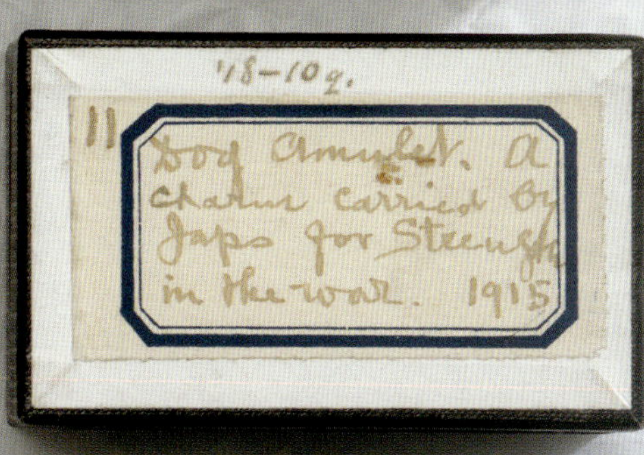

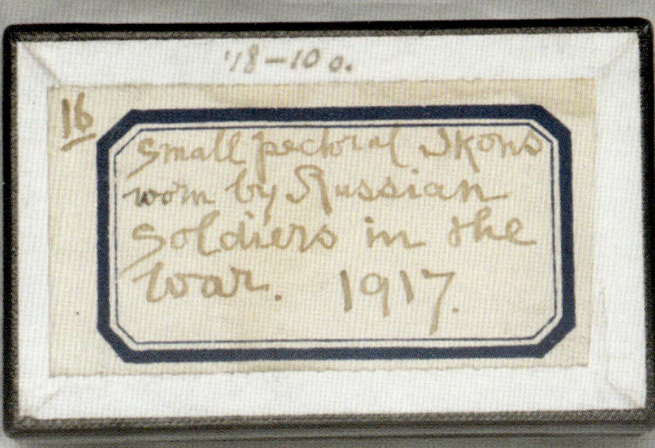

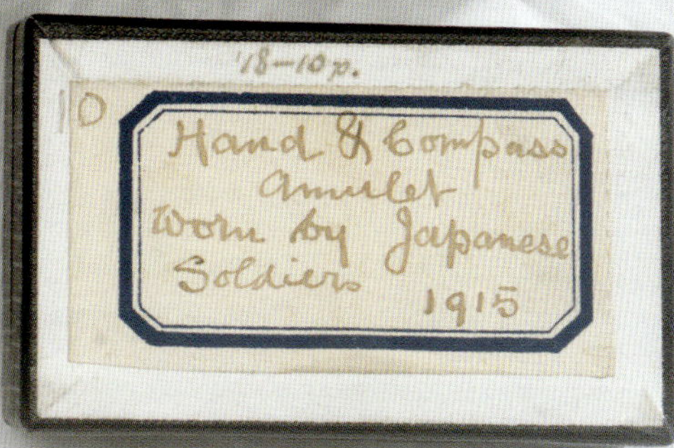

⬠ Twelve boxes for World War I charms and amulets, inscribed by the collector Edward Lovett in about 1914–18.

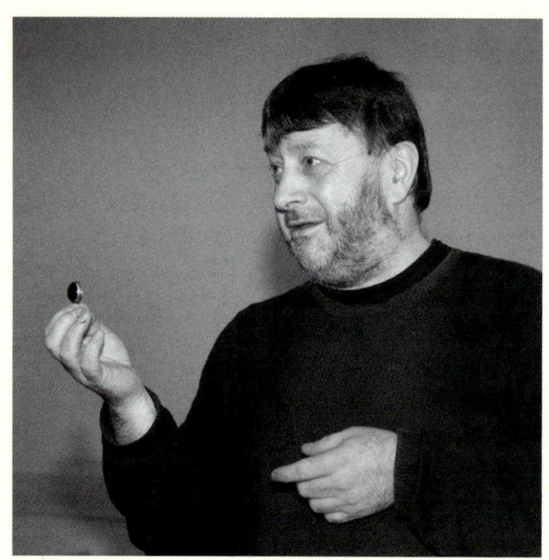

Francis McKee showing an amulet from his own collection at the *Doubtful Occasion* symposium.

A Level of Protection

FRANCIS MCKEE

Amulets suggest an arcane world: ancient, possibly mythical and probably populated by mages or superheroes such as Marvel Comics' Dr Strange. It is true that amulets have a long history, but their use has never been restricted to a 'magical' elite and today amulets remain a powerful force in daily life even if they exist in a more commonplace way.

The term 'amulet' often appears in tandem with 'talisman', but it is important to distinguish the two things. An amulet is more likely to be a natural stone, a herb or a simple figure; a talisman is an object that is frequently inscribed or carries an engraved sign. The amulet protects the wearer from evil, while the talisman is more active and emits its own power.

Today amulets are still popular in many countries and can be bought everywhere from specialist markets to ordinary supermarkets. They also live on in a decorative role – the charm bracelet is a direct descendant of the protective amulet, an example of supernaturally charged objects surviving simply as accessories.

Even in the early history of the amulet, when it functioned within societies dominated by magical beliefs, its ornamental aspect was important. In Viking culture, for example, personal amulets were common: small pendants in the shape of the hammer of Thor, thunderbolts, swords, shields or anchors. Some were crude and functional but others drew on the finest skills of Viking craftsmen. The quality of an amulet might reflect the status of its owner, but it could also signal the importance of gift giving – an amulet's power could be based not only in the protective power of the object but also in the good will or love of the donator.

If Viking and Roman amulets reflected the fears of warriors and soldiers in growing empires, some Ancient Egyptian amulets pointed to a more esoteric concern: the afterlife. Small amulets of various gods were made as part of the elaborate embalming process for mummies, with different amulets embedded in key locations around a wrapped body to provide very specific protection to the deceased in his or her journey through death. However, even in cultures where amulets held such significant power at high levels, it was the plethora of small, personal charms that demonstrated the ways in which belief in their protection permeated society.

These are small objects that save lives and we remain heavily invested in their power today. Anything, as we can see from objects in Glasgow Museums' World War I collection, can function as an amulet in times of danger or fear. Daily objects often assume a magical function, as our superstitious minds associate good luck with the presence of a certain item regularly in our pockets or even an article of clothing. Often it is what the object is made of that lends it power, unusual materials that link us back to nature: feathers, leather, sea shells and gemstones are among our favourites.

Rather than supernatural power, it is this human response to the object that counts most. The strangeness of the amulet and its appearance take us out of our habitual world. We are thrown slightly off-centre: we are more alert and conscious of our immediate situation. Humans with heightened senses perform better. Typically we ascribe this to the power of the amulet, which means we are reassured when it is close to us. The amulet creates a feedback loop. We believe it helps us and that belief builds confidence and success in our lives.

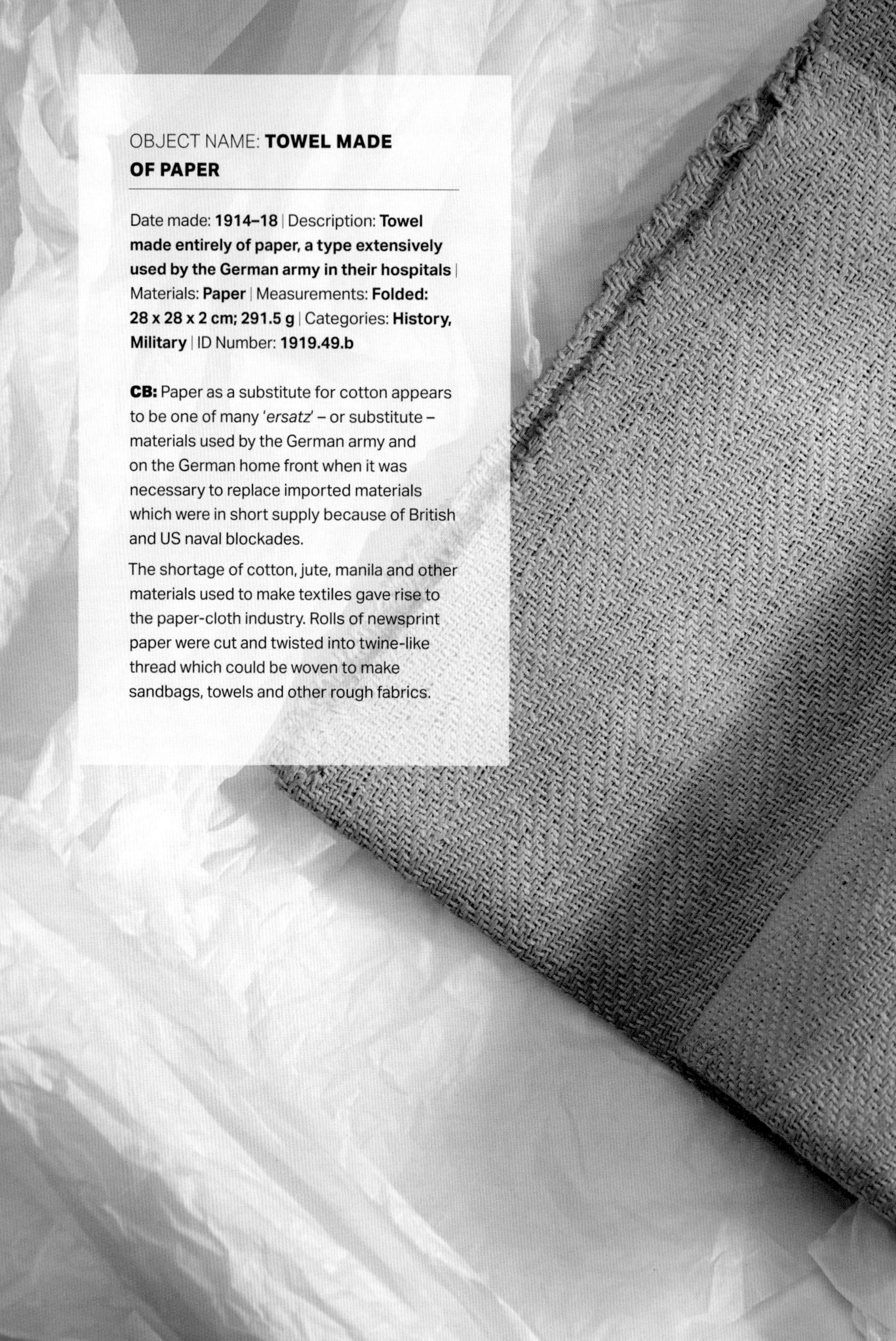

OBJECT NAME: **TOWEL MADE OF PAPER**

Date made: **1914–18** | Description: **Towel made entirely of paper, a type extensively used by the German army in their hospitals** | Materials: **Paper** | Measurements: **Folded: 28 x 28 x 2 cm; 291.5 g** | Categories: **History, Military** | ID Number: **1919.49.b**

CB: Paper as a substitute for cotton appears to be one of many 'ersatz' – or substitute – materials used by the German army and on the German home front when it was necessary to replace imported materials which were in short supply because of British and US naval blockades.

The shortage of cotton, jute, manila and other materials used to make textiles gave rise to the paper-cloth industry. Rolls of newsprint paper were cut and twisted into twine-like thread which could be woven to make sandbags, towels and other rough fabrics.

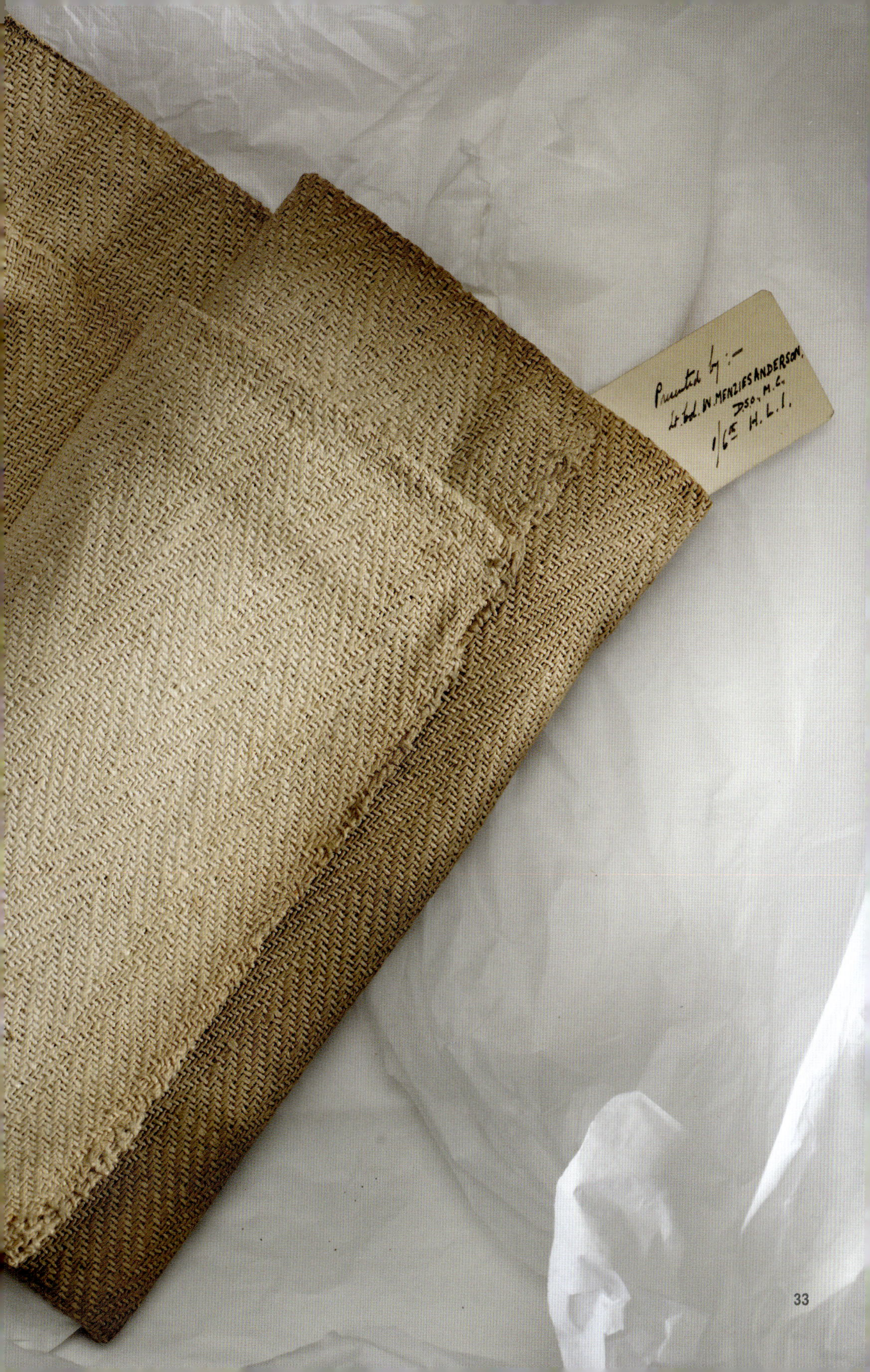
Presented by :-
Lt Col. W. MENZIES ANDERSON,
DSO, M.C.
1/6ᵗʰ H.L.I.

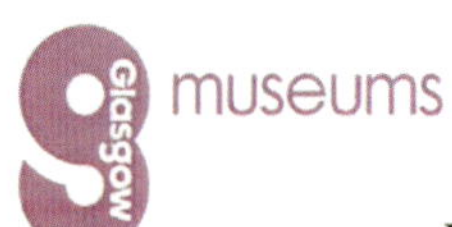

Preliminary Condition Report

Project/ Gallery		Story Title	
Registration Number E.1936.30.a		**Artist**	**Date**
Component German iron cross medal		**Title**	

Dimensions (mm):
H: 47   108 (cross + textile)
W: 45   38
D: 5   3
     cross   textile
Weight: kg

Examination Condition: visual macroscopic under storage lighting

Condition: fair
overall appears sound + stable. The textile is frayed at top and it appears that white yarn has worn away from weave.
Metal displays discolouration (tarnish)

Conservation Conversation:
Working with witnesses to the past

STEPHANIE DE ROEMER

A conservator's responsibilities concern the long-term preservation of our material heritage. They include the technical, practical examination and study of an object's physical state, the consideration of any associated construction techniques and technologies, writing condition assessments, making treatment recommendations, monitoring and maintaining environmental storage and display conditions, and advising on handling, packing and transport methods and practices. The role is comparable to that of a medical practitioner, as the conservator is concerned with the well-being of an object in order to make it accessible for study, research and appreciation by present and future generations.

The conservator seeks to determine an object's material composition, form and original nature, its function, who had owned and used it and the decay processes at work on it. The investigation of the physical and technical aspects will not only aid the diagnosis of the cause and extent of decay, but simultaneously provide a context and background into which to place the object for art historical or other interpretation.

Every object contains aspects that are definable as being of both aesthetic and historical interest. As a manifestation of consciously made and/or selected shape, colour and texture, created or chosen from a limitless range of possibilities by the maker or collector, an object is an aesthetic entity which provides an aesthetic experience for everyone who senses – sees, feels, touches, smells or hears – it. The aesthetic entity is that aspect of the object deliberately created by the artist or maker or chosen by the collector in order to communicate with the user or viewer and as such can be considered the physical manifestation of artistic intent.[1]

Alongside other conservation considerations, the conservator employs scientific and archaeological methodologies to identify, record and document aspects of the object's aesthetic entity and aspects that make it a historical 'document'. Now akin to a forensic scientist tasked to reconstruct conditions, events and environments from scientific observations and an examination of a body, the conservator employs a similar repertoire of scientific and analytical investigative techniques to retrieve evidence from an object to answer questions of 'why', 'how', 'by whom', 'when' and 'where' it was made, used, and/or altered.

The conservation encounter with an object as a witness to the past is a dynamic process of perception, observation, recording and decision-making with the objective of achieving the three aims of conservation: revelation, investigation and preservation (the RIP balance). Equipped with the parameters of the RIP balance (compass), a methodology of informed decision-making processes (coordinates), and a repertoire of treatment options (direction), the conservator embarks on a journey alongside the object, to 'listen to' and make audible the 'voices' of all those who have been involved with or encountered the object as part of their own and our shared narrative.

1. Chris Caple (2000) *Conservation Skills: Judgement, Method and Decision Making*, London, Routledge, p.36.

◐ A condition report written by Stephanie de Roemer for the German Iron Cross medal (p.37), shown at the *Doubtful Occasion* symposium.

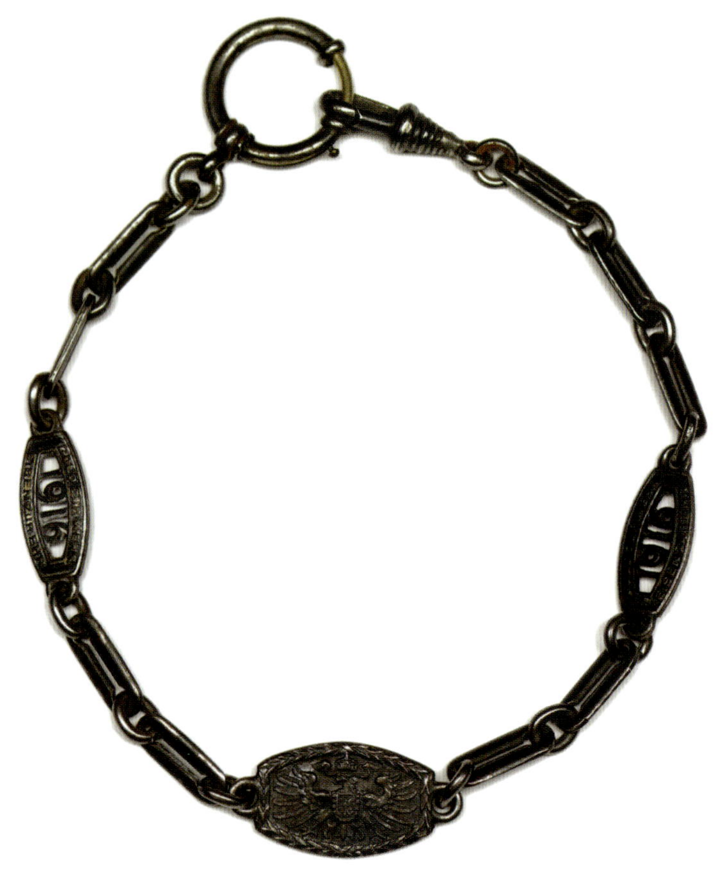

OBJECT NAME: **IRON JEWELLERY – WATCH CHAIN**

Date made: **About 1916** | Place Made: **Germany** | Description: **Watch chain with a centre link of a double-headed German eagle inscribed *'GOLD ZUR WEHR'* / 1916 / *'EISEN ZUR EHR'* ('GOLD FOR DEFENCE' / 1916 / 'IRON FOR HONOUR')** | Materials: **Cast iron** | Measurements: **Overall: 15.5 x 2.2 x 0.5 cm; Length when unclasped: 29.7 cm; Bolt ring: 2 cm; 21 g** | Categories: **History, Jewellery** | ID Number: **E.1976.1.328**

CB: The voluntary giving of gold for the war effort began in Prussia in the early nineteenth century with iron jewellery – inscribed *'Gold gab ich für Eisen'* ('I gave gold for iron'), or *'Für das Wohl des Vaterlands'* ('For the Welfare of our Fatherland') – given in exchange for gold and silver jewellery donated by citizens.

Germany had a strong link to iron as a wartime metal, both literally and metaphorically: 'iron rations' was the name given to the preserved food carried in his pack by a soldier in the field for times of emergency; it could only be eaten after he had been on half, third and quarter rations, and when the order was given by a commanding officer.

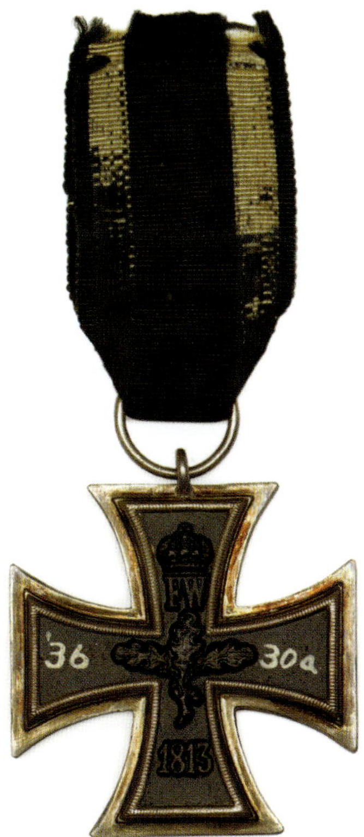

OBJECT NAME: **GERMAN IRON CROSS MEDAL**

Date made: **About 1914–18** | Place Made: **Germany (place associated)** | Description: **German Iron Cross medal: black cross with silver outline and black ribbon with two white stripes; obverse has a crown over 'W' over '1914'; reverse has a crown over oak leaves over '1813'** | Materials: **Iron, silver, cotton** | Measurements: **Overall: 10.4 x 4.3 x 0.6 cm; 20 g** | Categories: **Military, Numismatics** | ID Number: **E.1936.30.a**

CB: The Prussian Royal Foundry, which made German iron jewellery, also produced the Iron Cross, the German medal of honour awarded in various conflicts between 1813 and 1945, with some small changes in design occurring during that time. Adolf Hitler was awarded the Iron Cross Second Class in 1914 and the Iron Cross First Class in 1918; the awarding of the First Class Iron Cross was recommended by Lieutenant Hugo Gutmann, a Jewish adjutant in the List Regiment. In 1957 the West German government authorized a replacement World War II Iron Cross, with an oak leaf cluster in place of the swastika.

The Train Starts – it Stops – it Starts Again –

CHRIS DORSETT

For five years I shared my daily train to Newcastle with two geneticists who enthused about the difficulties of researching the human genome. I would respond with stories about working in an art school, often describing the challenge of pursuing contemporary art practices within the museum environment – my own interest as an artist-curator. Curiously, we found ourselves debating complementary ideas.

It turns out that a sizeable segment of the clustered genetic material known as a genome is inactive and we speculated that these 'non-coding' elements were not simply the junk-like residue of past DNA activity, as was then the prevailing view. Rather, my fellow commuters were of the opinion, now more widely favoured, that DNA code is active precisely because its components sit in contrast to a surrounding surface that could be code but is no longer operative. In this way biological information becomes an effective signal. 'Junk DNA turns out not to be junk at all', said one of the geneticists. Well, yes, and when it comes to the momentum of contemporary cultural life perhaps knowing that museum collections are kept in storerooms is enough to keep cultural messages 'live'.

Remember that these conversations took place on a commuter train which, like the on–off signals of biological code, started and stopped and started again all the way to its destination. This experience transformed my thinking about the interface between contemporary art and our museum culture. As a result, when Christine Borland knew that many of the delegates attending the symposium *Doubtful Occasion* would travel by train to Glasgow Museums Resource Centre, she saw an opportunity for a similar en route debate about the storage of the City's collection of World War I material. This she invited me to lead.

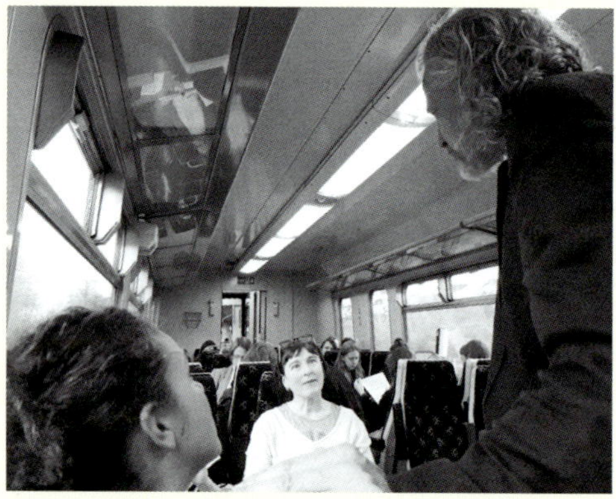

Once we had left Glasgow Central Station, I quoted a story told by the French philosopher Bruno Latour in an essay called 'Trains of Thought'.[1] He describes two twins, one of whom travelled by rail in order to attend a conference. We are told that this twin, twin one, sat quietly in a comfortable carriage and read a newspaper, paying no attention to the many places passed by the speeding vehicle. Indeed, the landscape outside the window made less of an impact on him than the projected images he would later view at the conference. On arrival virtually no trace of the twin's journey remained: some clothing

may have been creased, but, overall, what persisted were his thoughts and reflections on the articles he had perused in the newspaper.

In contrast, twin two sets off through dense jungle, cutting a path with a hatchet along a trail that was barely visible. This twin sweats profusely as each metre of pathway is gained. Cuts and bruises proliferate because, when you proceed like this traces are left over the entire body. Furthermore, as Latour points out, twin two suffers amongst other suffering bodies. The habitat which is traversed is full of creatures and plants that have competing needs. To make any kind of path must involve conflicting attempts to survive. There is no way that twin two can forget this excruciating journey.

The contrasting experiences of the two siblings draws attention to the way in which the contemporary world likes to conceal the effort involved in all transformational actions. For example, twin two is bodily changed by the journey undertaken, and ages much more than twin one. It would take a strike by the railway company's employees to make twin one even vaguely aware of what it cost the second twin to move a few feet. Latour puts it dramatically – someone travelling comfortably by train would have to accidentally fall out of the carriage to achieve a comparable sense of environmental engagement.

This was, I proposed to the delegates, the kind of thought that had the power to transform a suburban train journey to Glasgow Museums Resource Centre. No one travelling to the symposium should think themselves unaffected by the ongoing life of objects from World War I just because they have been in storage for a hundred years. Like an artist negotiating a dauntingly inert medium or process, our contact with historic material outside the context of exhibition display would be, in the first instance at least, a provocatively pathless prospect. But the two geneticists thought that pathlessness, in providing the necessary background noise for the active DNA signals to be read, galvanized the passage of information across the generations. And so, whilst nobody would have wanted any delegates to physically fall off the 9.27am train to Nitshill, it seemed appropriate that once we had alighted at the station our visit to the museum stores should be conducted more in the spirit of twin two than twin one.

1. Bruno Latour (1997) 'Trains of Thought: Piaget, Formalism, and the Fifth Dimension', in *Common Knowledge*, Winter 1997, Vol. 6, no. 3, pp.170 – 91.

2. Chris Dorsett (2013) 'trainslidingtalk', projection piece for *Extraordinary Renditions: the cultural negotiation of science*, Gateshead: BALTIC Centre for Contemporary Art, 2013.

◗ Chris Dorsett distributing text to be read by *Doubtful Occasion* participants on their train journey to Glasgow Museums Resource Centre.

Description: **Three mule hooves, from the Battle of Cambrai, France** | Materials: **Hoof, metal** | Measurements: **Largest hoof: 6.5 x 9.5 x 12 cm; Middle hoof: 7.5 x 7 x 10.6 cm; Smallest hoof: 7.1 x 6.5 x 10.6 cm** | Categories: **History, Natural History** | ID Number: **TEMP.16393**

CB: During World War I, the British Army purchased a large number of mules from the United States of America. Because of its stamina, the mule was better suited for use at the Front than the horse; both were used to move ammunitions and general supplies and as ambulances. By the final year of the war, the British army owned 213,000 mules.

These three hooves have distinct differences in size, suggesting they are not from the same animal; mules can vary considerably in size depending on the parents. One of the metal shoes has a hole pierced through the base. The animal wearing it may have been brought down by a caltrop – an antipersonnel weapon comprising four iron spikes, one of which always remains facing up when thrown (there are several caltrops in storage at GMRC).

I have read anecdotes suggesting that, in order to claim compensation, a hoof needed to be removed as a form of proof when an animal died, which could be the case for these examples.

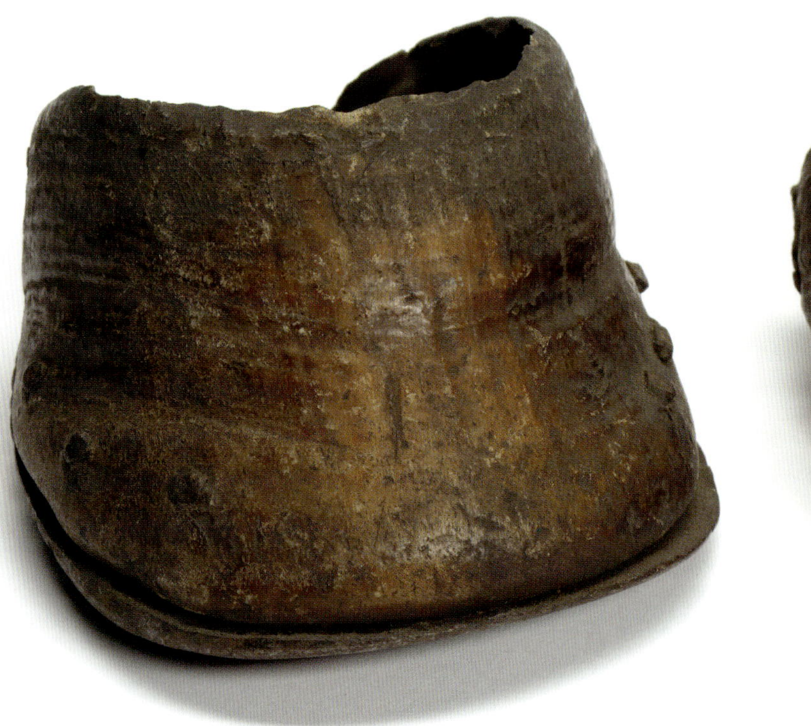

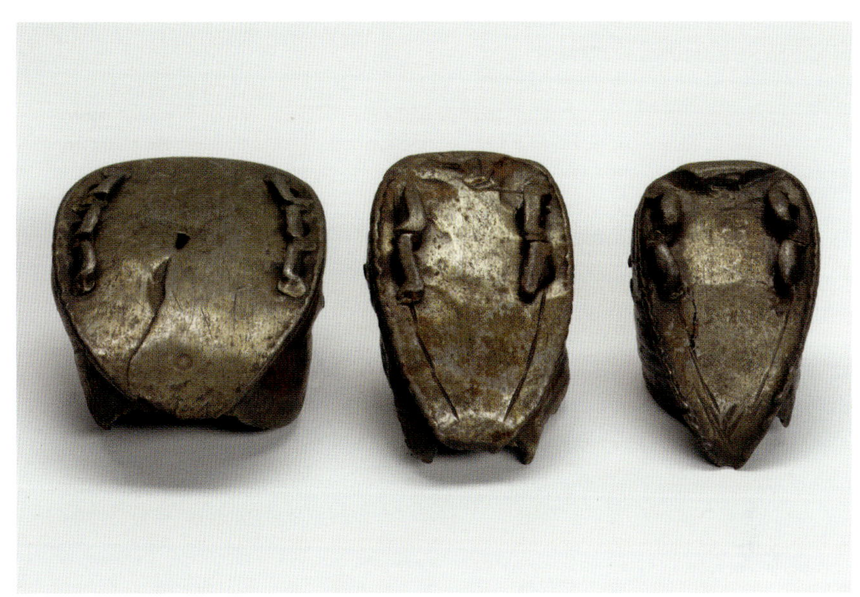

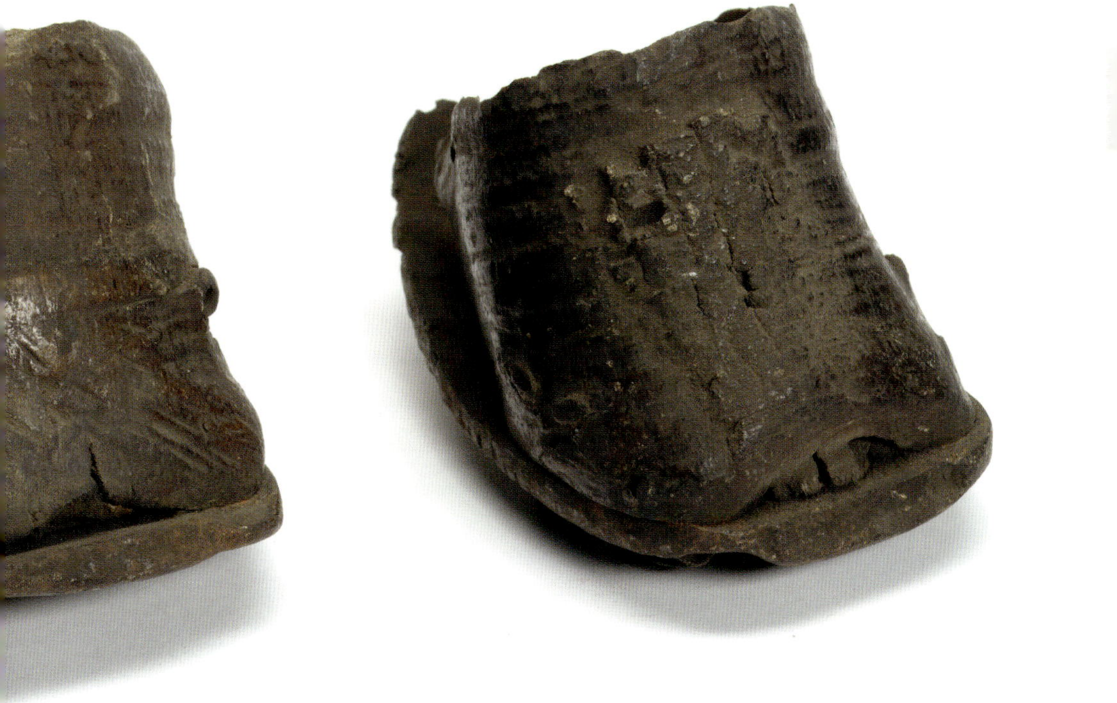

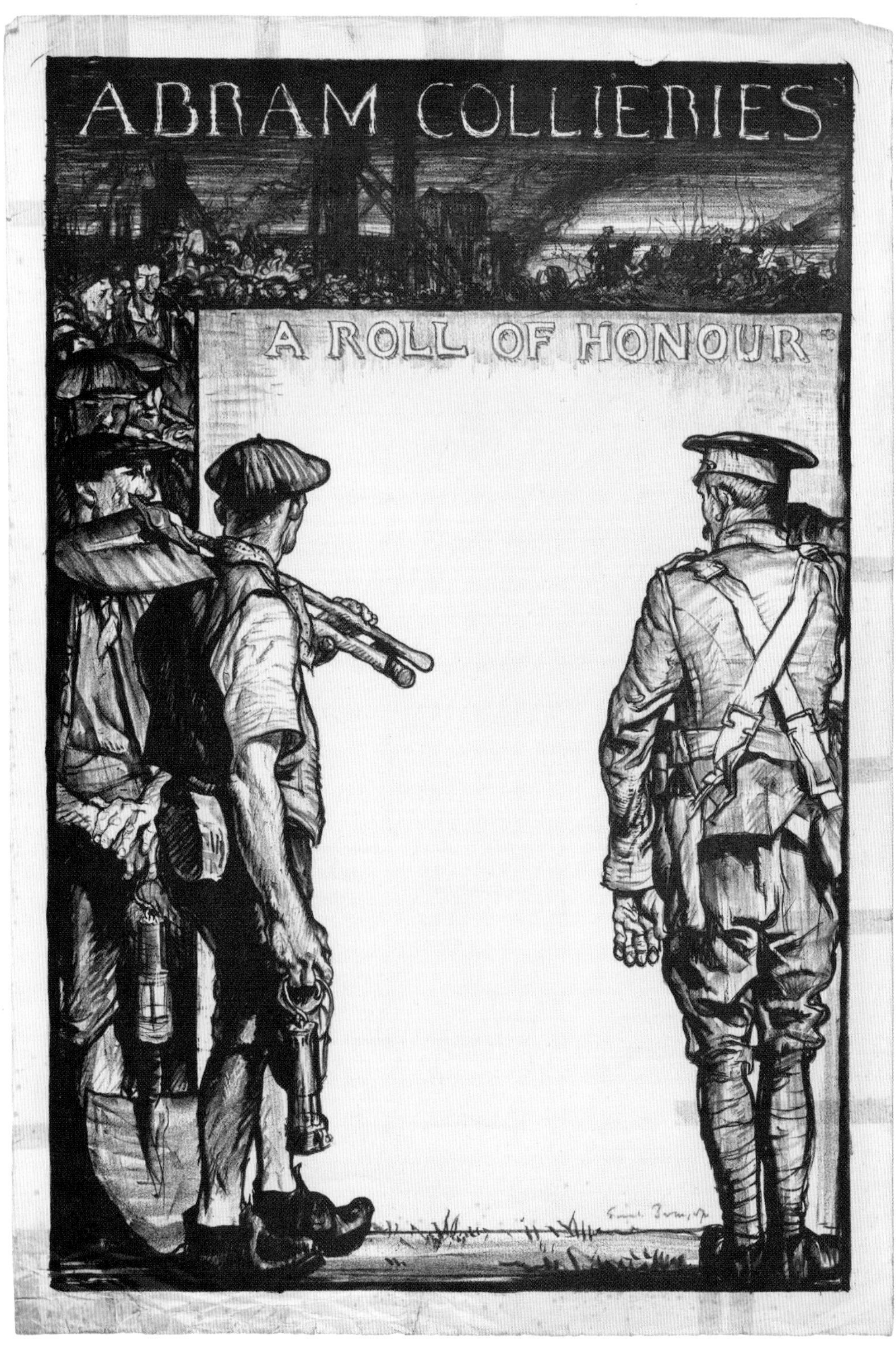

ABRAM COLLIERIES
A ROLL OF HONOUR

OBJECT NAME: **ROLL OF HONOUR** |
TITLE: **A ROLL OF HONOUR:
ABRAM COLLIERIES**

Date made: **About 1916** | Maker: **Sir Frank
Brangwyn (1867–1956, British)** | Place
Made: **London** | Description: **World War I
roll of honour created for Abram Colliery,
near Wigan. The central space is left
blank for names. On the left miners with
lamps and equipment pay their tributes
and on the right an officer salutes fallen
comrades. Pithead winding gear and a
slag heap at the top left and soldiers on
the front line at the top right.** | Materials:
Lithograph on paper | Measurements:
Unframed: 77 x 51.8 cm | Category: **Prints** |
ID Number: **PR.1944.2.h**

CB: This blank roll of honour was donated
to Glasgow Museums by artist Frank
Brangwyn in 1944.

From an index of all local men and women
who died during World War I, Wigan
Archives and Local Studies has been able
to find twenty names listed under Abram
Colliery; these names could potentially
have been inscribed on the colliery's roll
of honour, filling the blank space.

OBJECT NAME: **INDENTIFICATION
DISC FOR A GERMAN SOLDIER**

Date made: **about 1914–18** | Place Made:
Germany (place of manufacture) |
Description: **Identification disc for Martin
Vicktor, inscribed with his date and
place of birth: 6–8–99 (6 August 1899),
Murschnitz, near Sonneberg** | Materials:
Metal | Measurements: **5 x 6.5 x 0.1 cm;
13g** | Categories: **History, Military** |
ID Number: **1926.68.s**

CB: Army Order 287 of September 1916
required the British Army to provide all
soldiers with two official tags, commonly
referred to as 'dog tags'. There were four
types of official identification discs used
by German soldiers; in 1916 they started
using the kind of disc that can be broken
in two, one part to be left with the body,
the other used as an identification record
for notifications.

Items taken from the dead bodies of
the enemy were widely accepted by
soldiers as a valid form of trophy. It is clear
that the desire to acquire trophies was
endemic. Indeed, some officers evidently
perceived it as a threat to discipline. In
April 1917, the commanding officer of
the 15th Durham Light Infantry included
the following warning in his operational
orders: 'Many instances have accrued of
men searching for souvenirs instead of
instantly consolidating their position and
in consequence being unready to meet the
enemy's counter attack. It is therefore to be
distinctly understood that any officer, NCO
or man in possession of any such souvenir,
will be tried by court martial.'

From *Contested Objects: Material
Memories of the Great War*[1]

1. Nicolas J Saunders and Paul Cornish, eds
(2009) *Contested Objects: Material Memories
of the Great War*, Oxford, Routledge

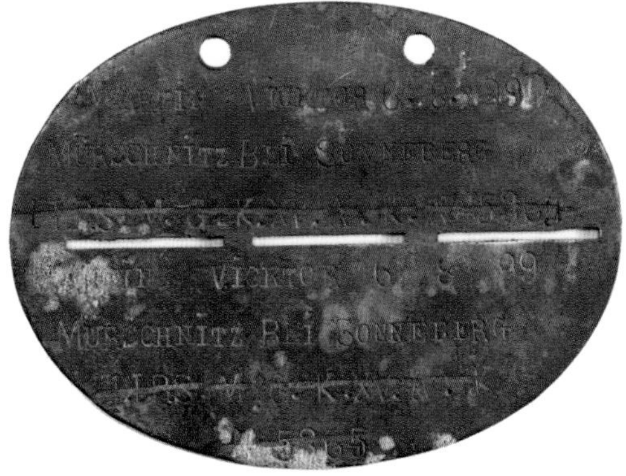

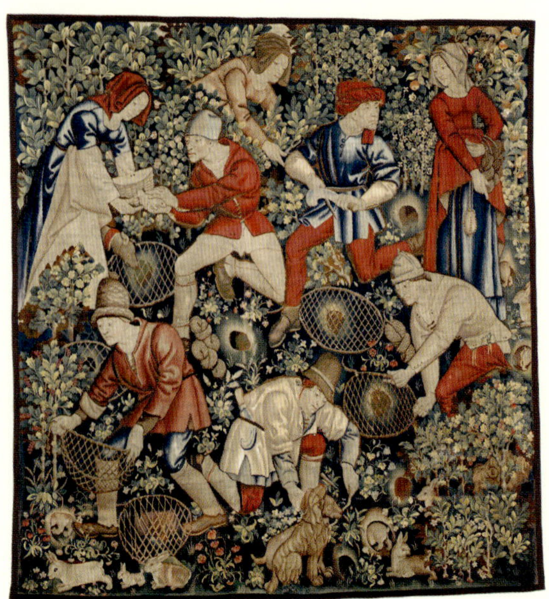

⬤ ***Peasants Preparing to Hunt Rabbits with Ferrets,*** tapestry
woven in the Southern Netherlands, about 1470–90, 323 x 300 cm,
gifted by Sir William and Lady Burrell to the City of Glasgow, 1944,
accession no. 46.56.

Thing Biographies and Missingness

BETTINA BILDHAUER

Things have their stories, too. Their materials come from somewhere; they are made or grow into something; they can be bought, stolen, loved, lost, broken, discarded, even collected in a museum. We humans tend to see the world from our perspective, as made up of humans' lives, intentions, actions, relationships and wars. But what would the story of World War I look like from the perspective of its bullets, its amulets, its booty, medals, warships, books, towels?

Things are not passive objects as opposed to active human subjects. It is an illusion that they do nothing and we do everything, intentionally, consciously, rationally. This goes not just for the amulets that some soldiers carried. Things make a difference in the course of some other agent's action, as the philosopher and sociologist Bruno Latour's famous definition of the agency of things has it.[1] What would the story of World War I be without bombs, uniforms, ambulances, telephones? Glasgow Museums' World War I collection includes a French grammar book, damaged by gunfire, which was found in a dugout at Givenchy – could this have saved a soldier's life?

Boxes for storing soldiers' amulets, hollow green glass balls used to float torpedo nets, torpedo nets full of holes: emptiness can be as essential to the functioning of a thing as the solid components of cardboard, glass and rope. The whole point of a box is to be an empty container for something else; glass balls only float because their empty cavity is filled with air; many nets only work because their large meshes make them invisible and stretchable.

And these vacancies attract their own stories. Some of the boxes are now empty, but still meticulously labelled with descriptions of charms, including an 'I say nothing' monkey. Things can speak to us, even in German, through the noiseless language of inscription, like the Berlin iron jewellery that replaced family gold jewellery donated to the war effort: '*Gold zur Wehr, Eisen zur Ehr*' ('Gold for Defence, Iron for Honour'). When things are held in a museum, their labels are meant to speak for them. But are the stories of provenance that the labels tell true, or made up by clever dealers of souvenirs of suffering, or do the words cover empty boxes?

The emptiness inside glass balls, which makes them bob up in water, is filled with witches or spirits by the imagination. Nets also have long had stories attached to them, such as of the Roman god Vulcan forging a steel mosquito net so fine that his wife Venus could not see it and got trapped in it with her lover in bed. Glasgow Museums has in its collection a medieval tapestry showing the preparations for a rabbit hunt with nets: the nets are being spread over the rabbit holes so that the rabbits, chased out of their warrens by ferrets, will get trapped when trying to escape. The strings of the net are represented by the silk and wool threads of the tapestry, as are the holes in the net. Through the holes one sees more holes – the rabbit holes – highlighted by halos of bright colours, creating a sense of anticipation, of future filling.

Missing things are always productive: they invite stories and explanations that put them centre stage. We notice things the most when they are missing, broken, lost, when they resist being used as objects by us subjects. As the literary historian Michael Niehaus writes, 'A wandering thing is most immediately the subject of a story [...] if it is nobody's object, if it is lost or forgotten and needs to be found again.'[2]

1. Bruno Latour (2005) *Reassembling the Social: An Introduction to Actor-Network Theory*, Oxford, Clarendon, p.71.

2. Michael Niehaus (2009) *Das Buch der wandernden Dinge: Vom Ring des Polykrates bis zum entwendeten Brief*, Munich, Hanser, p.394 (extract translated by Bettina Bildhauer).

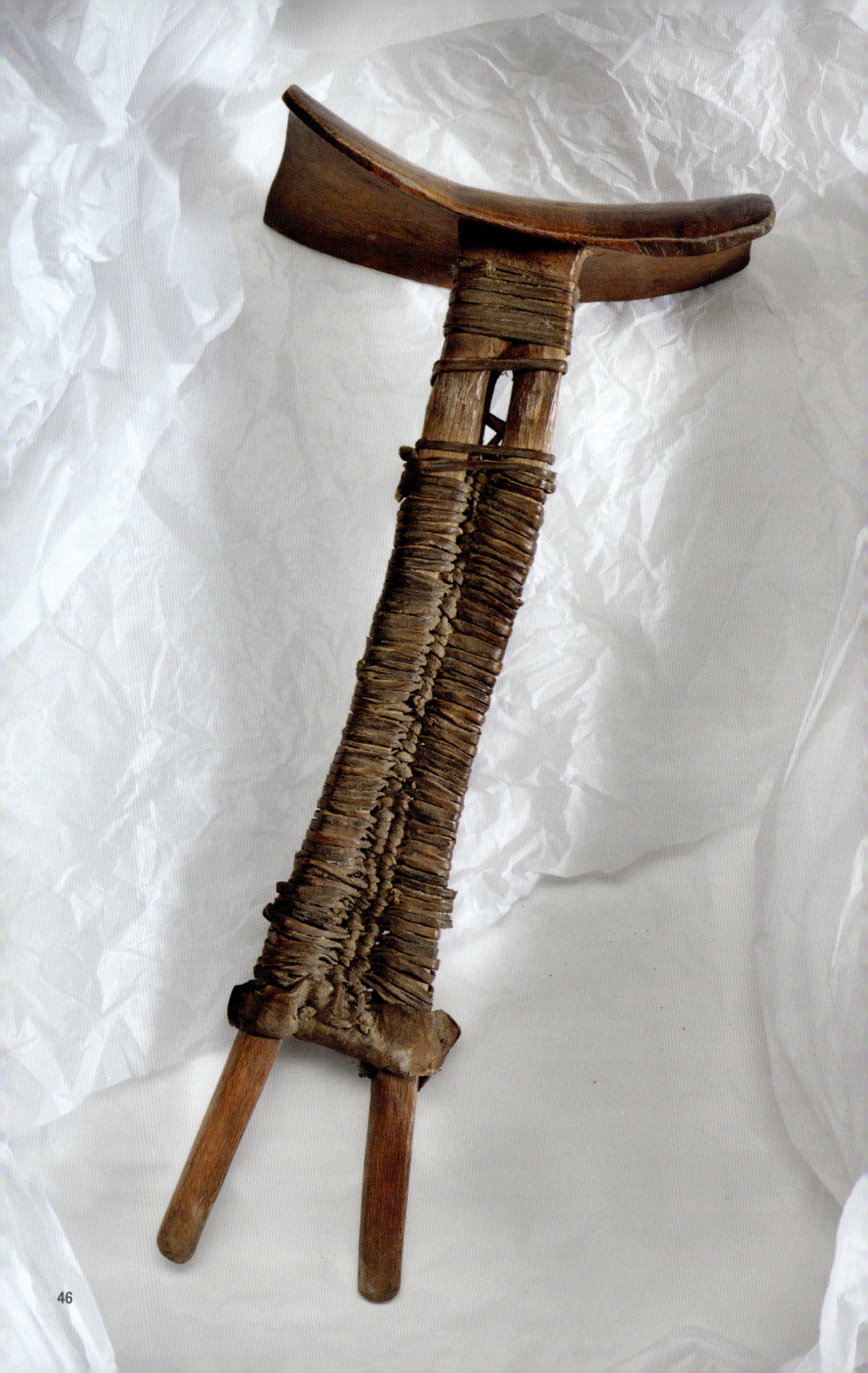

Date made: **Early 20th century** | Culture: **Suk-Pokot or Karamojong-Turkana** | Place Made: **Africa, East Africa, Uganda, Karamoja Region (place associated); East Africa, NW Kenya (place associated)** | Description: **Headrest, carved from one piece of wood, saddle-shaped top with two long spokes as stem, band with hide, thong lashings; used both as a stool and a headrest by nomadic pastoralists** | Materials: **Wood, hide** | Measurements: **32 x 13.8 x 6.3 cm** | Categories: **World Cultures, Furniture** | ID Number: **ETHNN.1407**

CB: Although the exact provenance is uncertain, the piece is thought to have been collected in East Africa around the time of World War I.

I wonder whether the tiny spider's web in the joint between the two wooden legs and the leather thong was spun in East Africa, on the journey back to Scotland with its collector, in the collector's house or during the time the headrest has been with Glasgow Museums (from 1985).

The form of the object as a support mechanism made me think of the structure of prosthesis developed during World War I, both more formally devised supports (like the revolutionary Erskine Leg – a prosthetic limb designed and pioneered by Sir William Macewen, co-founder of the hospital and Regius Professor of Surgery at the University of Glasgow[1]) and also informal improvised or experimental ones.

1. www.gla.ac.uk/news/archiveofnews/2015/november headline_433195_en.html (accessed 14 August 2018)

Descriptions: **Sample of moss used to stuff ambulance pillows, contained in a glass-topped box; two pillows of cotton stuffed with moss** | Materials: *Sphagnum* **moss; cotton,** *Sphagnum* **moss** | Measurements: **Sample box: 13 x 6 x 8 cm; 102.5 g; Each pillow: 14 x 22 x 3 cm; 17 g** | Categories: **History, Textiles** | ID Number: **TEMP.16217.13** and **TEMP.16217.14**

CB: Millions of wound dressings made from sphagnum moss – commonly known as bog moss – were used during World War I. When dried, sphagnum can absorb up to twenty times its own volume of liquids, and it acts as a mild antiseptic. The gathering, drying and cleaning of sphagnum was carried out on the home front by women, children, those not drafted due to age or fitness and by imprisoned conscientious objectors. The whole enterprise might never have started and the benefits of sphagnum might have remained unrealized by the Allies if it had not been for the combined efforts of Lieutenant Colonel Charles Walker Cathcart, an Edinburgh surgeon, and his friend Professor Isaac Bayley Balfour, then Regius Keeper of the Royal Botanic Garden, Edinburgh, who brought its properties to public and official attention at the beginning of the war.

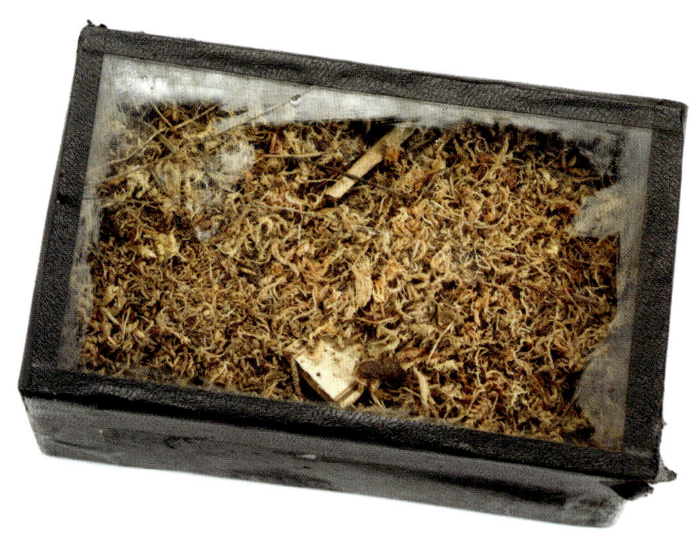

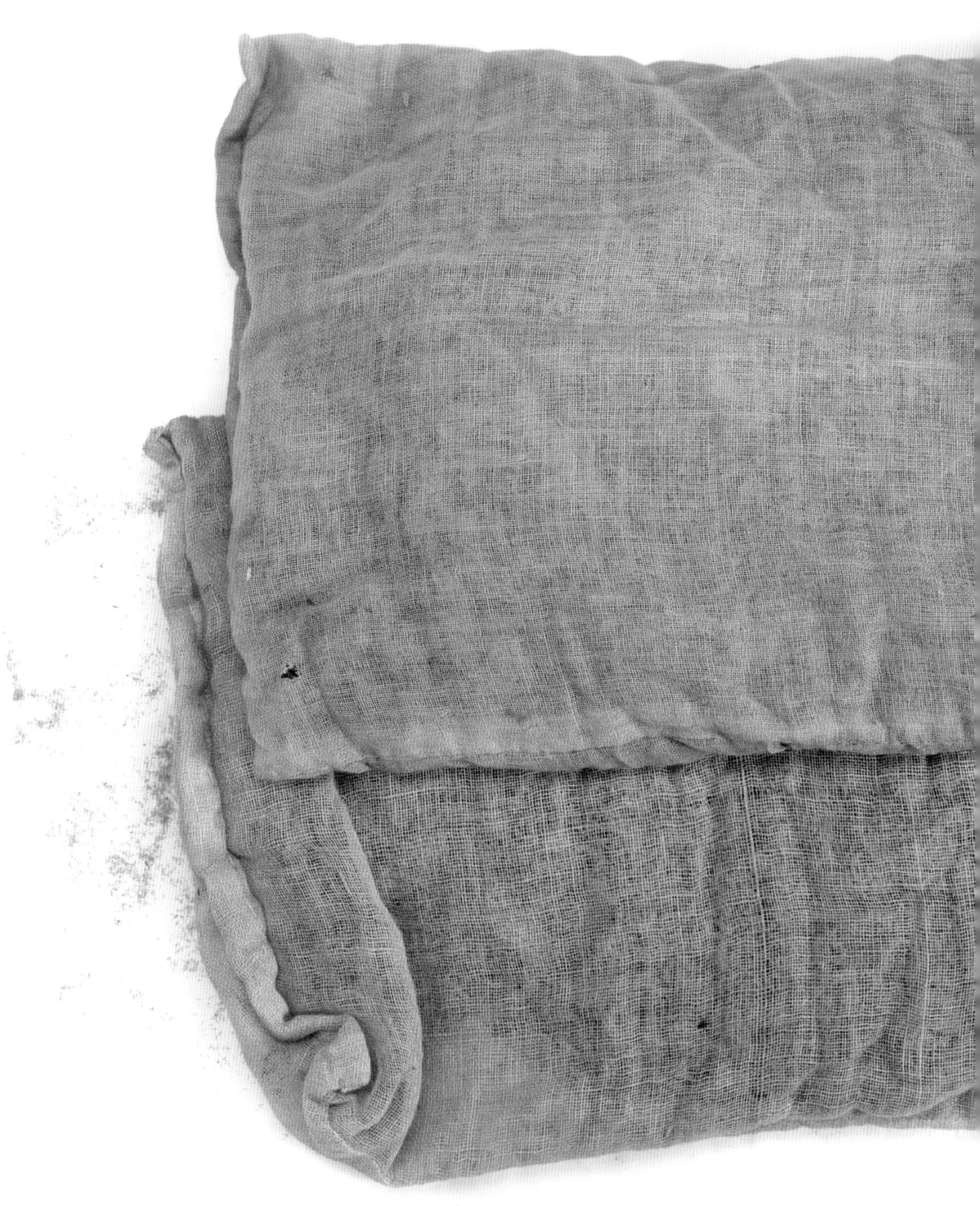

Date made: **Possibly about 1914–18** | Description: **Float, green glass, ball shaped with label stuck to it, reading 'For suspending torpedo nets during the Great War 1914–18, found on the Coldingham Shore, near St Abbs, Berwickshire'. 1 of 2.** | Materials: **Glass** | Measurements: **13 cm in diameter** | Category: **Military** | ID Number: **AANN.279.2**

CB: Floating glass buoys became associated with witches during witch-hunts in the late 17th century. In a like manner to the rule of trial by water – which was based on the idea that if someone suspected of witchcraft floated in water, rather than sank, it was proof of his or her guilt – these heavy glass fishing floats, all tied up in a net, could not be made to sink, perhaps contributing to their nickname: 'witch balls'.

Superstitious sailors valued the talismanic powers of the witch balls in protecting their homes. According to folk tales, witch balls would entice evil spirits away from inside the homes with their bright colours, so they were displayed on outside window ledges. Another tradition holds that the reflective qualities of witch balls prevented a witch from entering a room, because it would betray their lack of a reflection.

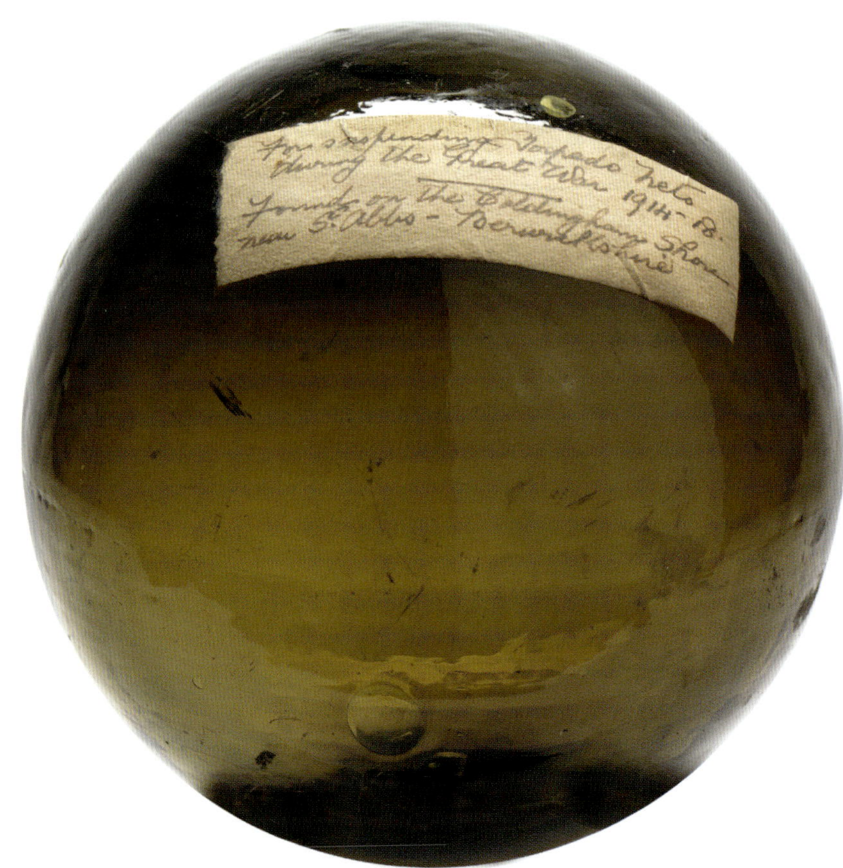

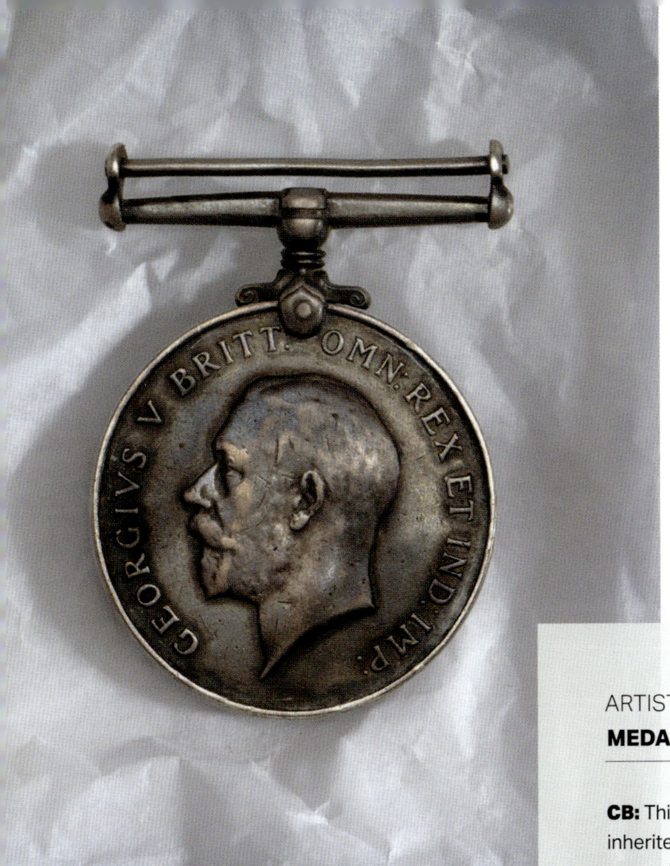

CB: This is an ordinary service medal, inherited from my grandfather, of which some six and a half million were issued after the end of World War I. It's made of bronze, which you would never know as it is completely black, and is missing its ribbon. I asked my mother how it had got in such a state, very clearly not treasured. She told me that my grandmother (maybe as a clever tactic to draw fire?) would leave it on the mantelpiece and that my grandad would later hurl it into the open fire when he got back from the pub on a Friday night. Next morning she would retrieve it from the grate and put it back on the mantelpiece, ready for Saturday night.

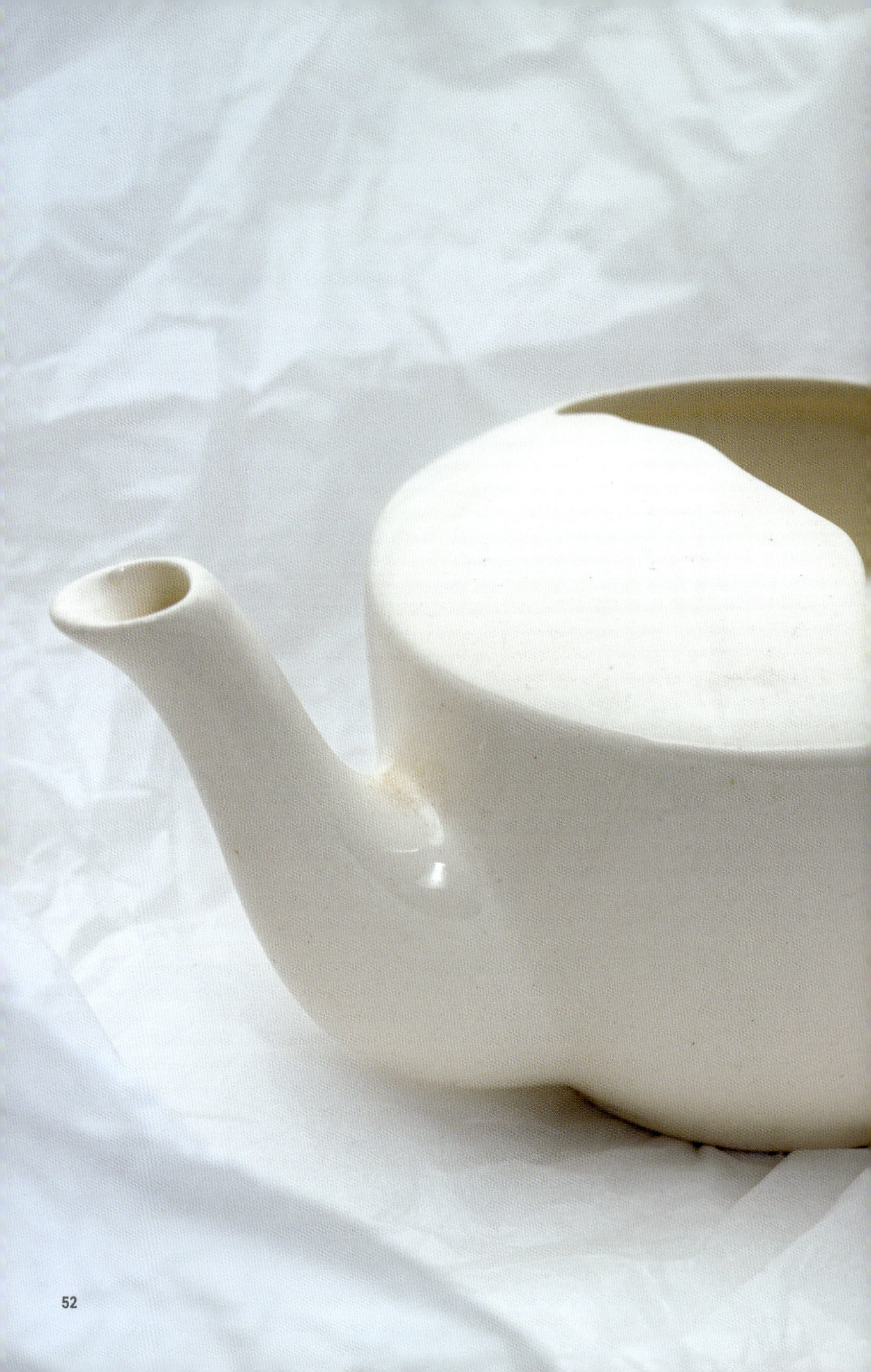

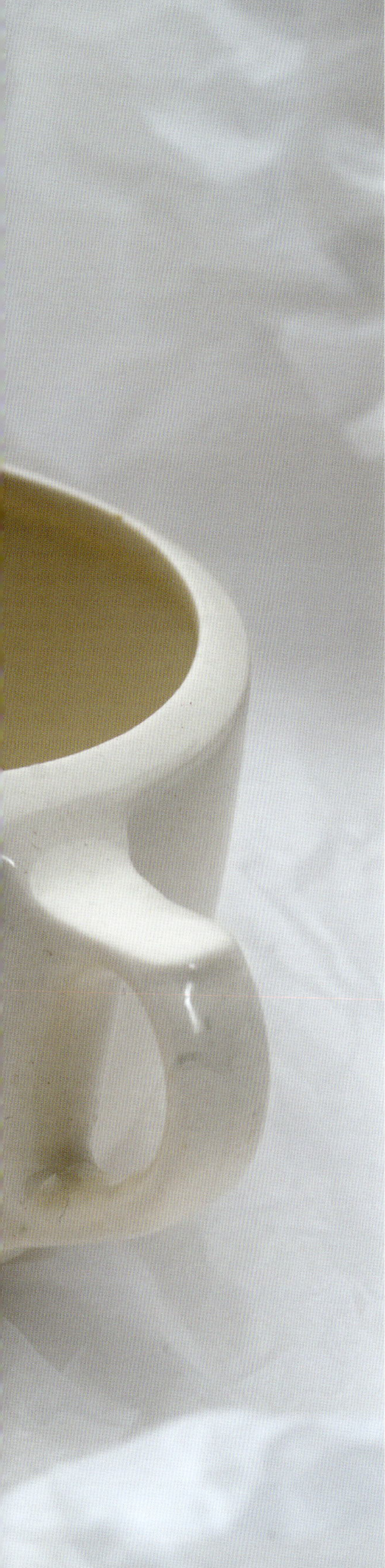

INVALID FEEDER CUP

CB: The ceramic cup is from the Open Museum's handling kit about World War I. The Open Museum is a part of Glasgow Museums – the team takes handling kits of objects to groups in the community. This feeder cup, therefore, can be held and its pouring function potentially demonstrated or re-enacted by facilitators or members of the public; it leads a very different existence than a similar object kept in storage.

Cups like this were widely used in nursing during World War I but had been in use at least since the Victorian period for patients confined to bed, who were unable to feed themselves – the cups allowed liquid food to be poured into their mouths. As well as its use in nursing the sick generally, and specifically the war-wounded in World War I, I have come across references to the use of invalid cups in the force-feeding of hunger-striking suffragettes between 1909 and 1914. The hunger strike, and the brutal forcible feeding that was the considered medical response – following the Government directive to ensure that the hunger strikers did not die – often left women seriously ill and seemingly less capable of resistance. Yet, the suffragettes were able to transform this most vulnerable state into a form of 'passive resistance' – a triumph of the individual in the face of overwhelming institutional power.

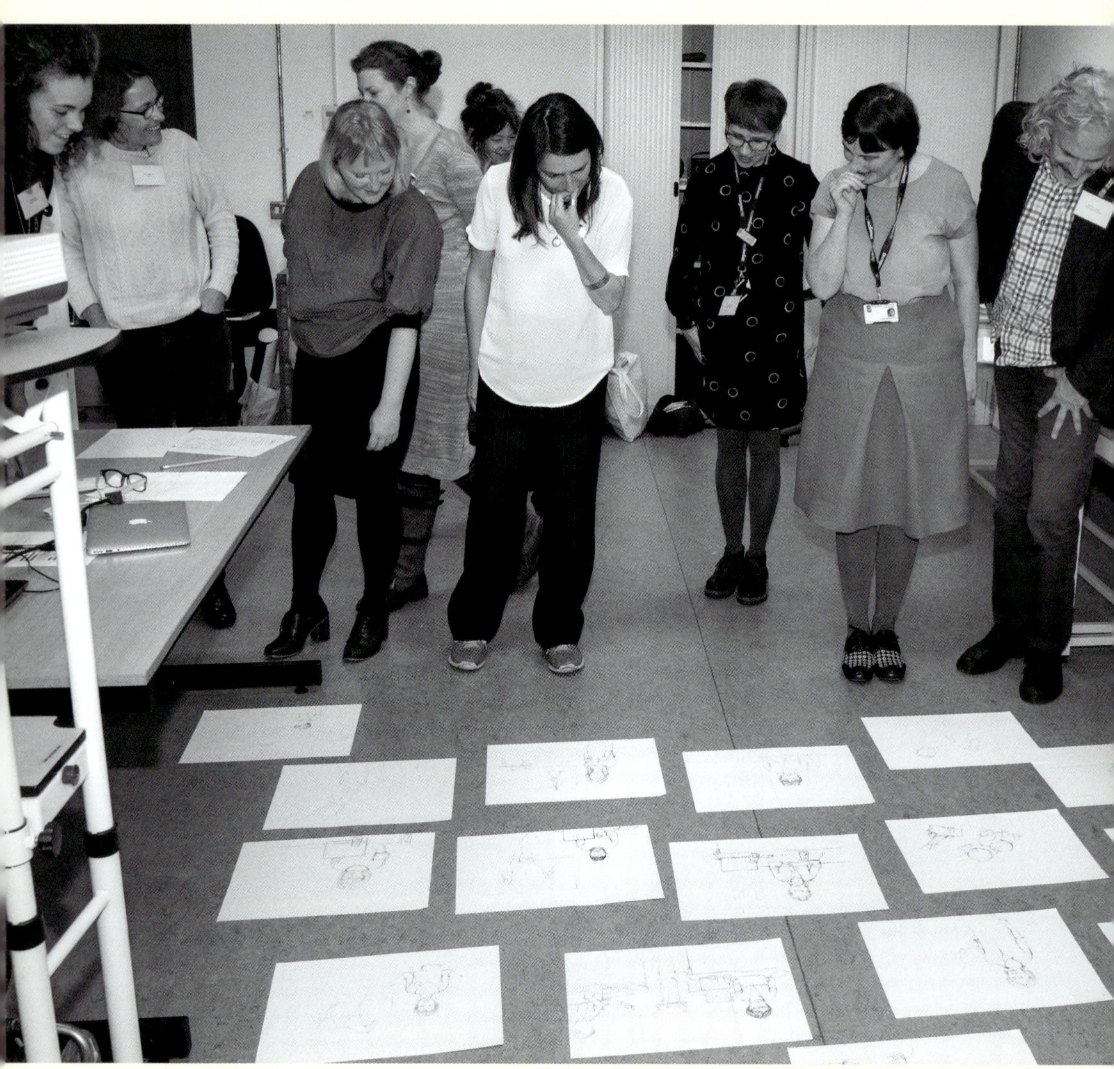

⬥ Participants at the *Doubtful Occasion* Symposium
looking at drawings by Birthe Jorgensen.

Doubtful: Glossary

DAISY LAFARGE

This glossary was composed during the *Doubtful Occasion* symposium, a day when artists, conservators and researchers from various disciplines were invited to share aspects of their own practice. At first these seemed disparate – varying from a discussion of non-coding DNA to the 'agentic' objects depicted in a certain medieval tapestry – but the day itself soon assembled a patchwork frame of reference. Unlikely pairings began to emerge between the objects and the presentations, stitched anarchically between descriptions entered on Mimsy (the collections management system used at Glasgow Museums) and the in-jokes and by-words that accumulated in the symposium's relaxed atmosphere.

The glossary's contents derive from poaching the day's chatter; to what extent it functions intelligibly outside of the symposium's context is unknown – the jokes are lost, the potency of a particular phrase or association impossible to gauge in retrospect. In this sense, the glossary enacts a mimetic solidarity with the World War I objects themselves, experienced by us as cut loose from their original contexts, which any amount of contextualization cannot reconcile them to, changed again by the circumstances of conservation, archiving and museum display. So the glossary's contents drift here, unanchored from the day they relate to, but with the hope – as on slow winter afternoons spent dawdling in museums – that some glint might catch the eye and resonate.

Absence: *spacingforpresence*

The interdependency of presence and absence
is long established, and dismissing something
as absent is often done through ignorance;
perhaps we don't yet have the tools to perceive
its presence, or grasp how it is bound up
with what we believe to be present. Here,
absence refers specifically to the non-
coding DNA discussed by Chris Dorsett
and the genetic scientists who share his
daily commute by train. Non-coding DNA,
sometimes called 'junk DNA', is scrambled
code attached to the 'pure' code that writes
us as genetic individuals. It was previously
understood as an accrual of generational waste;
more recently it has been discovered that this
is archived material, capable of reuse, waiting
to be stimulated by certain environmental
triggers. Non-coding DNA is in fact the space-
building material between the pure code, like
theindispensablespacesbetweenwords.

Drawings by Birthe Jorgensen of objects presented by
Christine Borland at the *Doubtful Occasion* symposium.

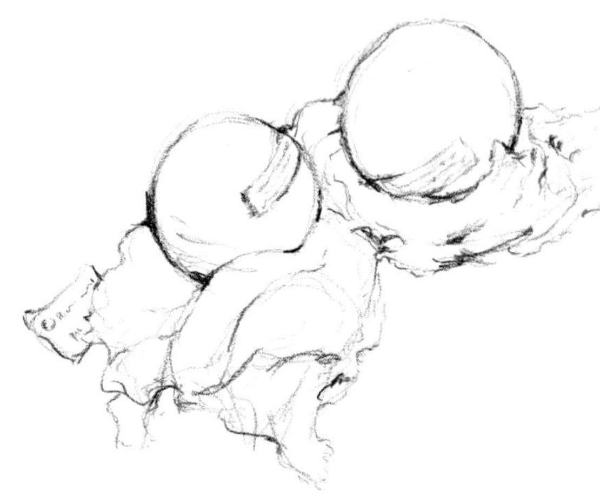

Assimilation: *where the spider spins its web*

Object: a handmade wooden headrest from East
Africa. Christine pointed out the remnants of a
spider's web woven between two sides of the
leather thong, and then raised the question of
where the web might have been spun. By a spider
in Africa? In Europe once it had made the journey
north? In Glasgow, during its conservation? Or
did the spinning happen in transit from Africa
to Europe, in the hold of a ship or plane? Each
possibility raises questions of identity and
assimilation – weaving oneself into a new culture –
and the latter, especially, of hybridity: what strange
ecology forms in the many-man's land through
which objects migrate? An entomologist might
be able to pin down the web's classification, but
we were content with its question left hanging,
imagining multiple points of origin.

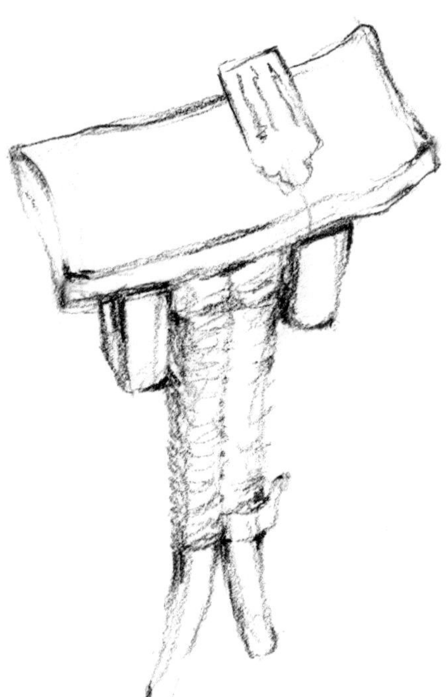

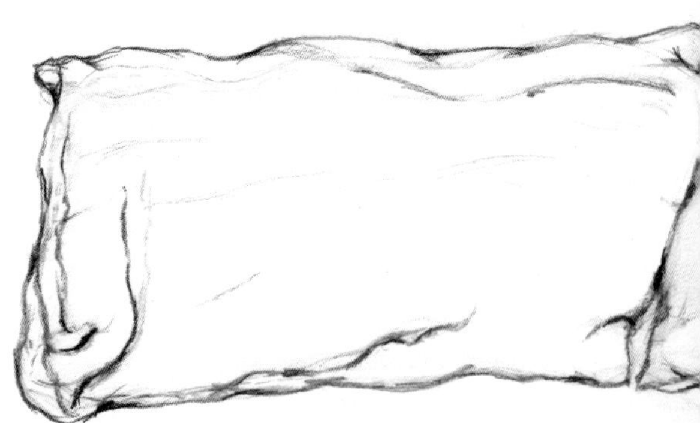

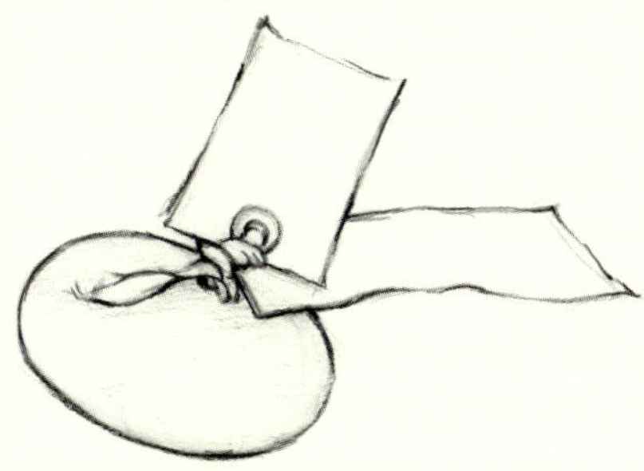

Ethics: *unidentified fluids on moss*

Object: a small, delicate-looking pillow, stuffed with sphagnum moss and used by ambulances that serviced the front line. Moss has antimicrobial and healing properties. It was gathered by women and children in Scotland and the thousand conscientious objectors imprisoned in Dartmoor, where there was even a moss depot for the pillows' production. This particular pillow, brown and frayed, was stained with 'unidentified fluids'. Likely human in origin, this fact troubles conservation ethics: how should the object be treated, and how does our relationship to it change, once we know it contains the material residue of a human life? Later in the day, Bettina Bildhauer posed a question that resonated: 'We have got used to animal rights, so why not object rights?' That we respect a pillow more for its proximity to human life – or death – suggests an acknowledgement, on some level, of the interwovenness of human, object and memory; it prompts a careful consideration of object ethics. Reading back, I find my notes from the day describe the pillow as 'the size of a child's face', perhaps an attempt at provoking my own object-empathy.

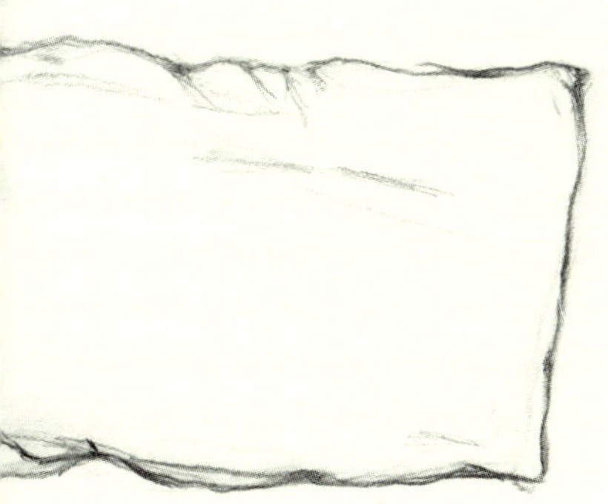

Freedom of movement: *'all movers are required to fill out an object movement form'*

Sleeves containing Object Movement Forms (OMFs) were pinned to the back of each door in GMRC's sprawl of storerooms. The fields on the forms include Object Description, ID, where the object is being moved from, and where it is moving to. This procedure makes an interesting companion to human movement: in addition to borders, states and citizenship, we also impose a scaled-down version of this order on objects, via classification.

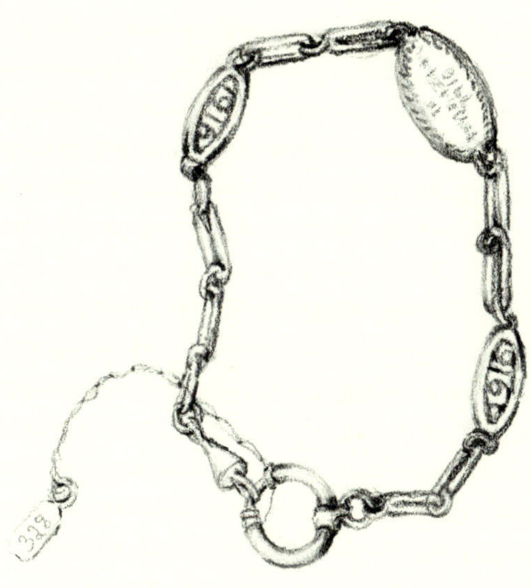

Hand grenade: *(verb) to obliterate an object with interpretation*

From a discussion about the interpretation of objects. Someone remarked: an object is not a hand grenade about to explode. Our encounters with objects are not always – nor should they be – vibrant with meaning. Sometimes the object just is, its 'real life' obscured to us, yet we should respect it all the same.

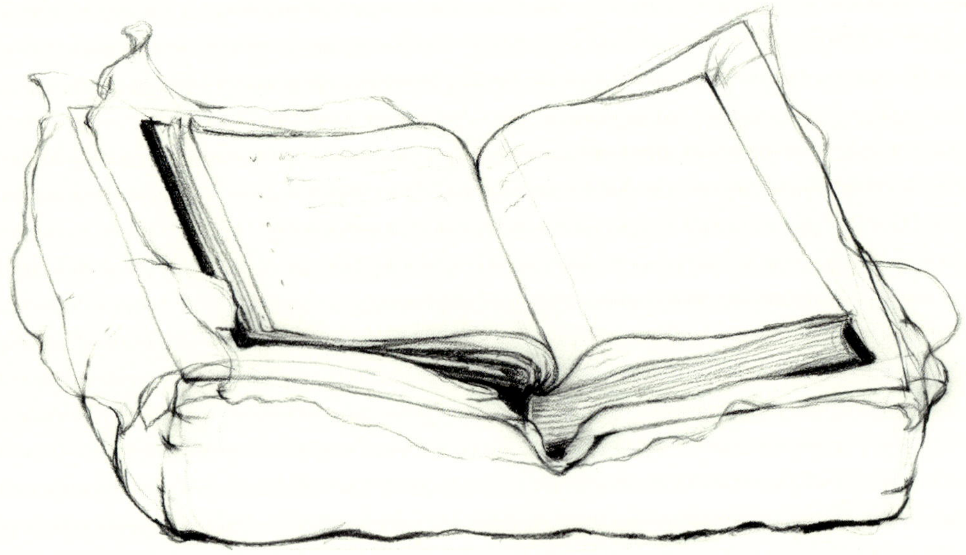

Punctuation: *the grammar of bullet-holes through tenses: past, perfect, and conditional*

Object: a French grammar book damaged by gunfire. A bluish green, worn cover; the holes look like the work of overambitious woodworm. Christine remarked that it seemed as if the book hadn't been opened since the holes were made; we speculated that its function was not located in its linguistic contents, but its physicality, taking a lethal hit for the person it belonged to. The holes form an alternative grammar, the language of impersonal violence. In his book *Camera Lucida*, the philosopher Roland Barthes discusses the 'punctum' of an image as that rare detail which overpowers the scene as a whole: 'that accident which pricks, bruises me', 'its mere presence changes my reading, that I am looking at a new photograph, marked in my eyes with a higher value.'[1] The holes are literally pricks and punctures, but they also overhaul the way we read – or are prevented from reading – the book.

1. Roland Barthes (1980), this edn translated by Richard Howard (1993) *Camera Lucida: Reflections on Photography*, London, Penguin Random House, p. 26–7.

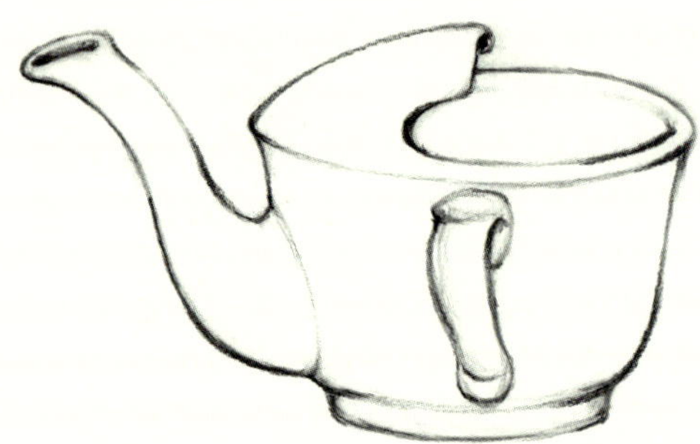

Reciprocity: *the silent care of an object for its keeper*

Watching a curator, conservator or collections assistant handle objects is like watching an exercise in more-than-human care. It has ritualistic, ceremonious aspects: the wearing of gloves, the percussion of tissue paper as the object is gently unwrapped and placed exactly on the table. There is also a reciprocity in these performative gestures; in their own way, the objects also care for their carers, preserving conservators, curators, academics and artists.

Retirement: *an object that's earned its pillow*

Each object brought out of the store and shown at the symposium rested on a soft white pillow. It seemed like a kind of care, or tenderness, or the object equivalent of a hospice: making the object comfortable now that it's no longer expected to 'function' in the outside world. This display feature was particularly striking in the case of the ambulance moss pillow: a cushion for a cushion.

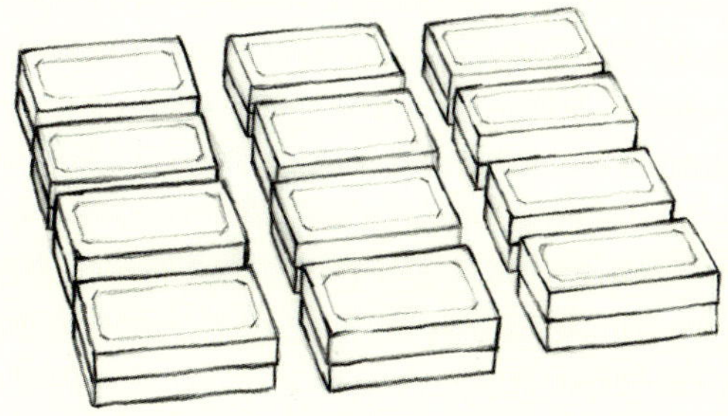

Wisdom: *never ask a direct question*

Indirectness and feigned ignorance were amongst the techniques of Edward Lovett, banker and folklorist who collected charms, amulets and other superstitious objects in early twentieth-century England. The material for his book *Magic in Modern London* (1925) was gleaned through a proto-qualitative style of research, using the pedestrian sources of commonplace gossip and rumour. He found that assuming a knowledgeable or inquisitive position would often make people shut down, and so he maintained a faux naivety to keep the anecdotes coming. The assumption of this role is an interesting one to compare to the artist in the archive, never asking direct, exacting questions of the objects, but 'skirting around the narrative' (Christine's phrase), to pick up on what might be whispered as an aside.

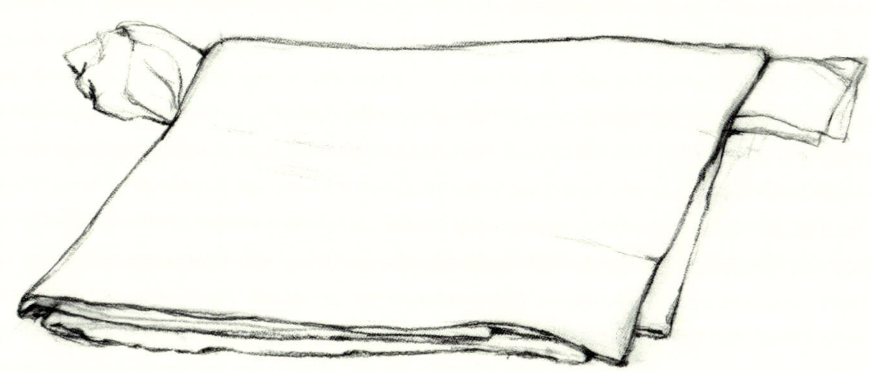

Drawings by Birthe Jorgensen of objects presented by Christine Borland at the *Doubtful Occasion* symposium.

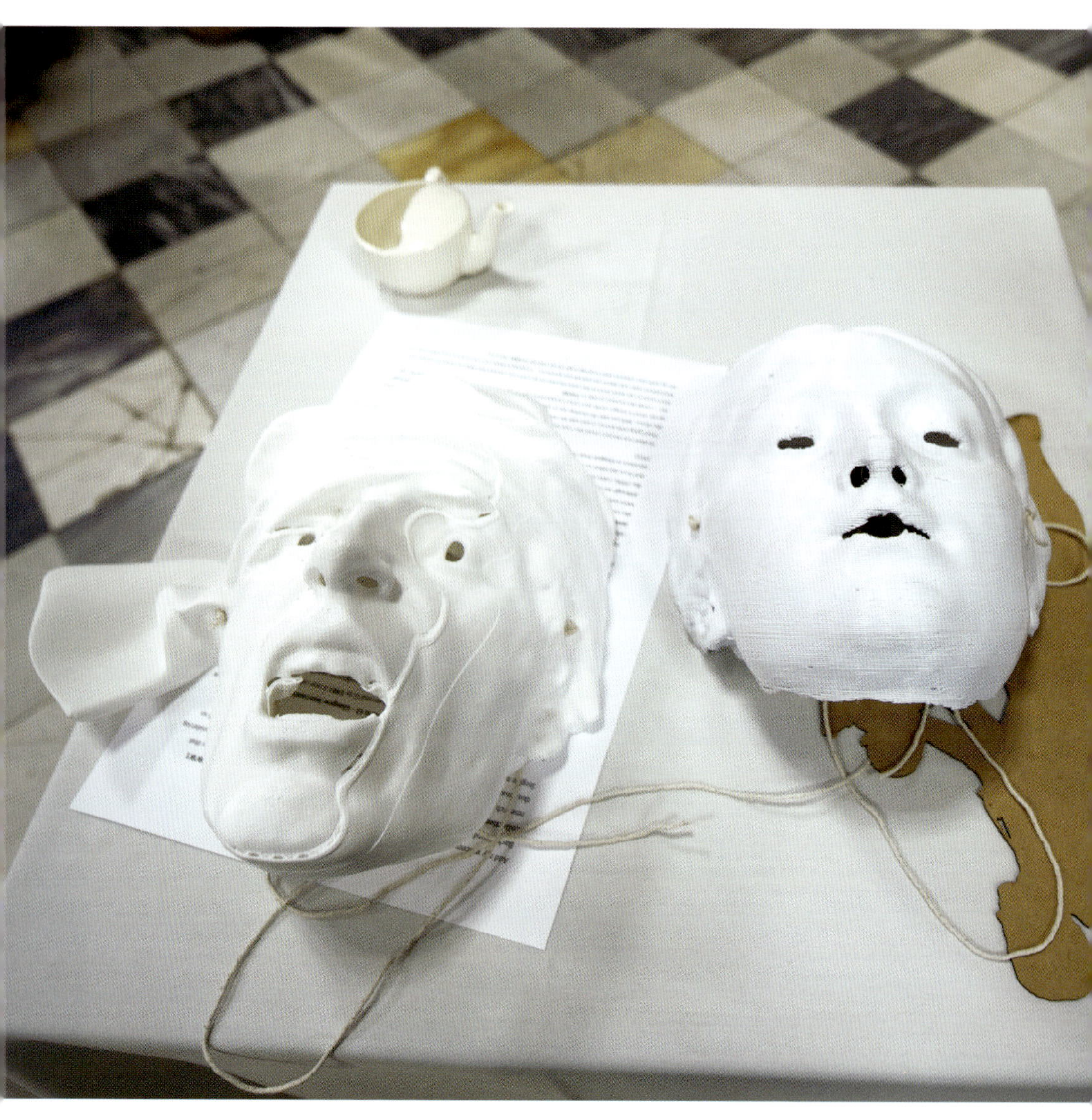

Masks created from 3D scans of the sculptures of *Peace* and *War* on Kelvin Way Bridge.

Doubtful Occasion
to
PhotoSculpture

RESEARCH AND PRACTICE
STUDIO AND KELVINGROVE ART GALLERY AND MUSEUM

OCTOBER 2017 – APRIL 2018

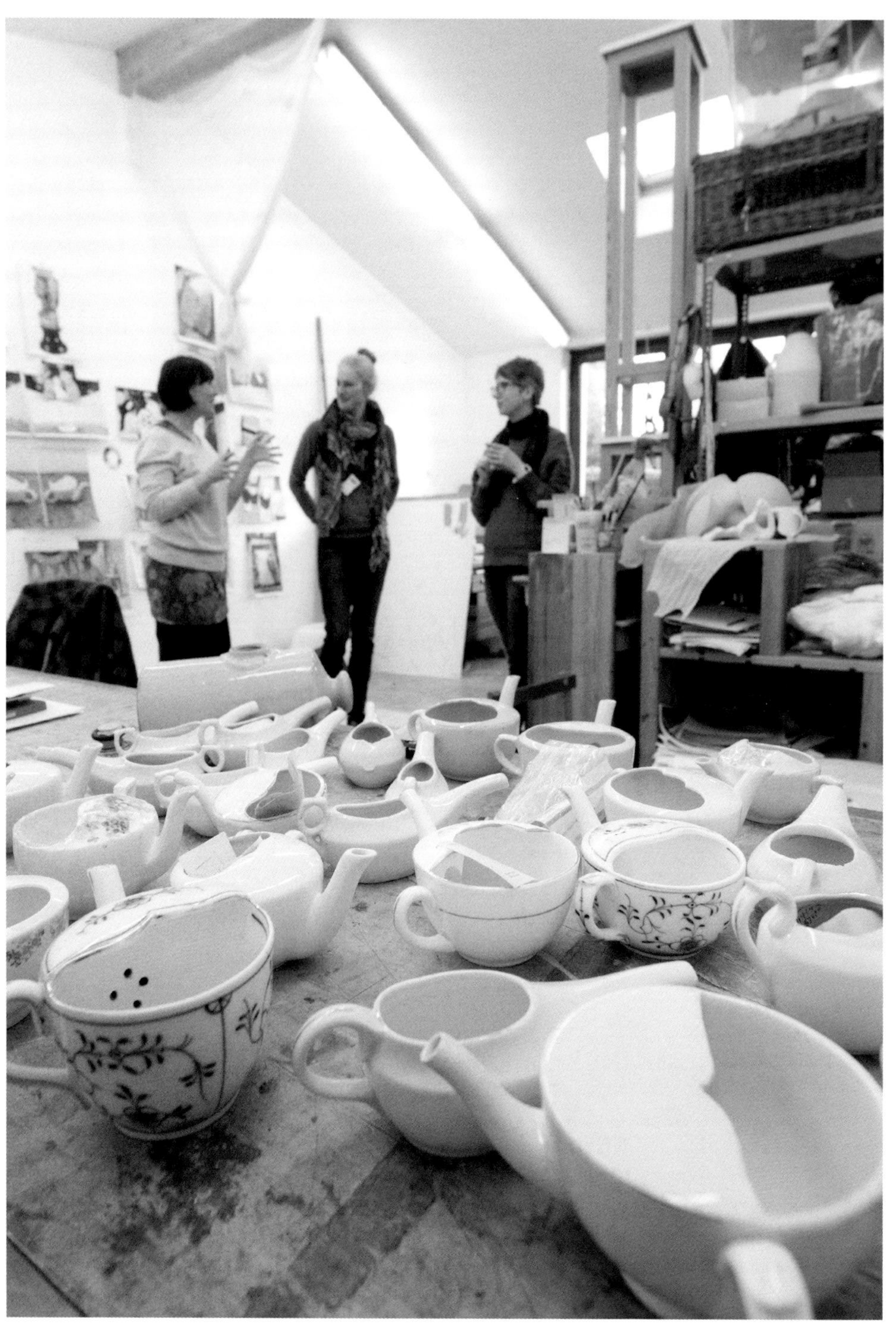

ARTIST'S NOTES:

Following the *Doubtful Occasion* symposium, time spent in the studio experimenting with archive photographs, copying and collage led to my increasing fascination with the performative potential of the small ceramic teacup-like object with spout: the invalid feeder cup. In tandem I came across the photo-sculpture studio of François Willème that operated in Sedan, France, during the mid nineteenth century. An extraordinary rotunda housed 24 concealed cameras to simultaneously capture a subject posed at its centre, a process which combined experimental photographic and sculptural methods to reproduce three-dimensional portraits. It was of immediate interest as a non-traditional means of representation which used a highly theatrical method. It led to *PhotoSculpture*, an event at Kelvingrove Art Gallery and Museum on 23 April 2018.

Working with models, I selected two poses to be reproduced using the photo-sculpture method: one representing 'invalid care', based on a German World War I photograph of nurses feeding a wounded soldier with an invalid feeder cup, and one based on a description of a feeder cup being used in the force-feeding of suffragettes. By posing the groups far beyond the central point of the circular structure, it was clear that images gathered from the event would not produce an accurate 'replica' of either of the poses, rather a creative distortion of reality which I wholly embraced.

The faces of the models playing the male and female subjects were covered by masks of the faces from a sculpture sited on Kelvin Way Bridge, facing the entrance to Kelvingrove Art Gallery and Museum. *Peace* and *War* by Paul Raphael Montford are one of four pairs of sculptures adorning the bridge; despite their title, they are not associated with war memorials. The faces of the sculptures were replicated by laser-scanning the originals and 3D printing them in ABS plastic in order to make the masks.

Glasgow Museums staff, participants from the *Doubtful Occasion* symposium, artists and friends were invited to be the 24 camera operators who simultaneously pressed their shutters to take the required images used to develop the work.

◀ Christine Borland in her studio, speaking with Glasgow Museums conservator Stephanie de Roemer and curator Jo Meacock.

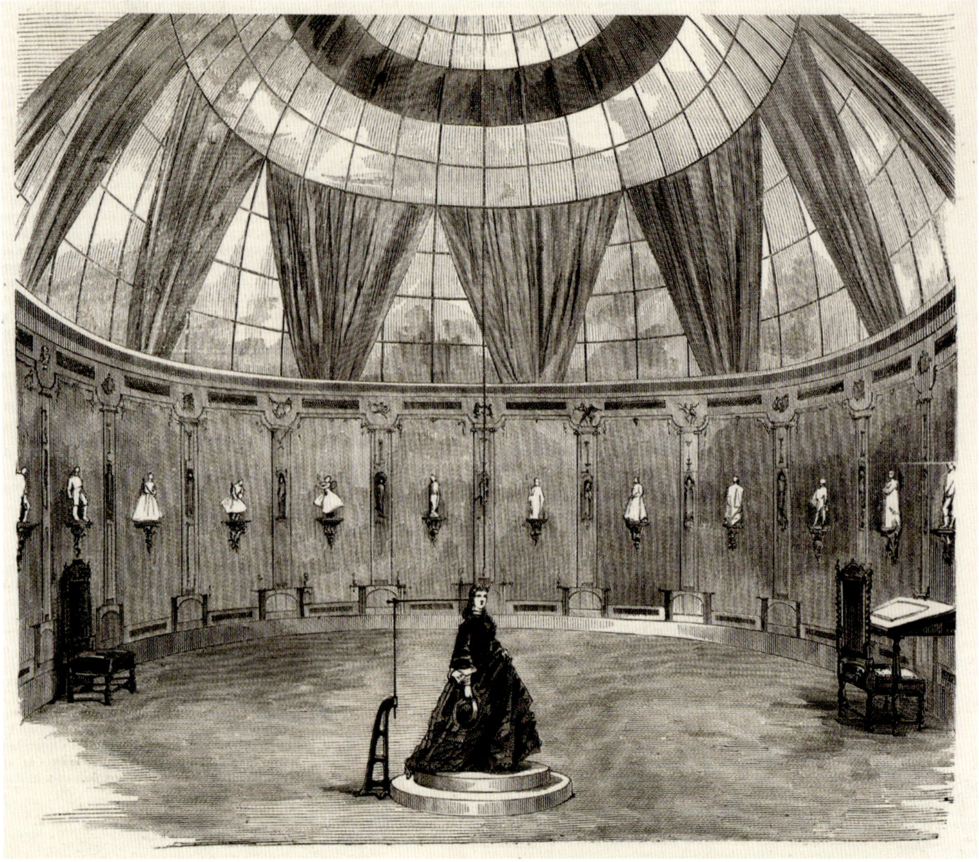

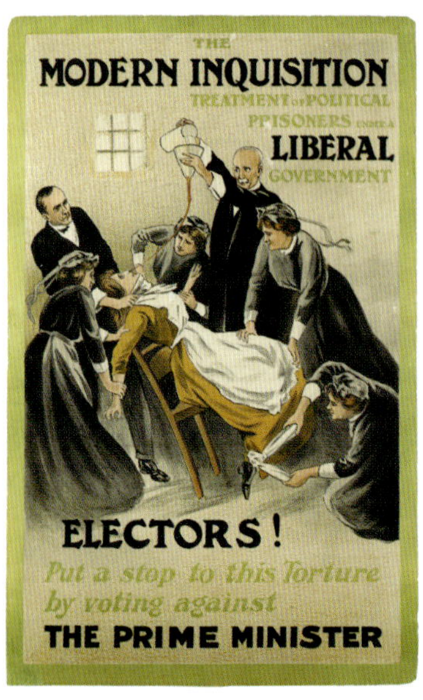

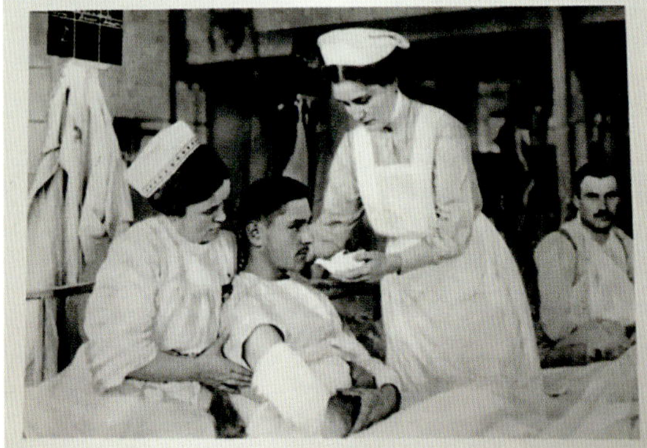

top: François Willème's photo-sculpture studio, rotunda serving as pose room (from *Le Monde Illustre*, 31 December 1864); © Bibliothèque nationale de France (BNF).

left: *The Modern Inquisition, c.*1910; © The Museum of London.

above: World War I military hospital, nurses of the Red Cross assist a wounded soldier with feeding; © DRK (Deutsches Rotes Kreuz).

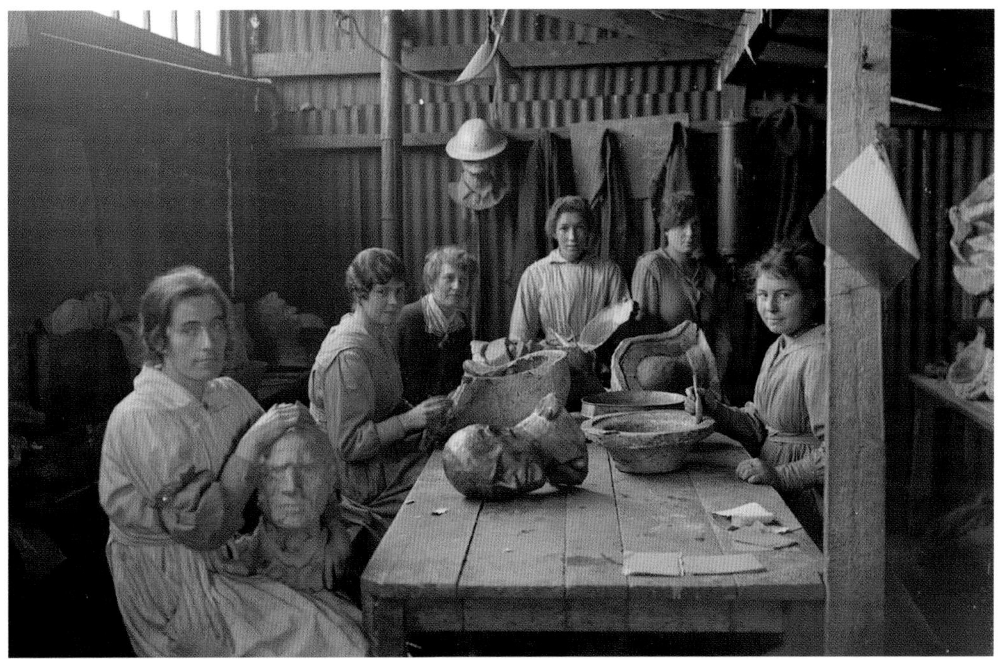

⬥ Women making papier mâché decoy heads, France, World War I. Image courtesy of Paul Reynolds/mediadrumworld.com.

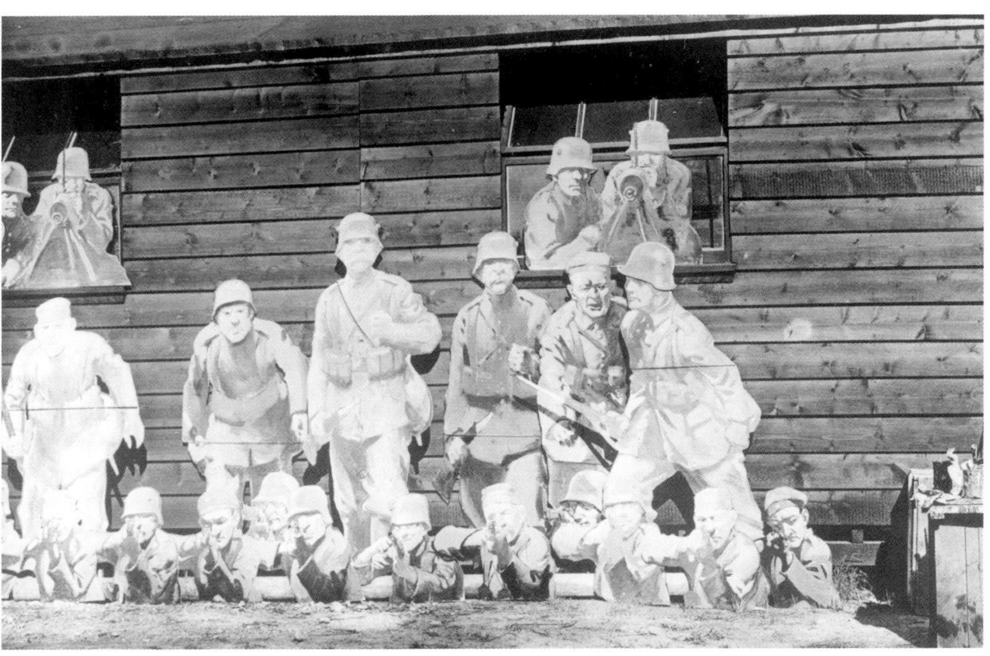

⬥ The British Army Camouflage School in Kensington, where cut-out soldiers were designed to mislead the enemy during attacks. © IWM (Q 95955).

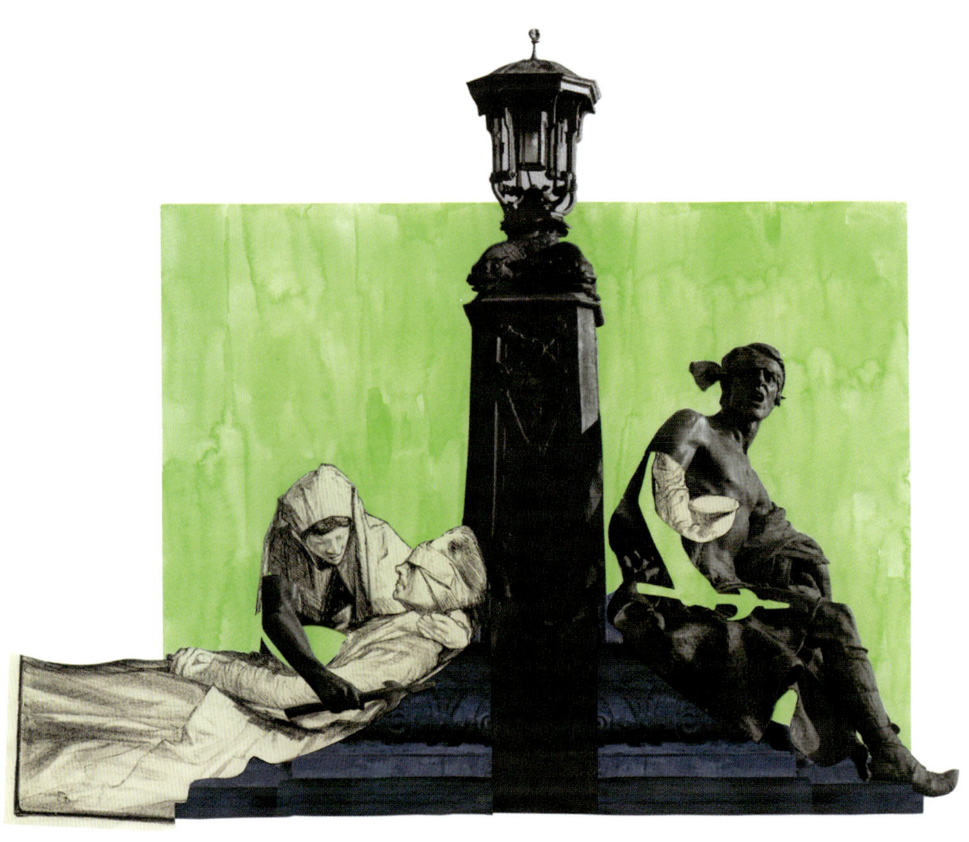

⬤ **Wrong Right Hand (Glasgow Museums Collection; Frank Brangwyn Print; nurse feeding blind soldier),** 2018
Christine Borland. Limited edition print on Hahnemuhle German etching paper (edition of twelve). Courtesy of the artist
and Patricia Fleming Projects, Glasgow.

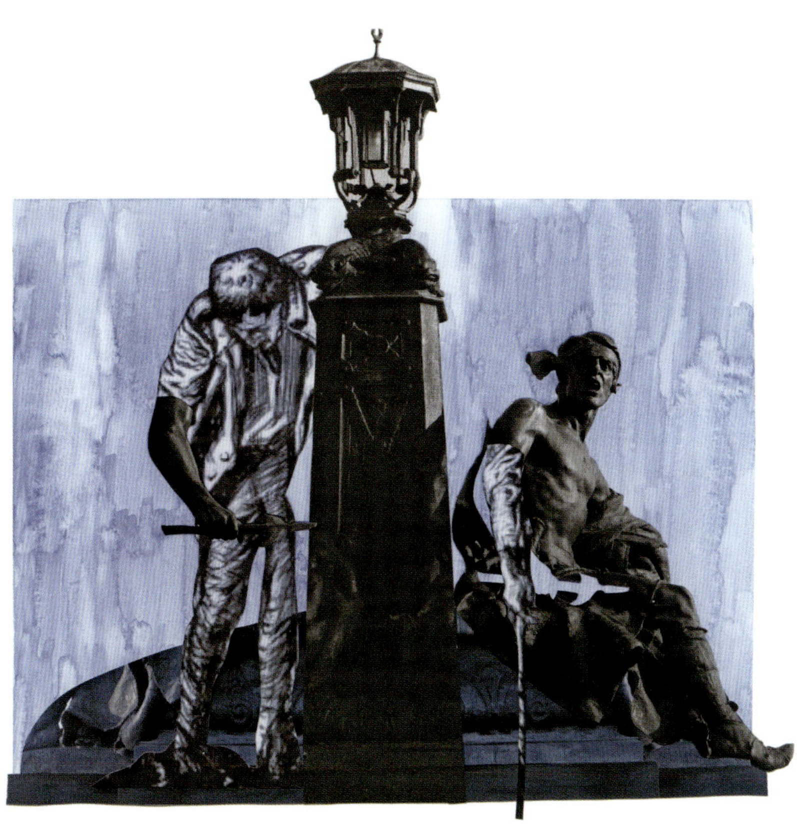

⬥ **Wrong Right Hand (Glasgow Museums Collection; Frank Brangwyn Print; soldier injured during battle),** 2018
Christine Borland. Limited edition print on Hahnemuhle German etching paper (edition of twelve). Courtesy of the artist
and Patricia Fleming Projects, Glasgow.

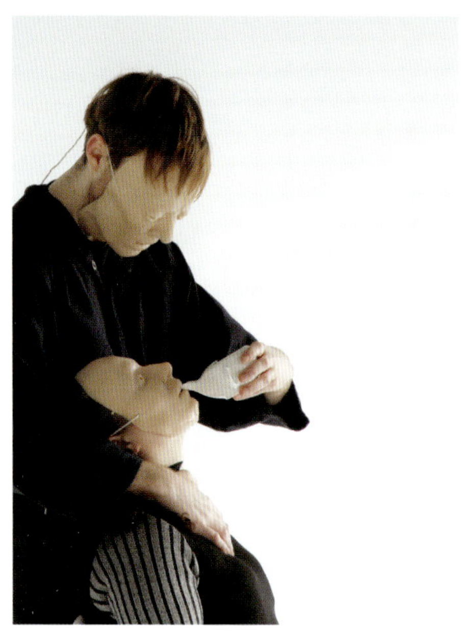
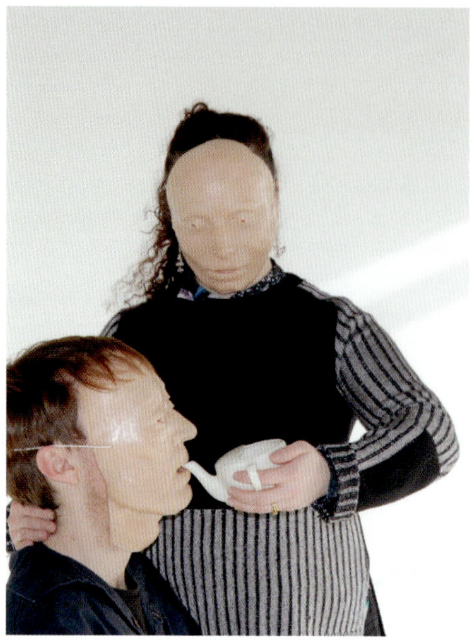
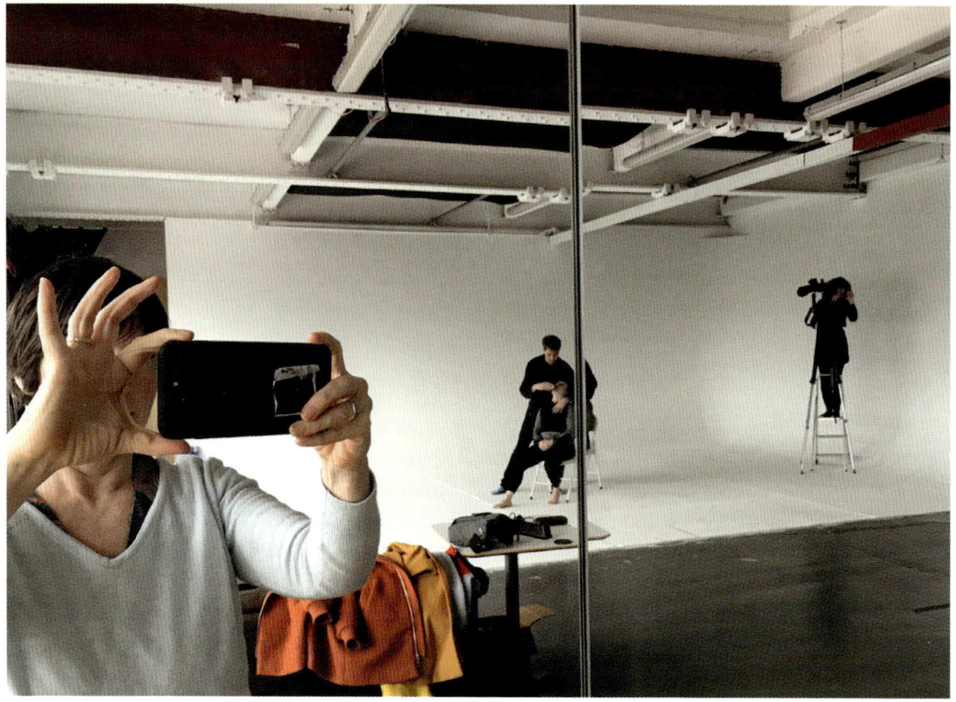

○ *PhotoSculpture* developmental work with models.

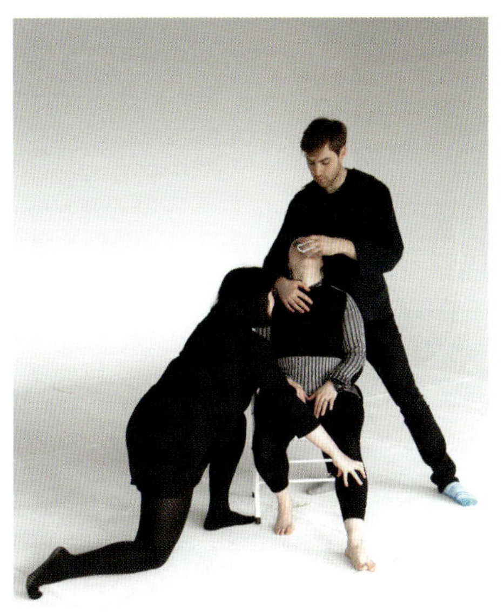
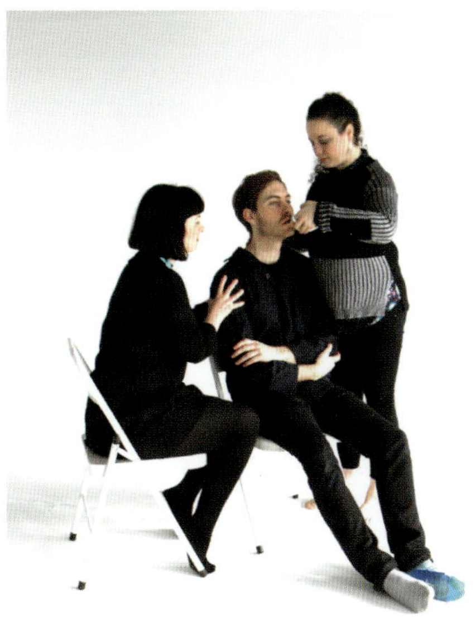
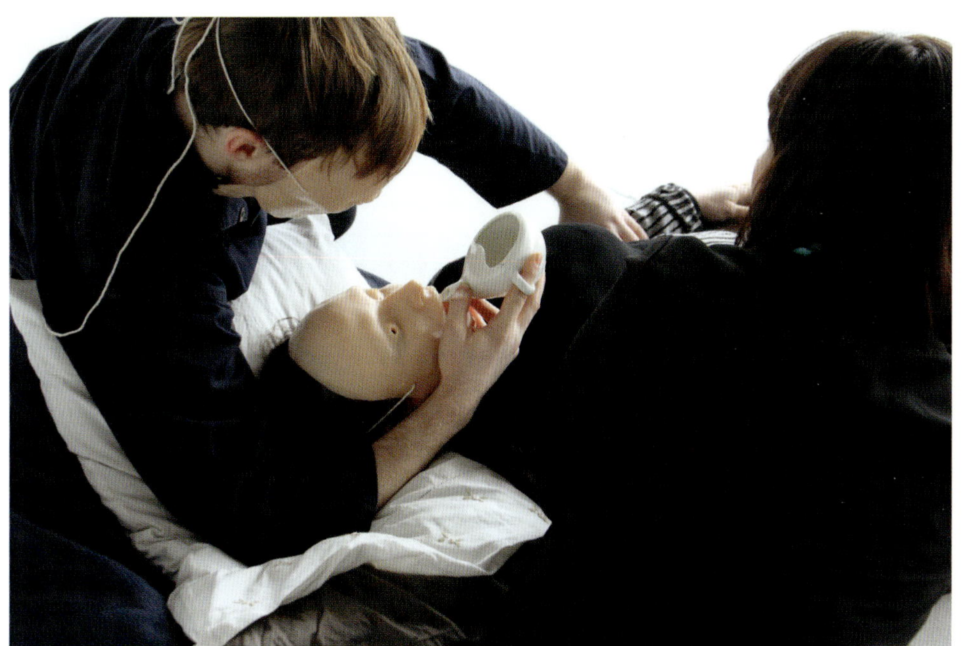

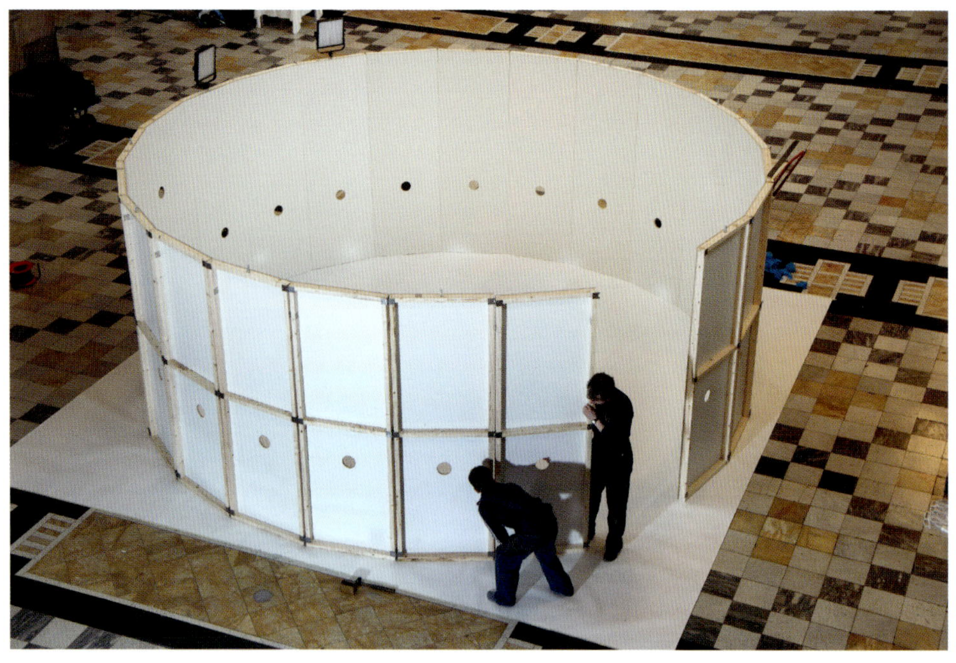

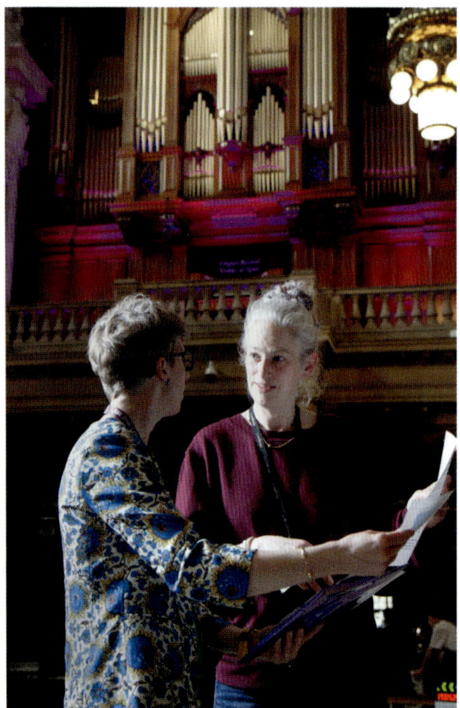

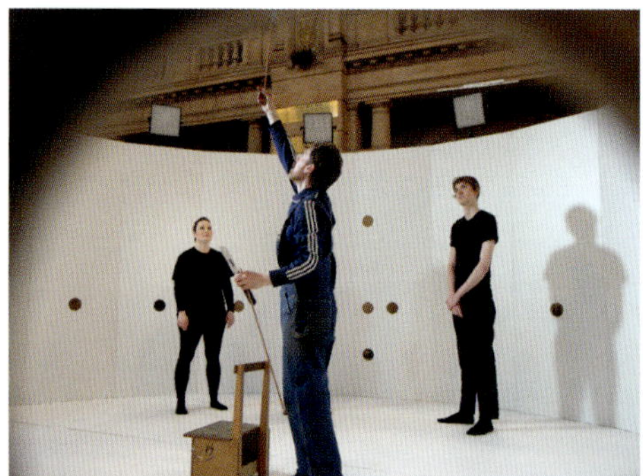

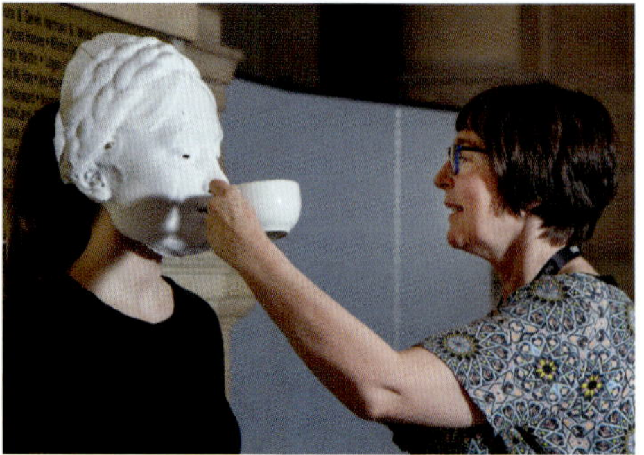

Pages 70–78: *PhotoSculpture* event in the Centre Hall at Kelvingrove Art Gallery and Museum.

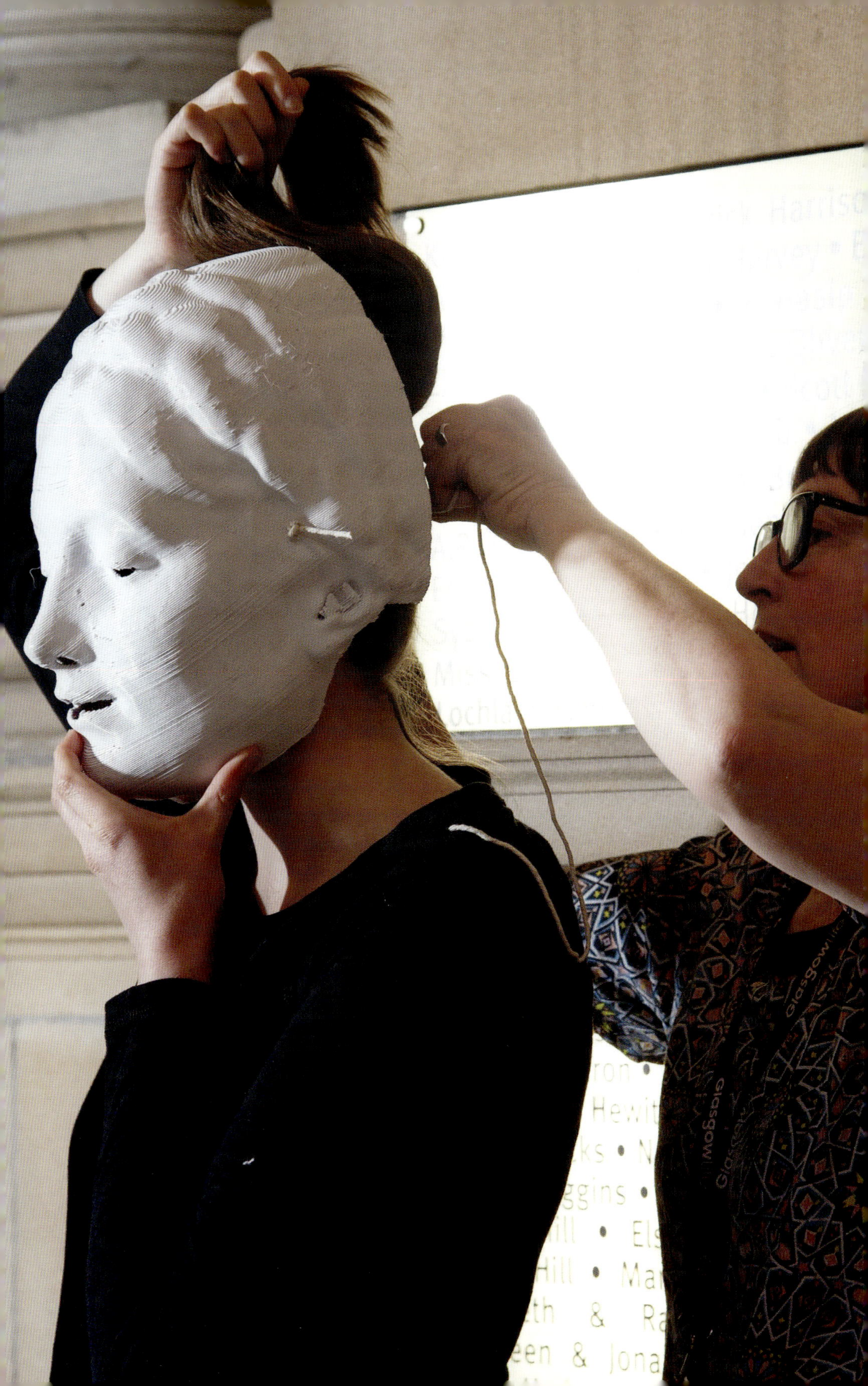

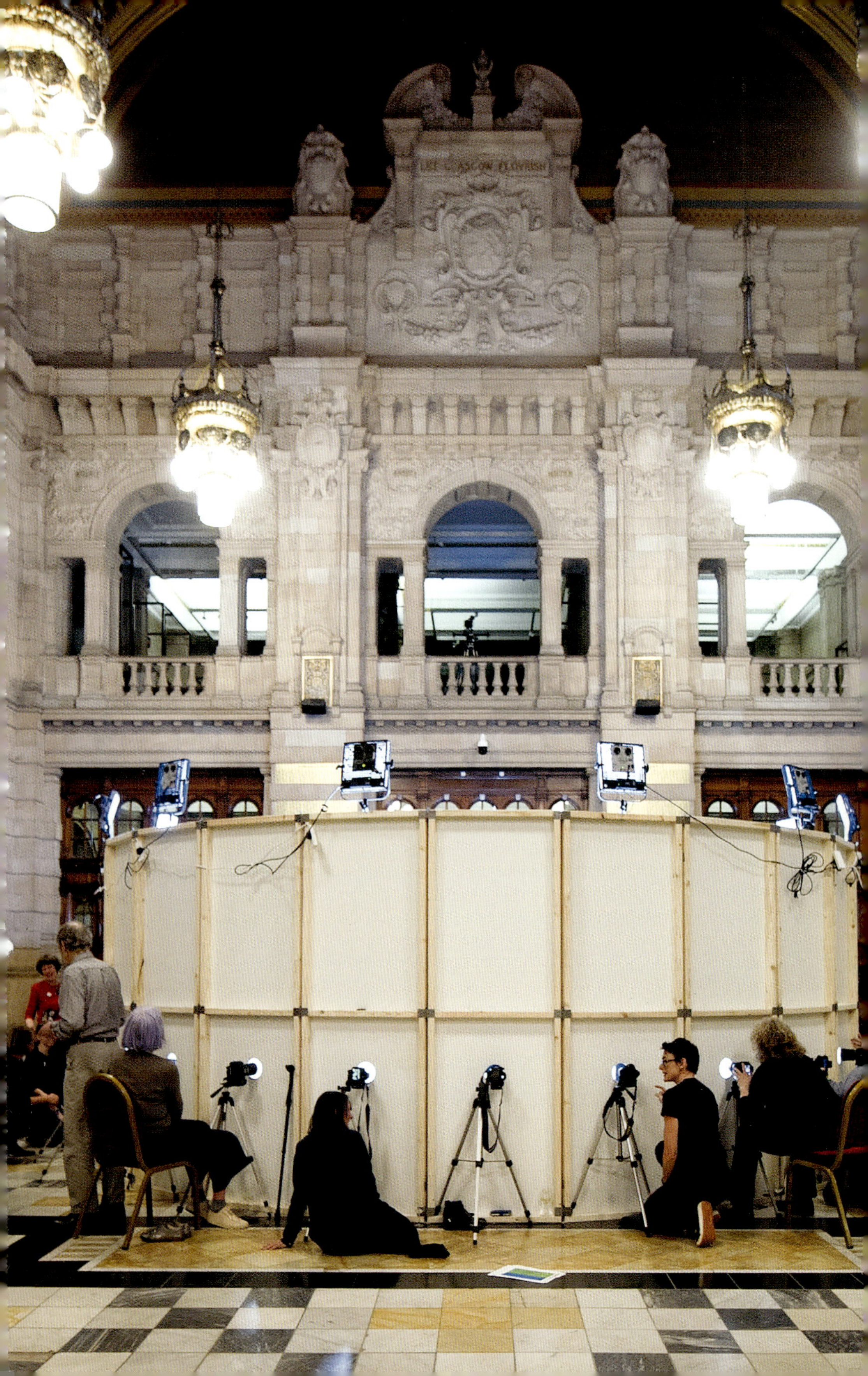

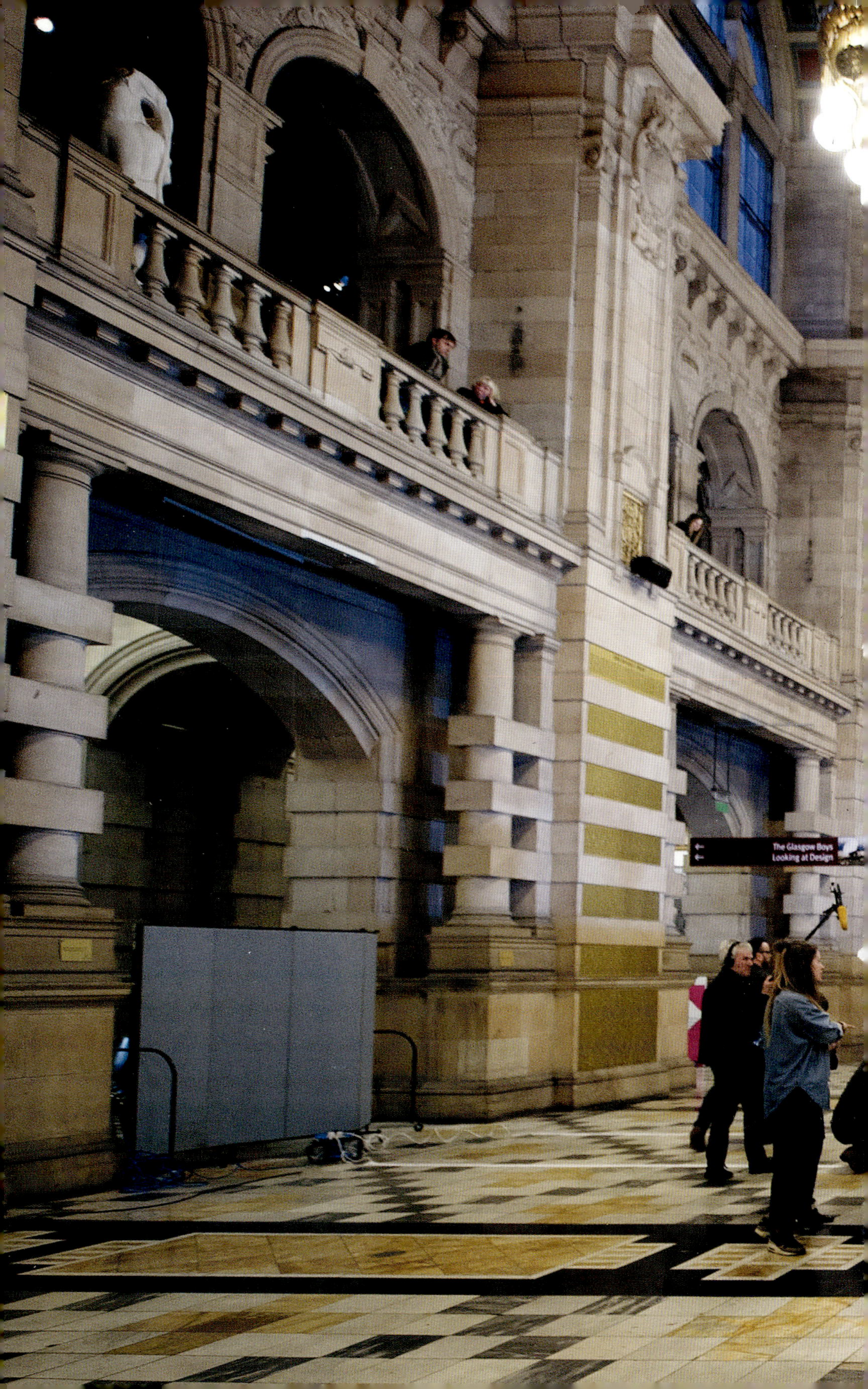
The Glasgow Boys
Looking at Design

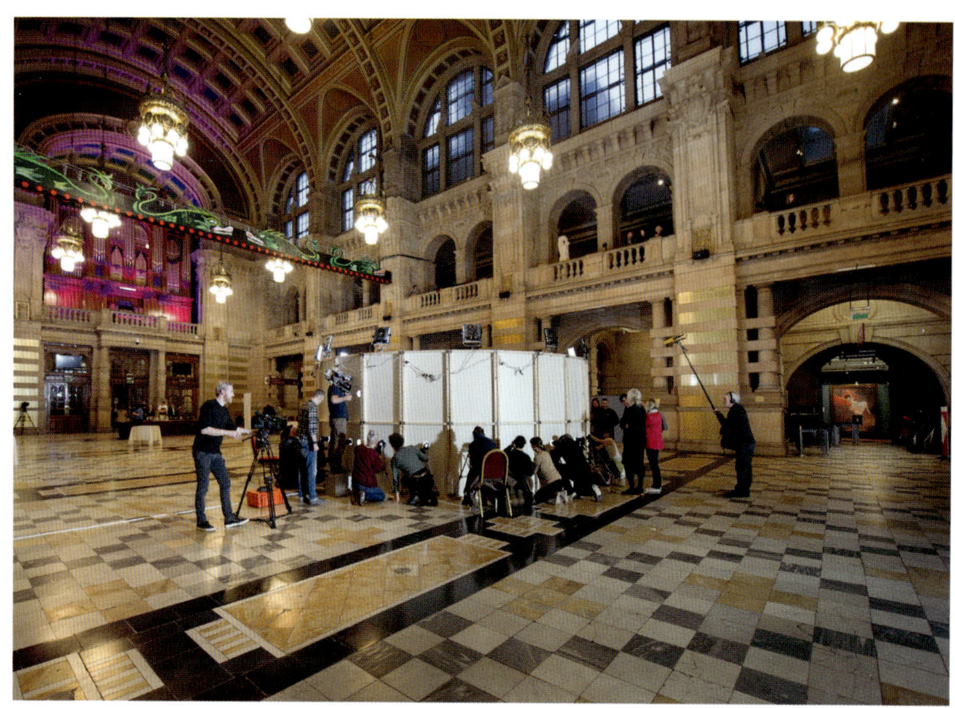

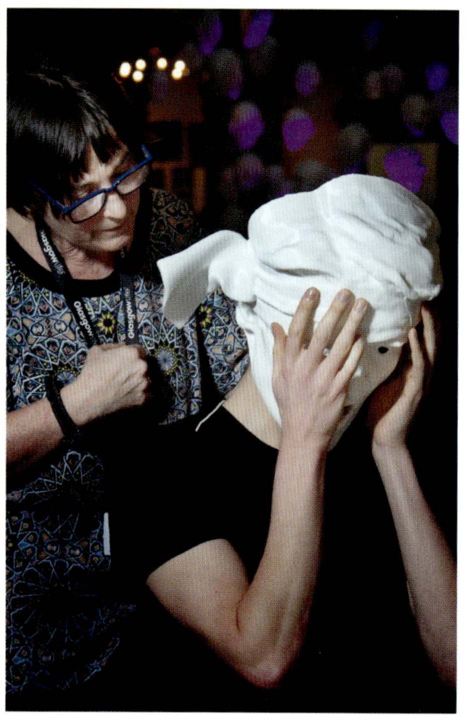

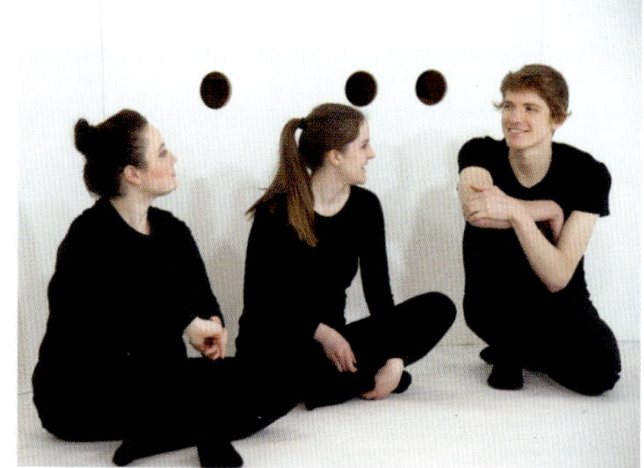

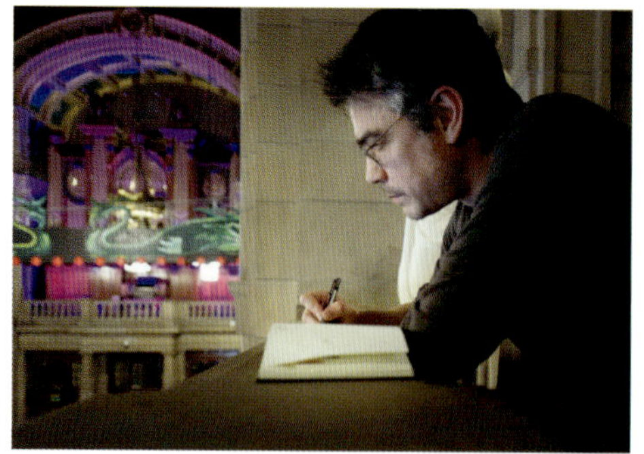

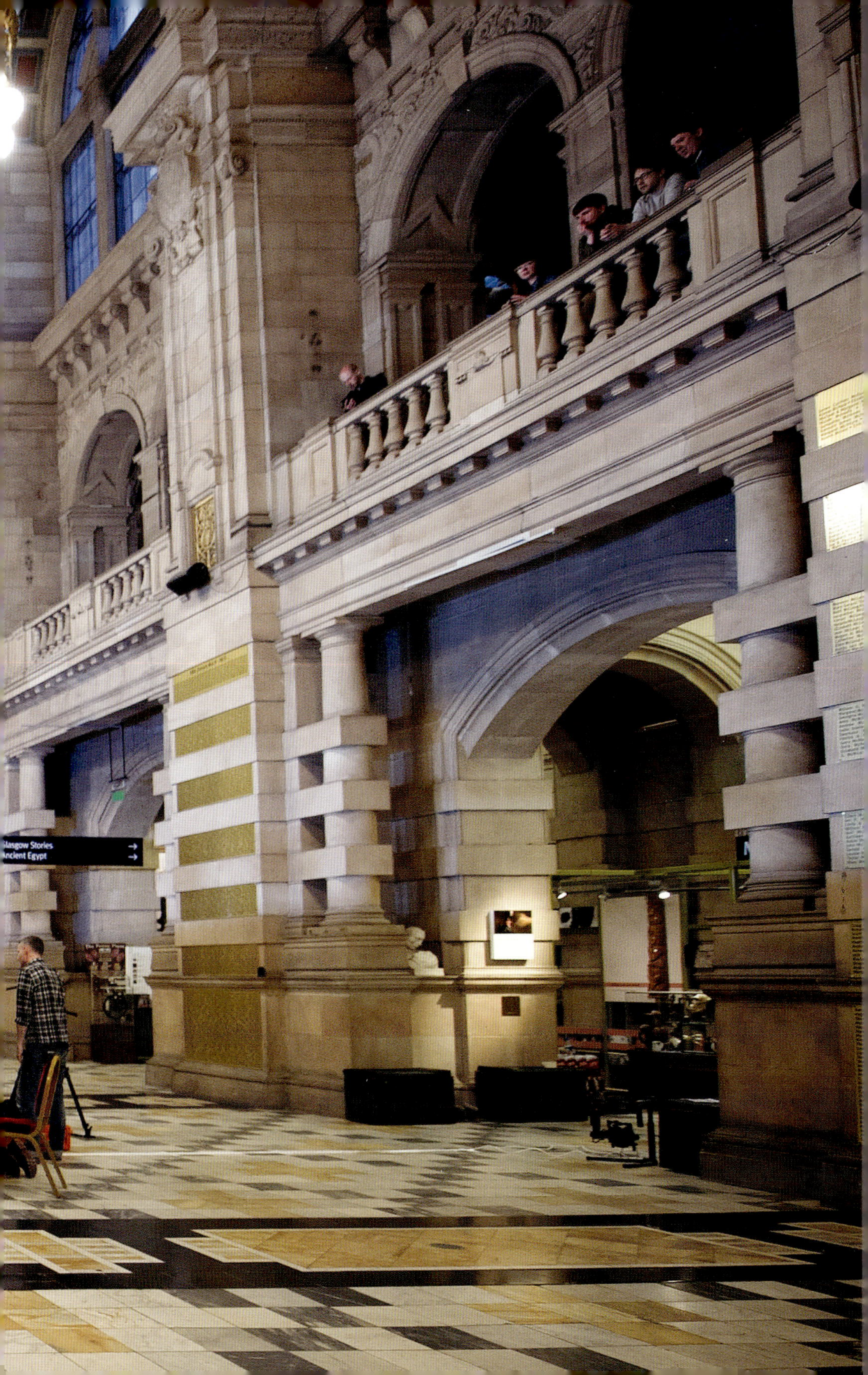

Glasgow Stories
Ancient Egypt

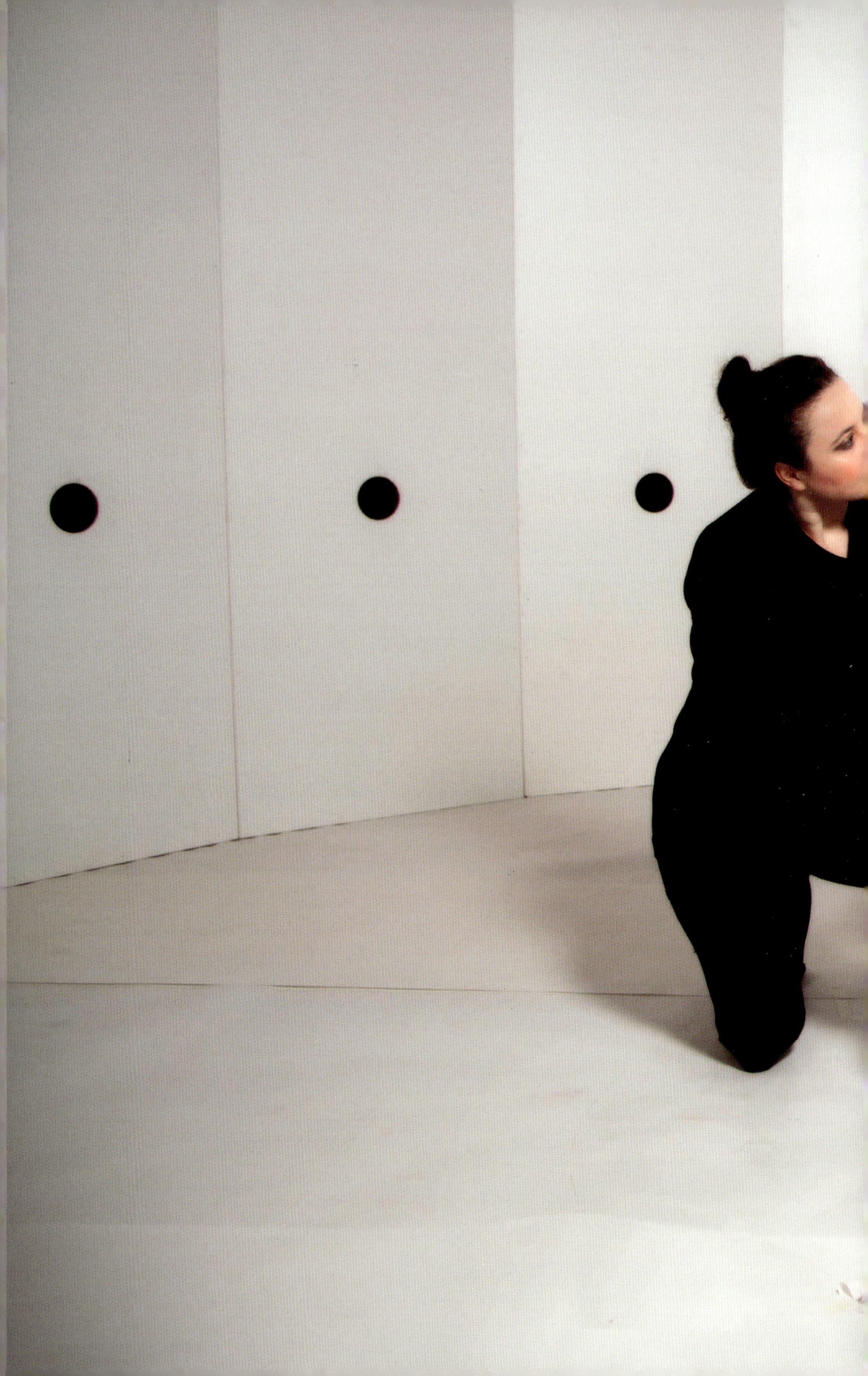

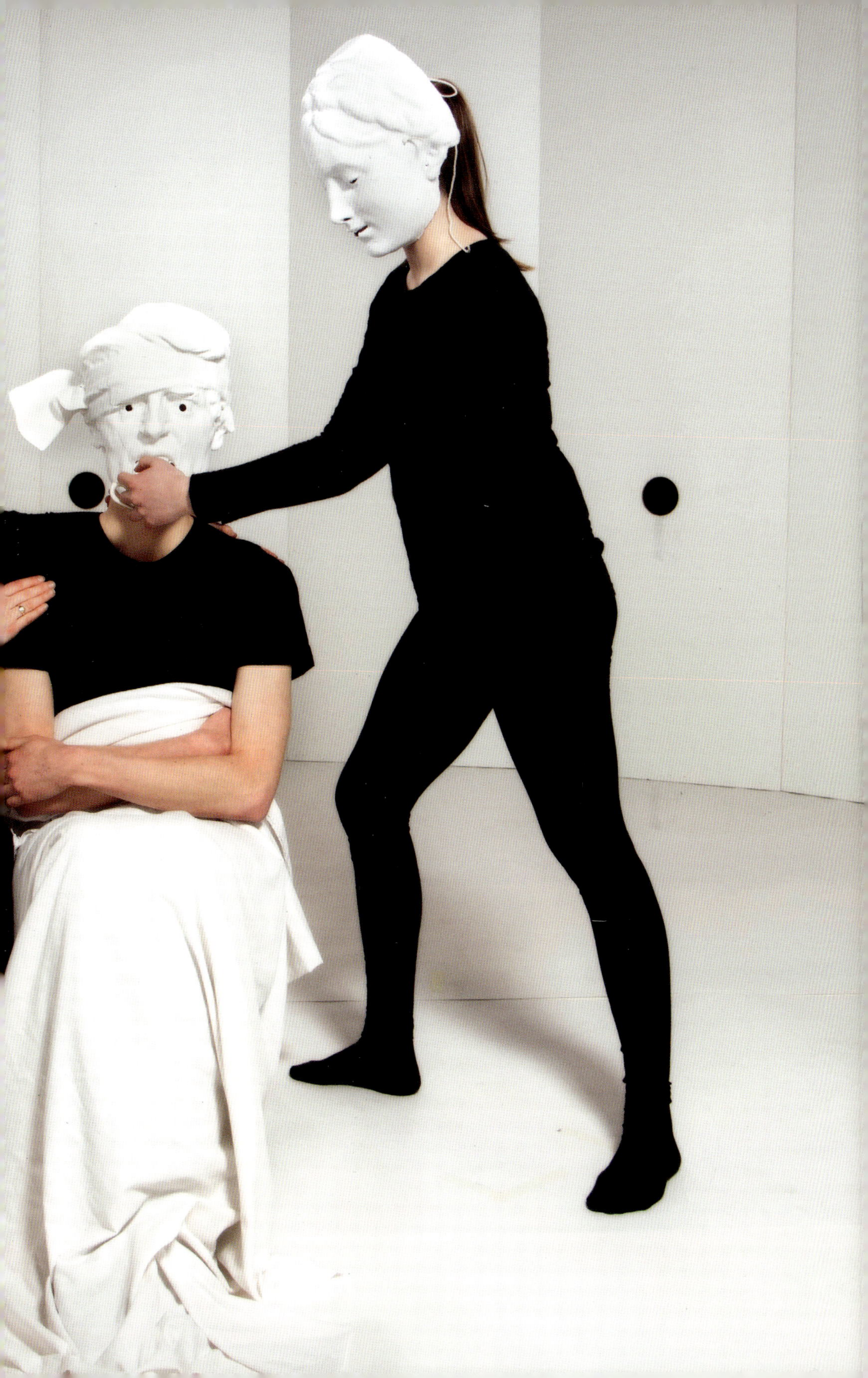

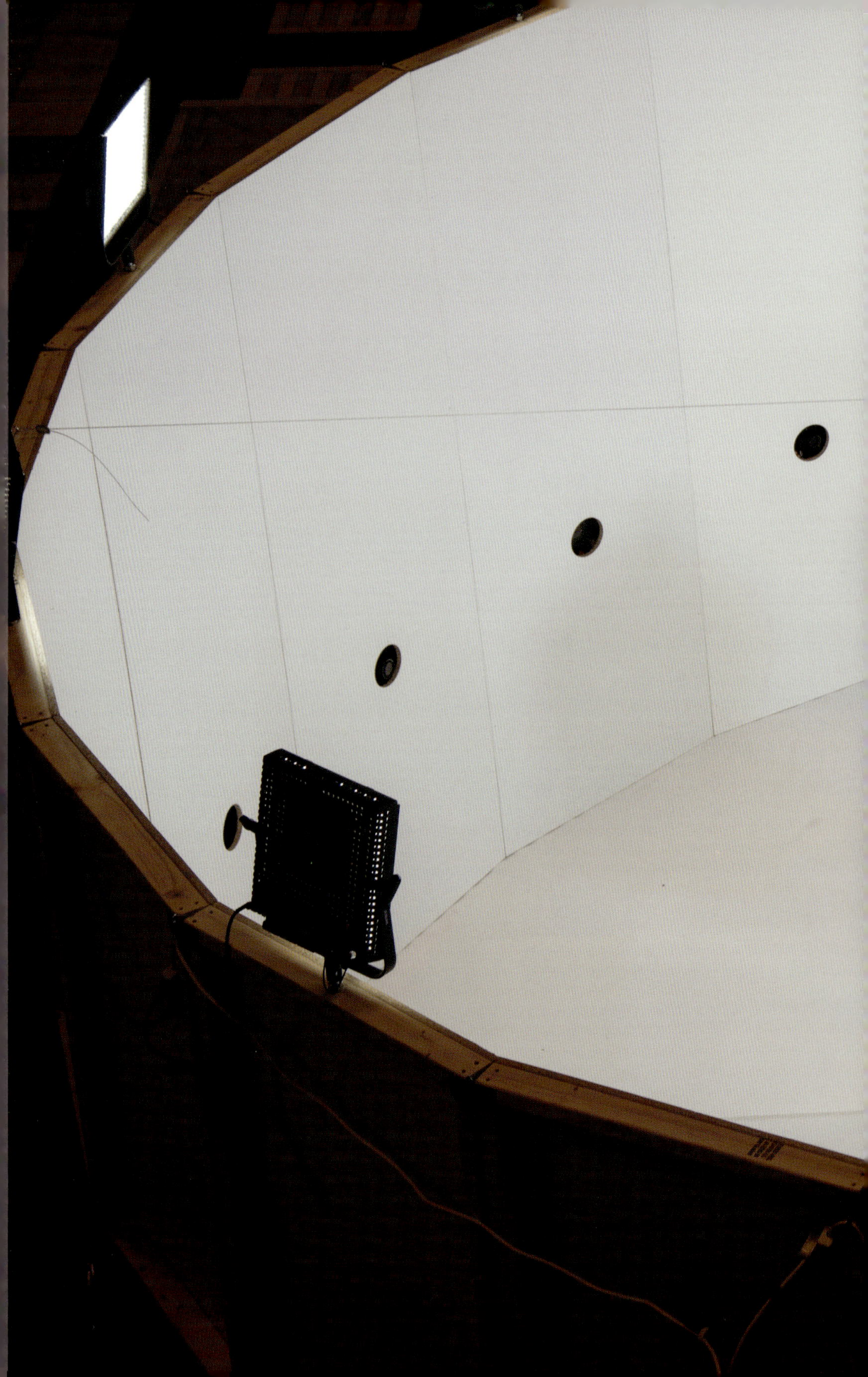

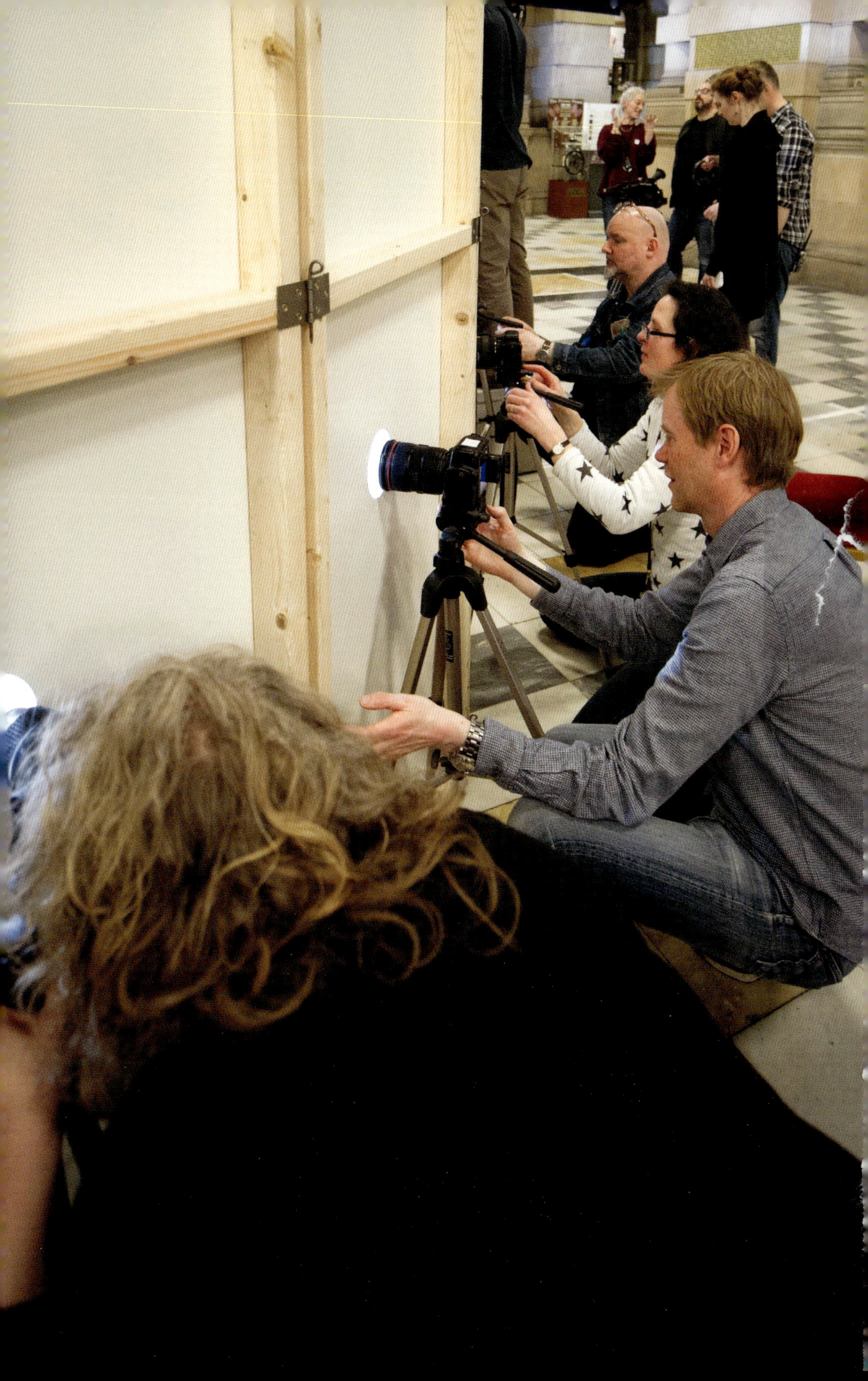

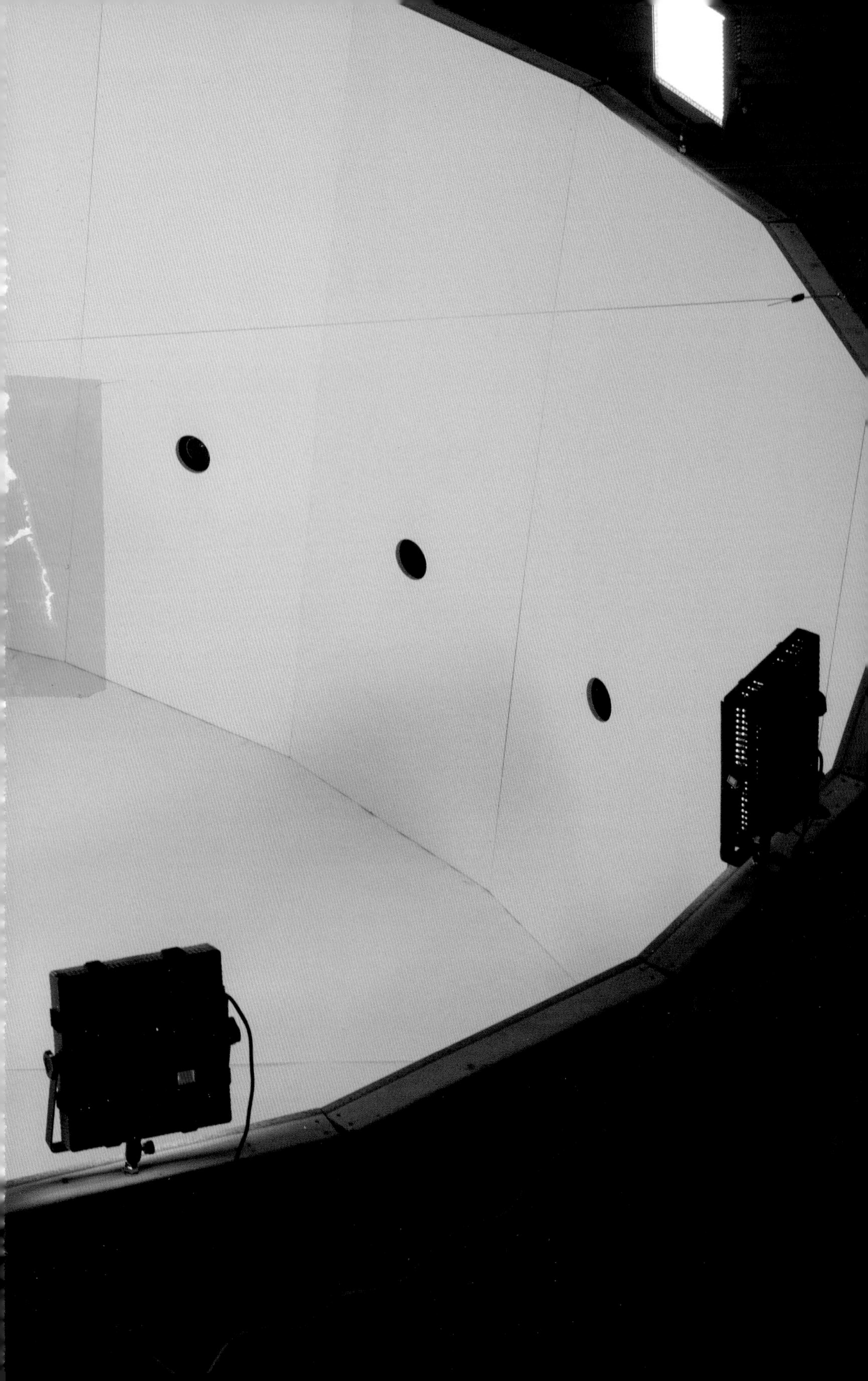

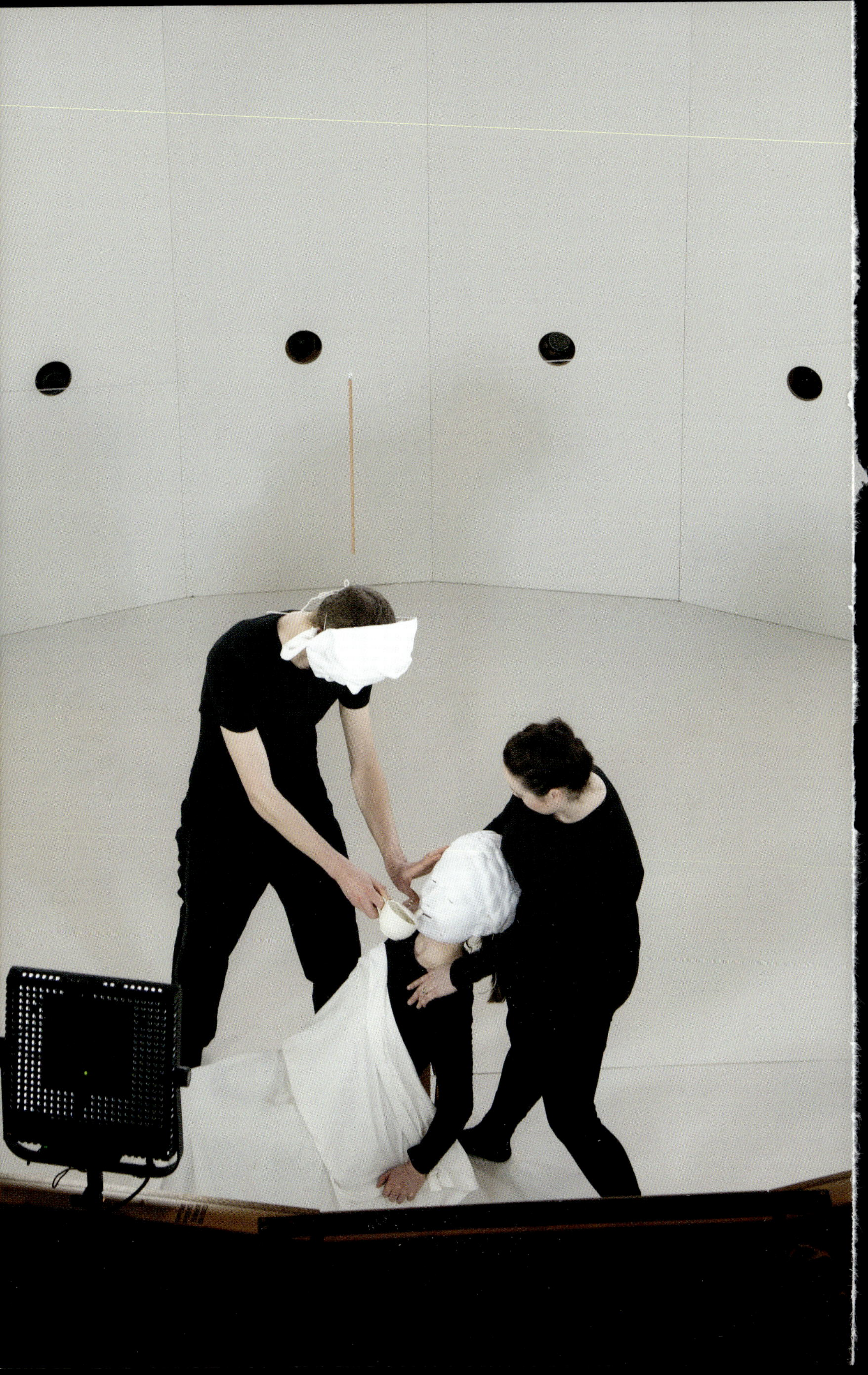

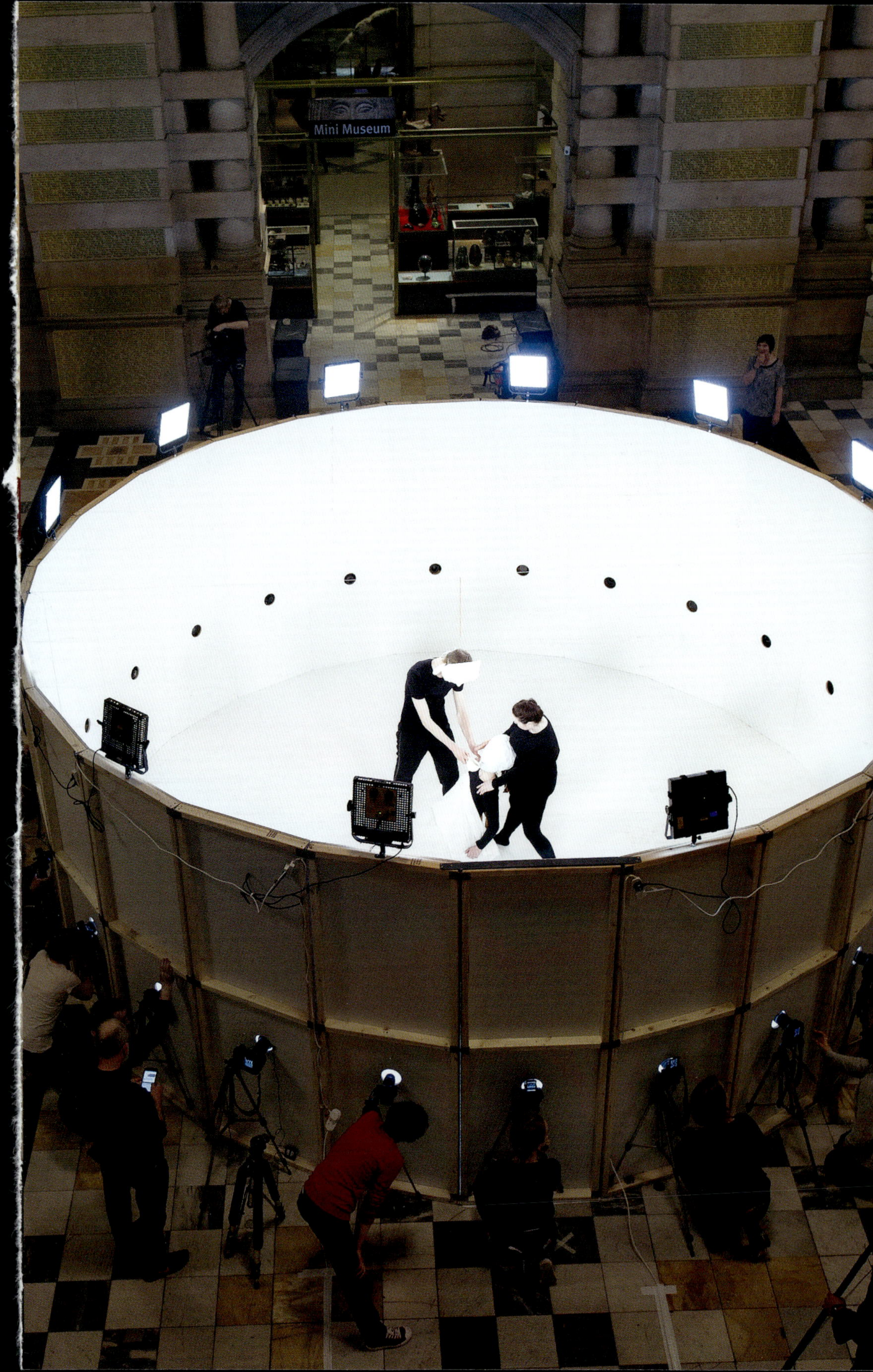
Mini Museum

PhotoSculpture
to
I Say Nothing

RESEARCH AND PRACTICE IN STUDIO, FLANDERS
AND GLASGOW MUSEUMS RESEARCH CENTRE

APRIL 2018 – OCTOBER 2018

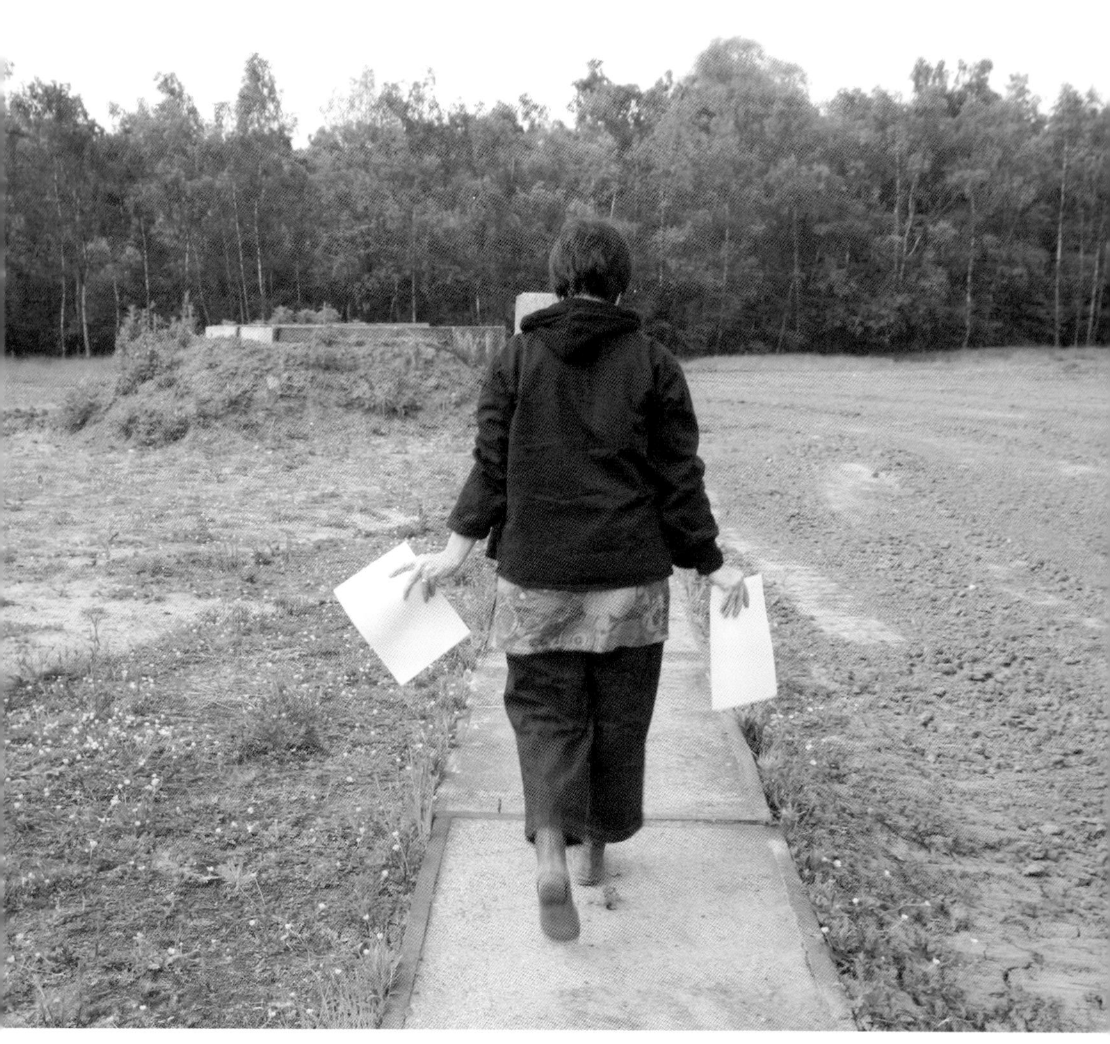

ARTIST'S NOTES:

The development of the project towards the finalized artwork was
based on experiments with the information and images produced at the
PhotoSculpture event, and a radical intervention with the invalid feeder cup.

The photographs taken during the *PhotoSculpture* event were turned
into silhouette 'cut-outs' of the figures posed within the photo-sculpture
structure and tested in a variety of materials from plaster to papier mâché.
The figures were distorted in form and scale, depending on their proximity
to the camera that captured them.

The invalid feeder cup which was first encountered at GMRC and then
used in the *PhotoSculpture* poses (an unaccessioned object purchased
by Glasgow Museums as part of a handling kit) was taken to Flanders and
subjected to a controlled explosion by the Belgian bomb disposal unit
DOVO-SEDEE. This feeder cup was then replaced in the handling kit by
a near identical one from my own collection.

The final production of the sculptures, including decisions in relation to
methods and materials, was undertaken in a conservator's studio turned
artist's studio, back at Glasgow Museums Resource Centre, where the
research for the project began in October 2016.

In keeping with the symmetry of the balcony space, the installation of
the work at Kelvingrove grew to accommodate elements from across
the timespan of the whole commission. This included the invalid feeder
cup, the *PhotoSculpture* structure – which simultaneously blocks off and
protects the sculptures – and pillar-mounted screens showing *Drone*,
two films created from footage shot via drones during the *PhotoSculpture*
event in the Centre Hall below.

◐ Christine Borland at the DOVO-SEDEE explosives range, Flanders, carrying prints
of drawings by Birthe Jorgensen from *Doubtful Occasion*, which will become witness
boards (see overleaf).

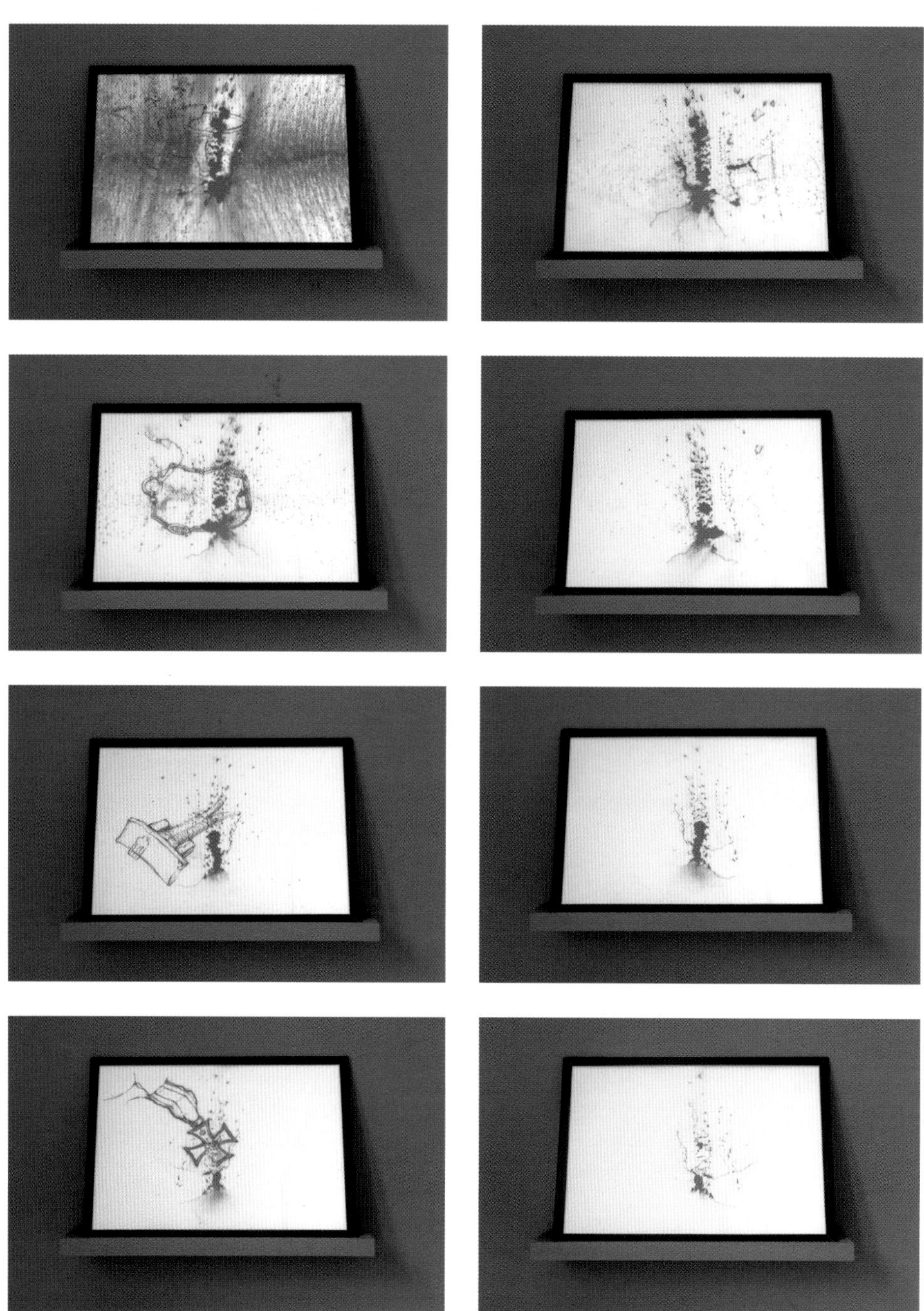

⭘ **Witness Board: Invalid feeder cup, Witness Board: Berlin iron watch chain, Witness Board: East African headrest, Witness Board: German Iron Cross medal** Giclée prints of Birthe Jorgensen drawings (unique). All Christine Borland, 2018. Courtesy of the artist, Birthe Jorgensen and Patricia Fleming Projects. The front (left) and reverse (right) of each work is shown. The witness boards were created during controlled explosion tests by DOVO-SEDEE.

Opposite: Close-ups of **Witness Board: Invalid feeder cup**, with the front above and reverse below.

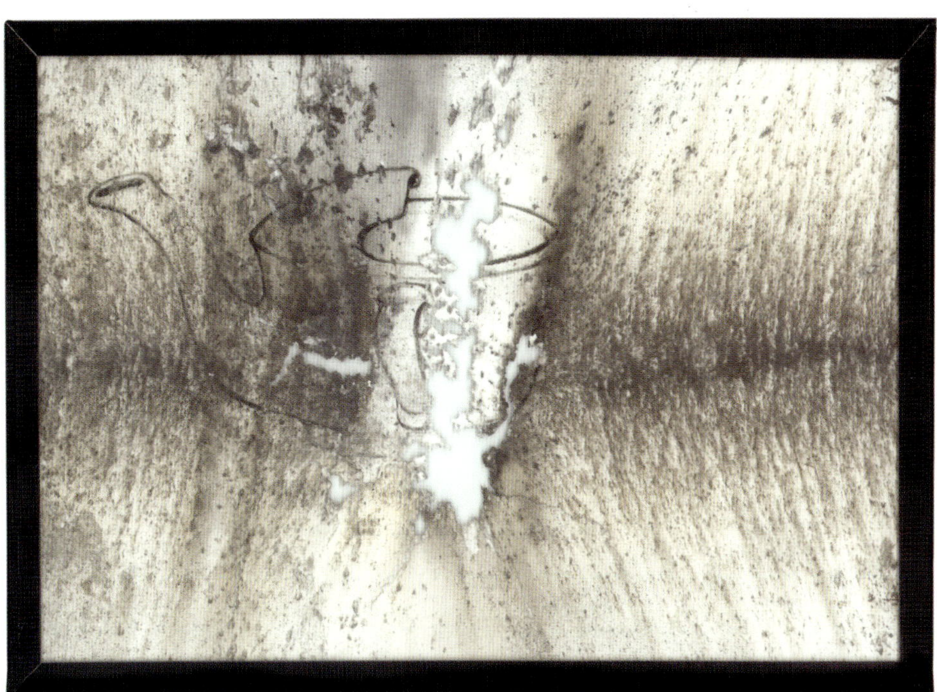

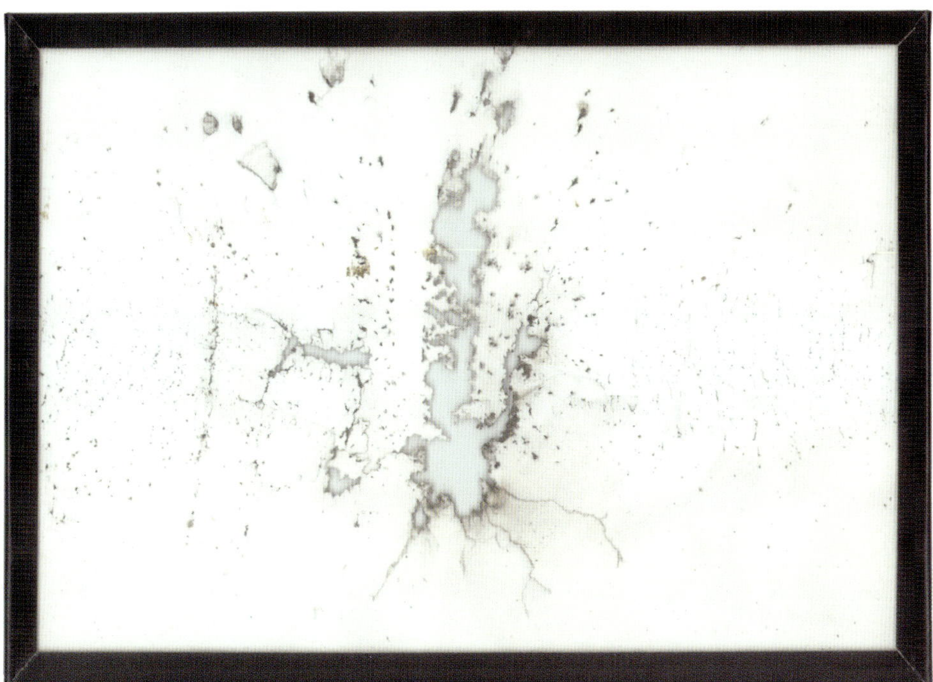

Overleaf, pages 84–5: Stills from video documentation of the invalid feeder cup being exploded by DOVO-SEDEE, with photographic witness boards to the right of the cup, May 2018.

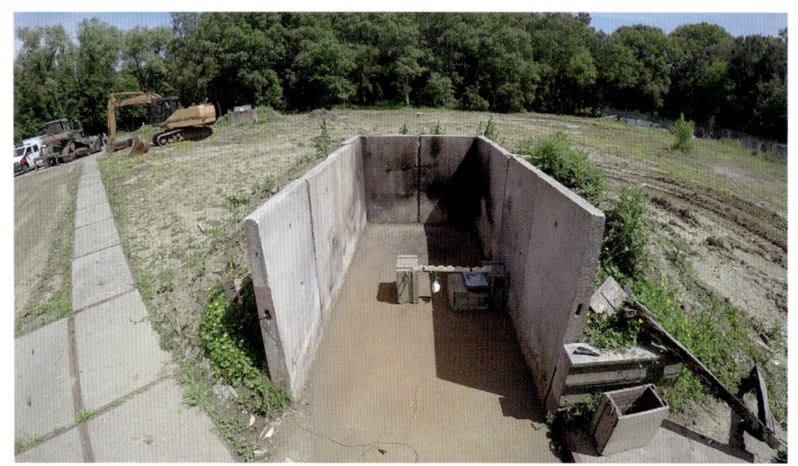

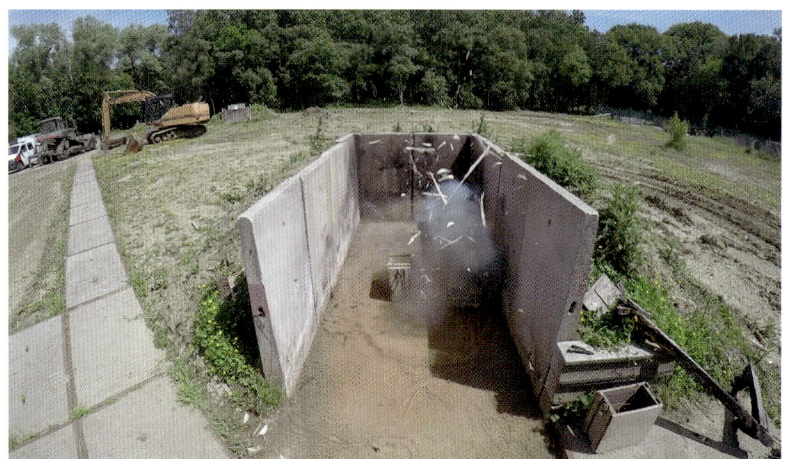

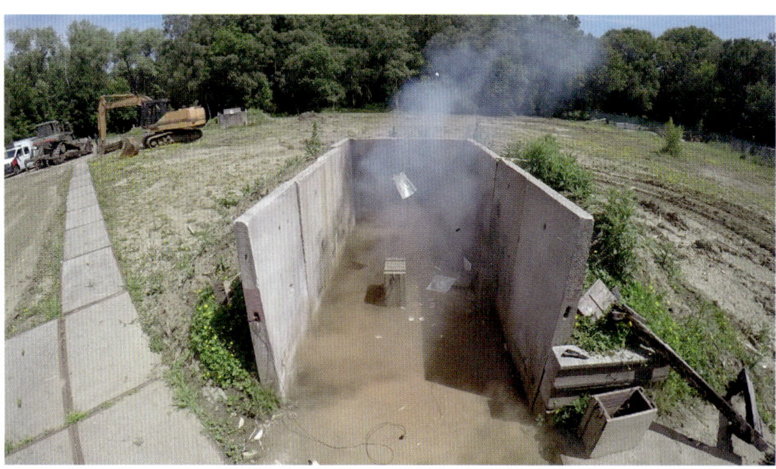

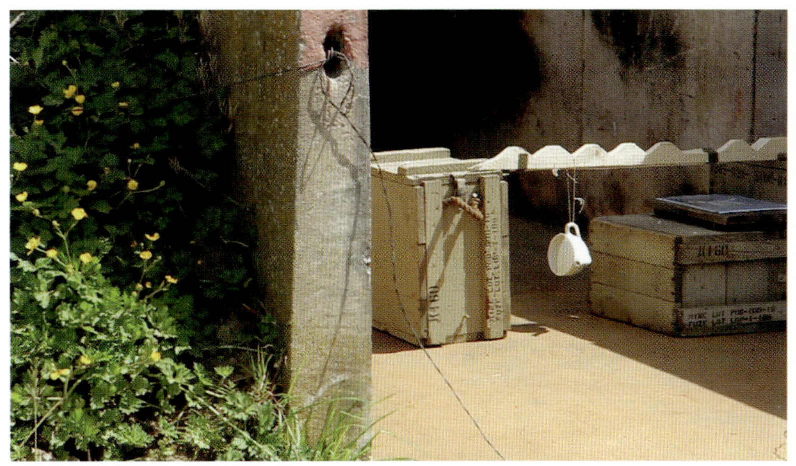

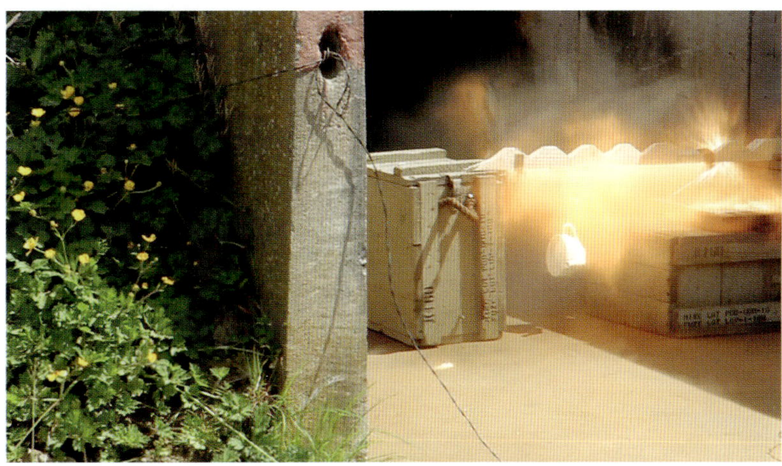

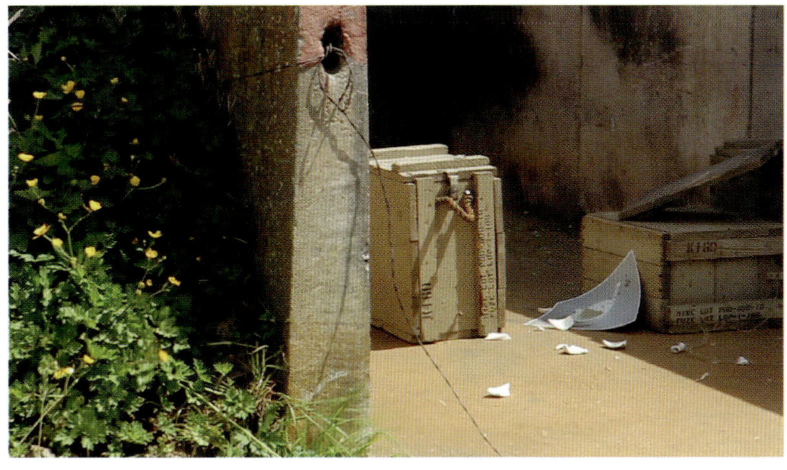

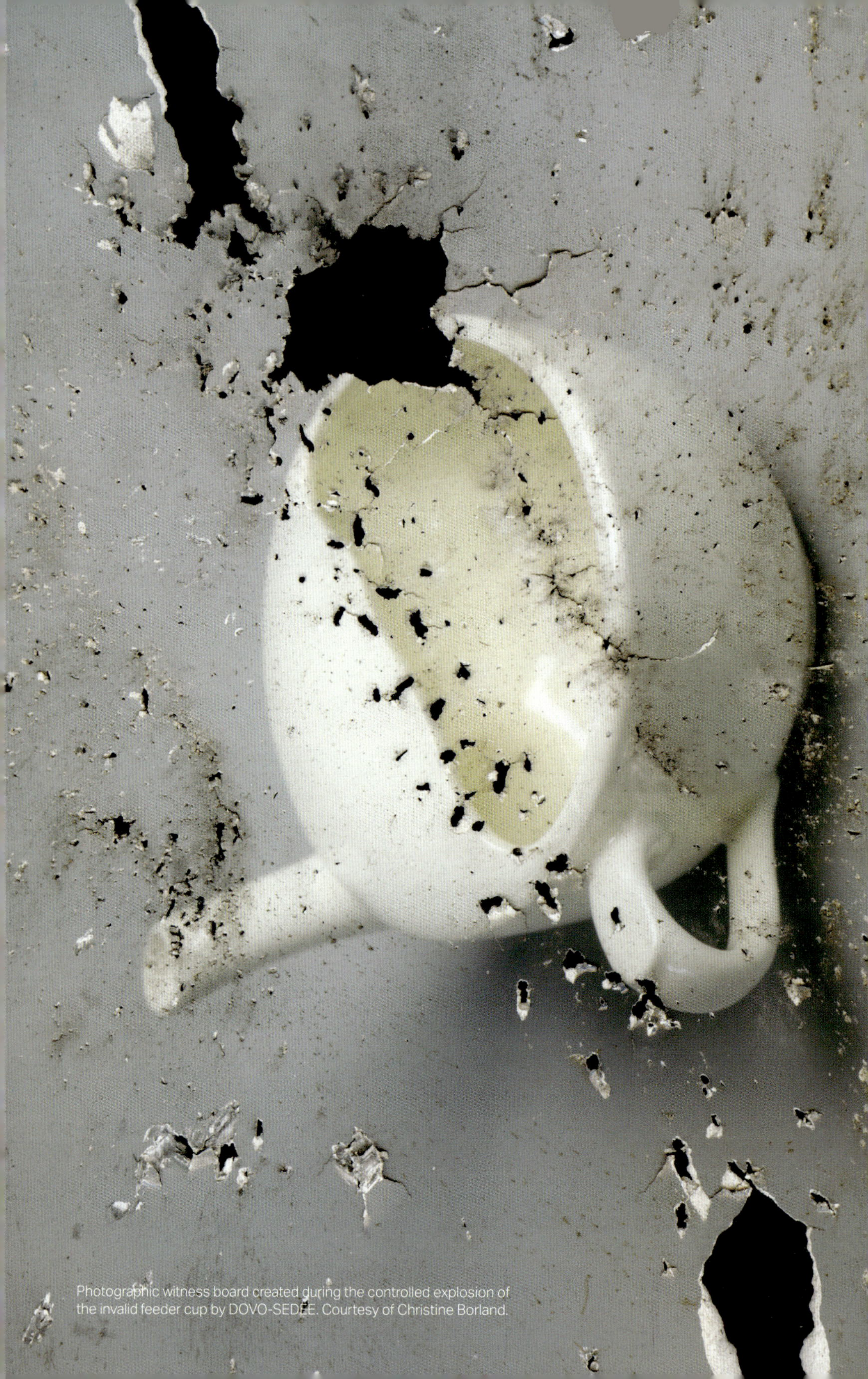

Photographic witness board created during the controlled explosion of the invalid feeder cup by DOVO-SEDEE. Courtesy of Christine Borland.

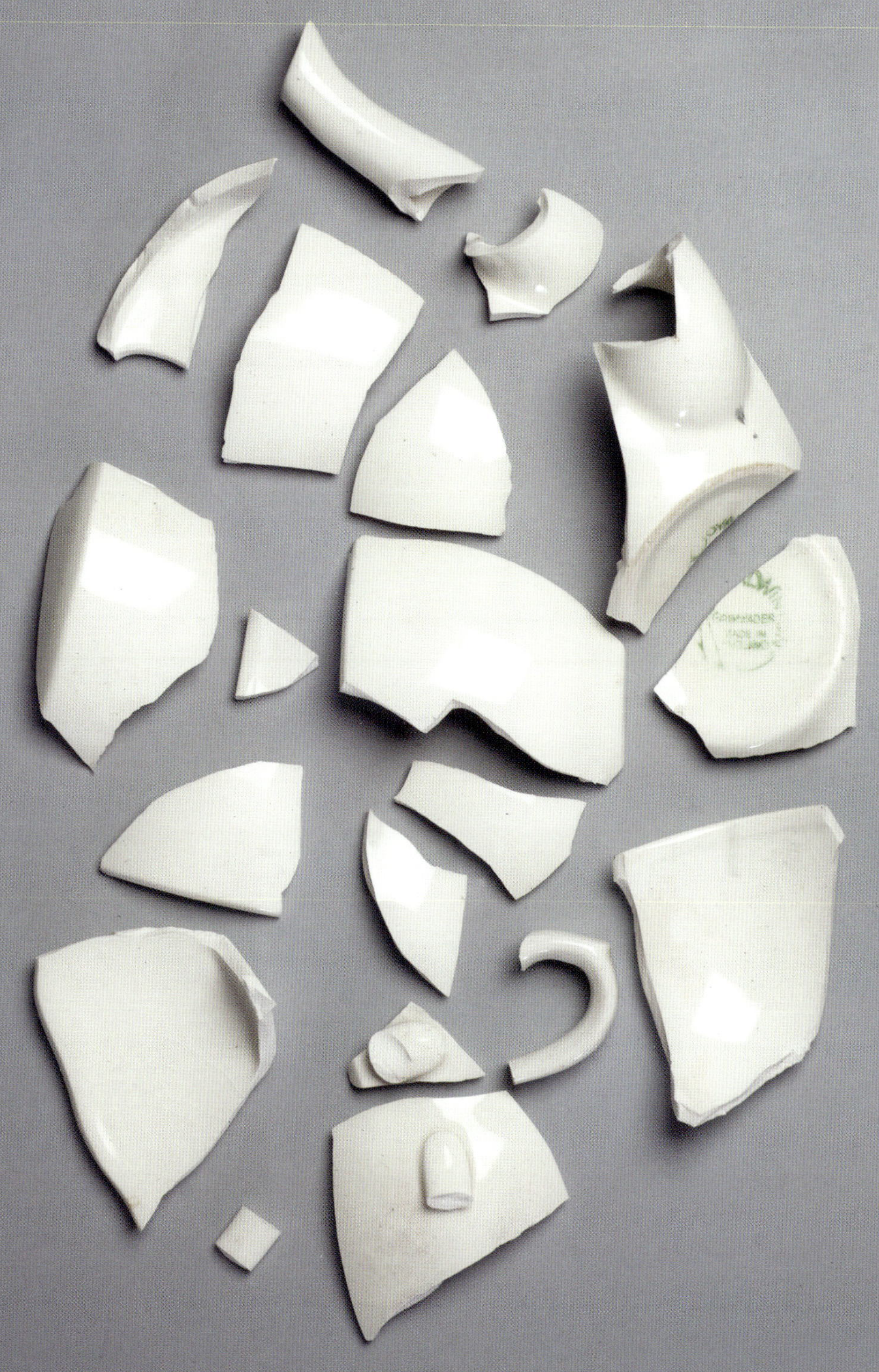

Nine fragments of the invalid feeder cup exploded by DOVO-SEDEE, 15 May 2018. Courtesy of Christine Borland.

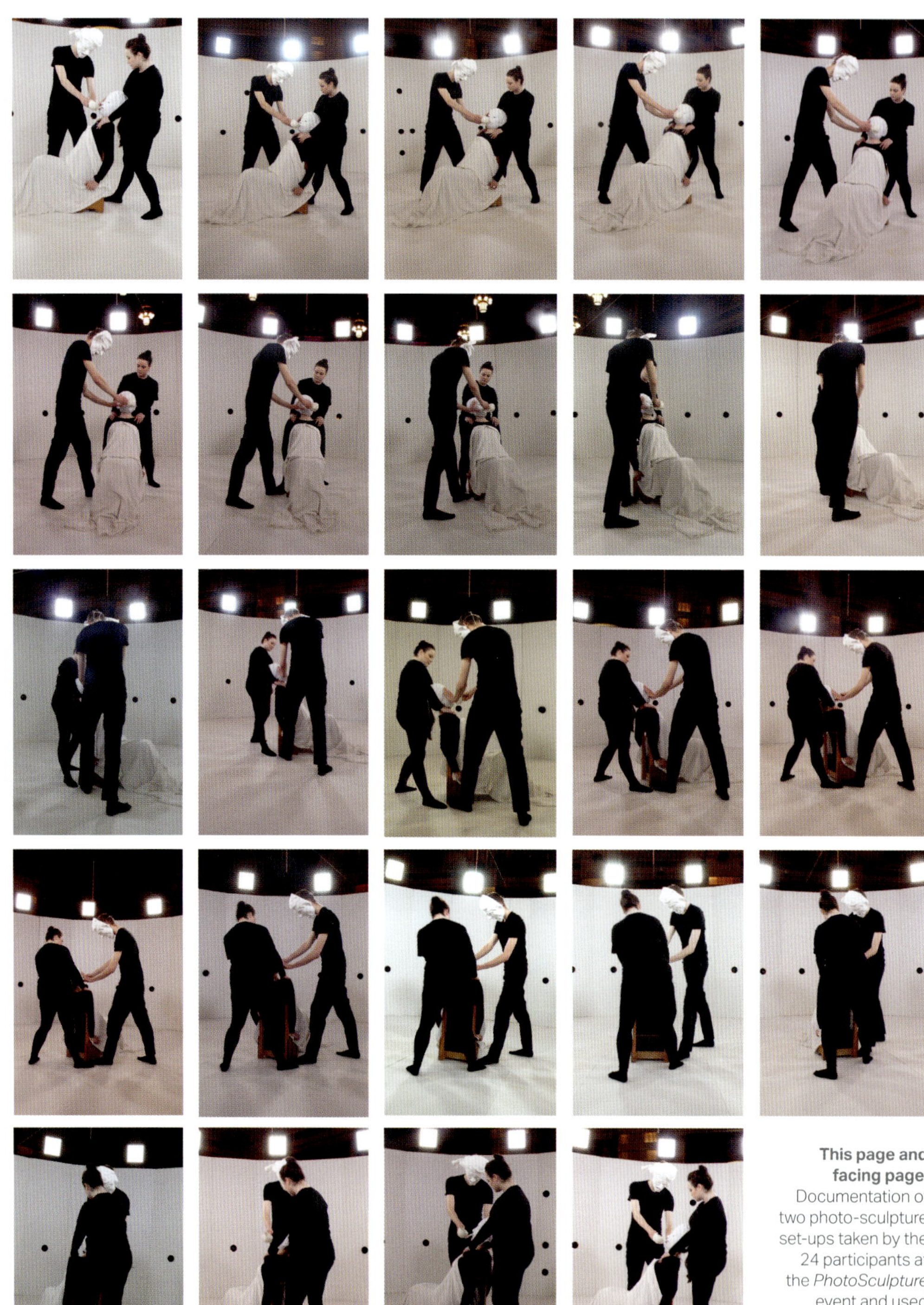

This page and
facing page:
Documentation of
two photo-sculpture
set-ups taken by the
24 participants at
the *PhotoSculpture*
event and used
as templates to
create the sculptural
silhouettes for
I Say Nothing.

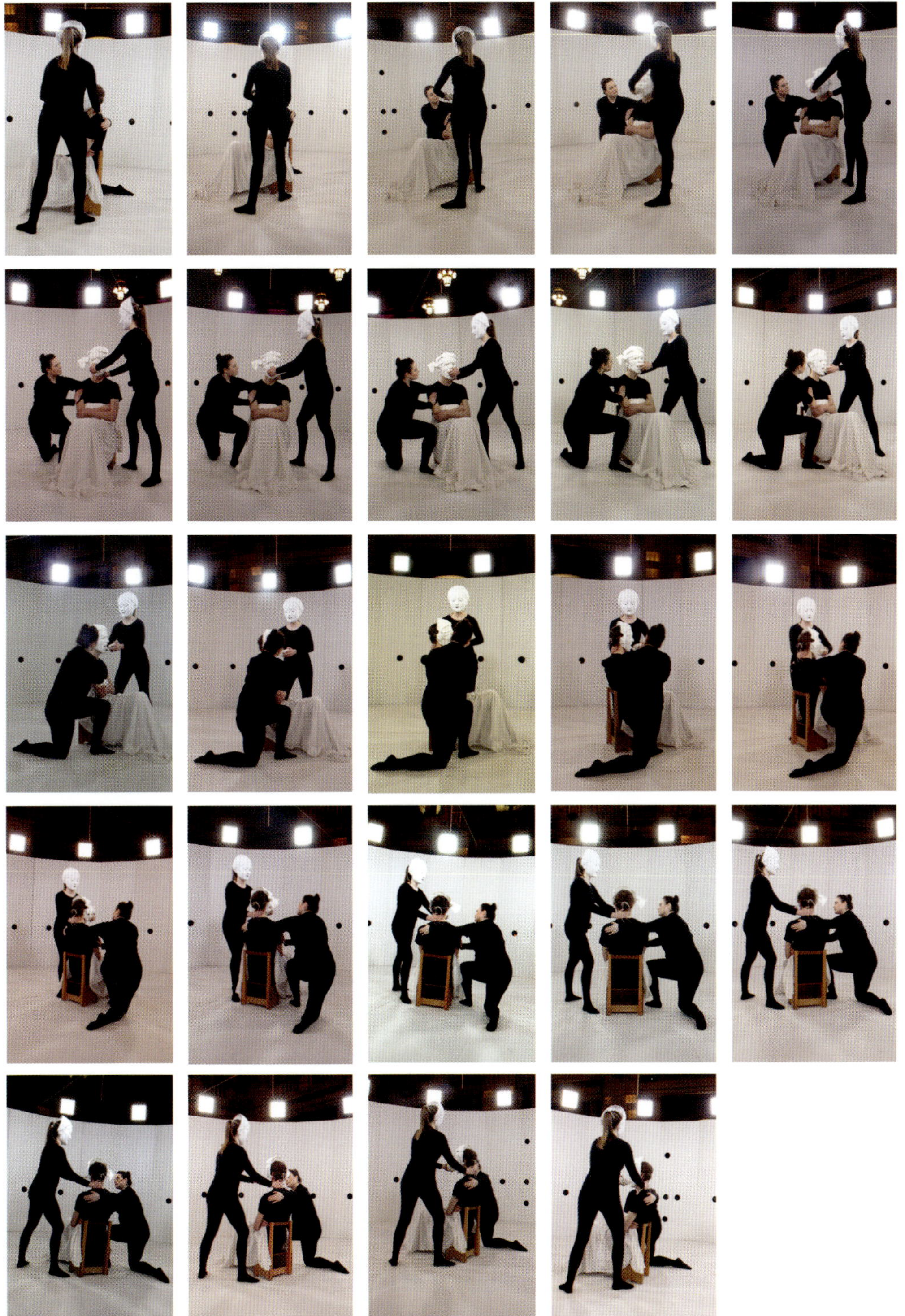

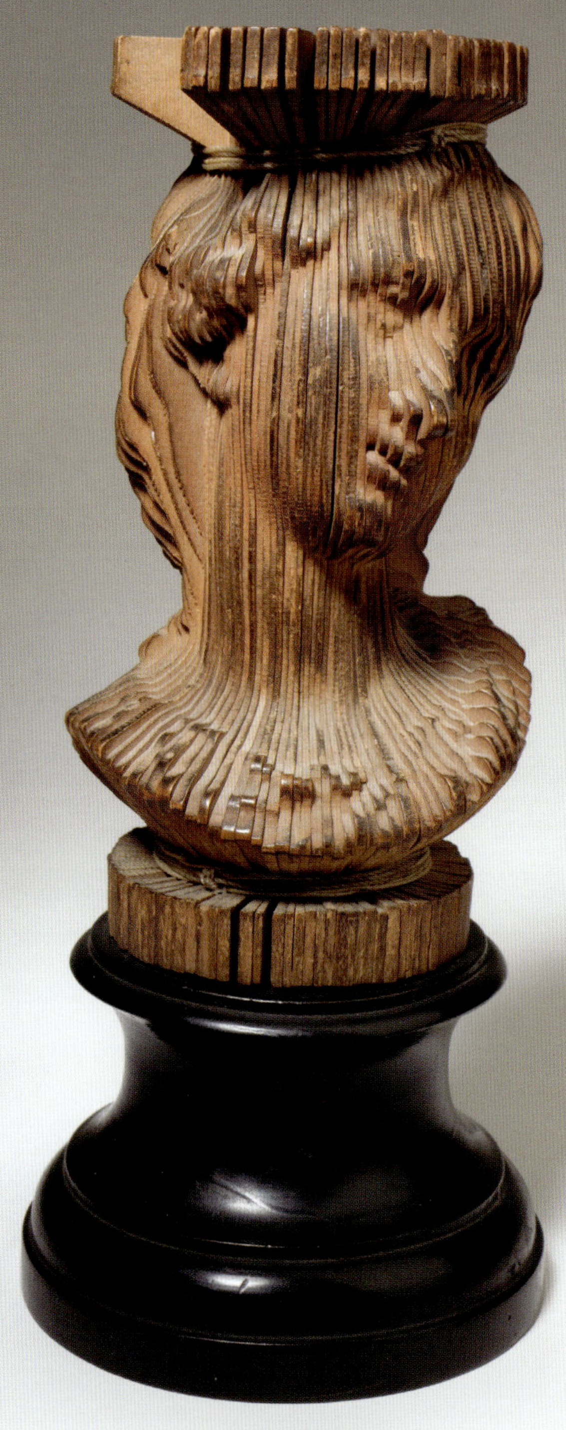

Unfinished photosculpture by François Willème, *c.*1865: portrait head of a woman, oak maquette on base. Courtesy of the George Eastman Collection.

I Say Nothing
Installation

PEACE

24 MDF cut-out figures painted black,
glassine, timber structure

WAR

24 MDF cut-out figures painted white,
glassine, timber structure

PHOTOSCULPTURE STRUCTURE

2 groups of 12 chipboard panels with
circular camera apertures

DRONE

2 digital videos on LED displays

SOURCE MATERIAL

MDF trestle table, invalid feeder cup fragments,
acrylic mounts, conservation report for the
cup prior to controlled explosion

SOUTH BALCONY

KELVINGROVE ART GALLERY AND MUSEUM

OCTOBER 2018

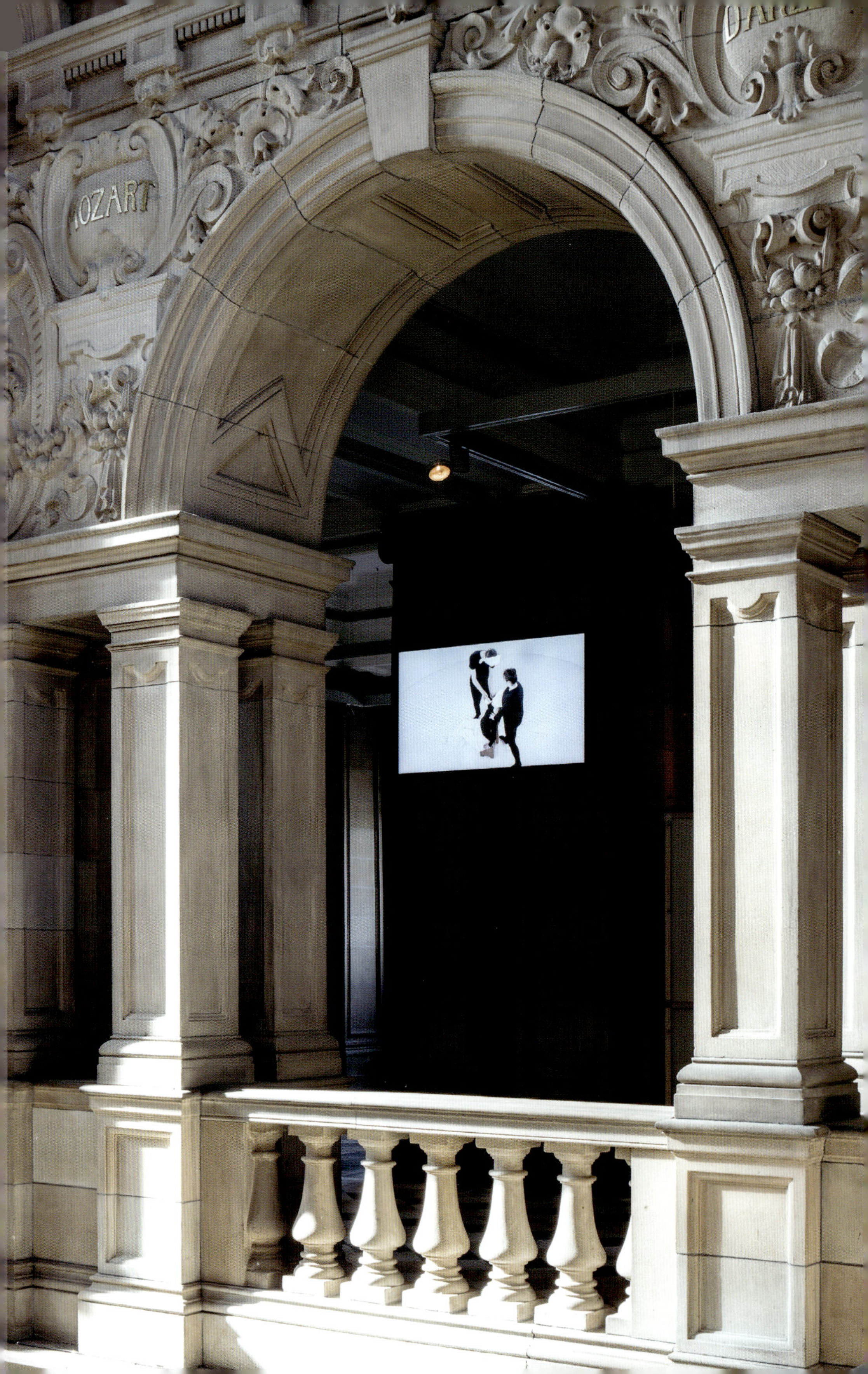

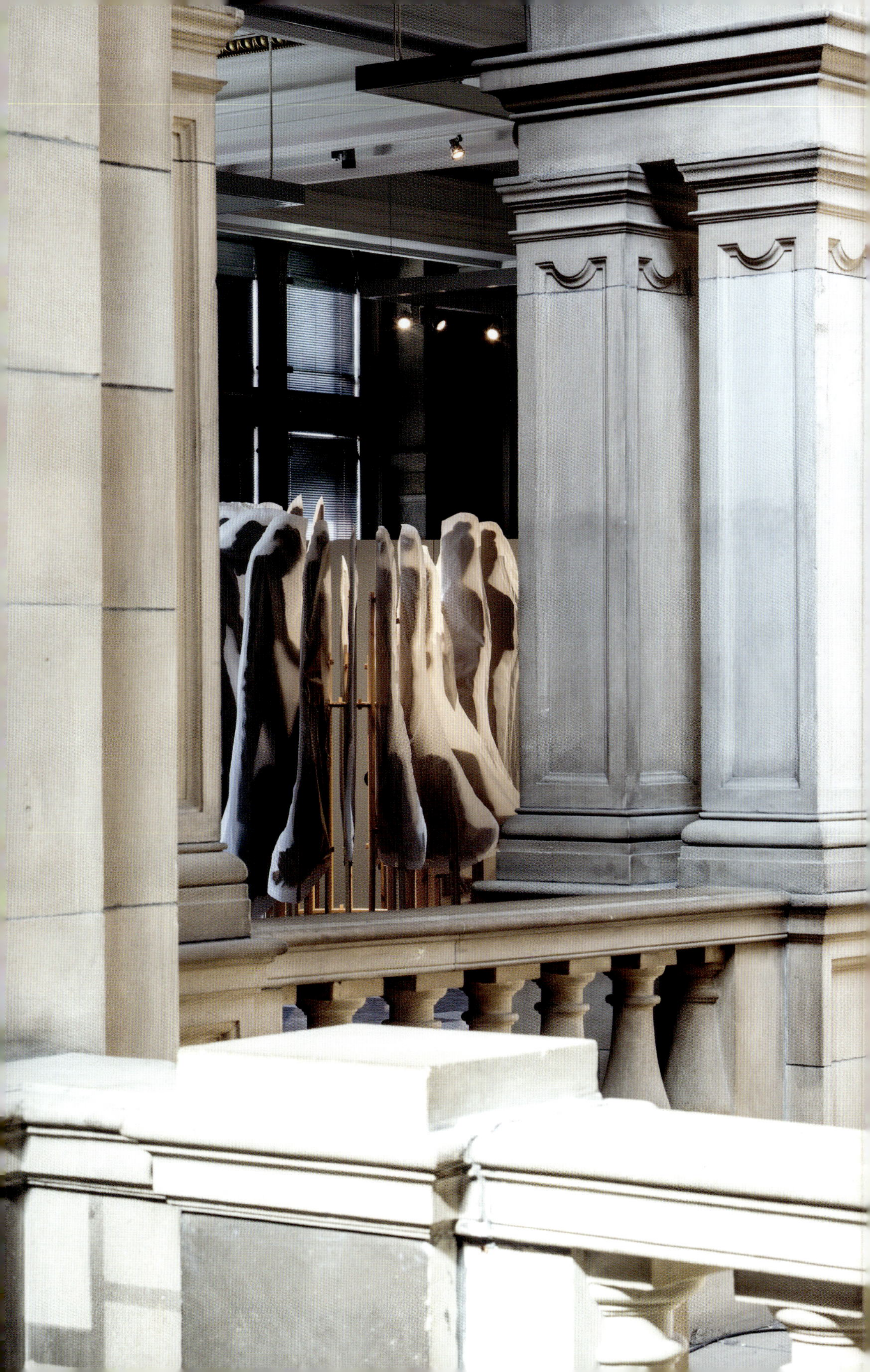

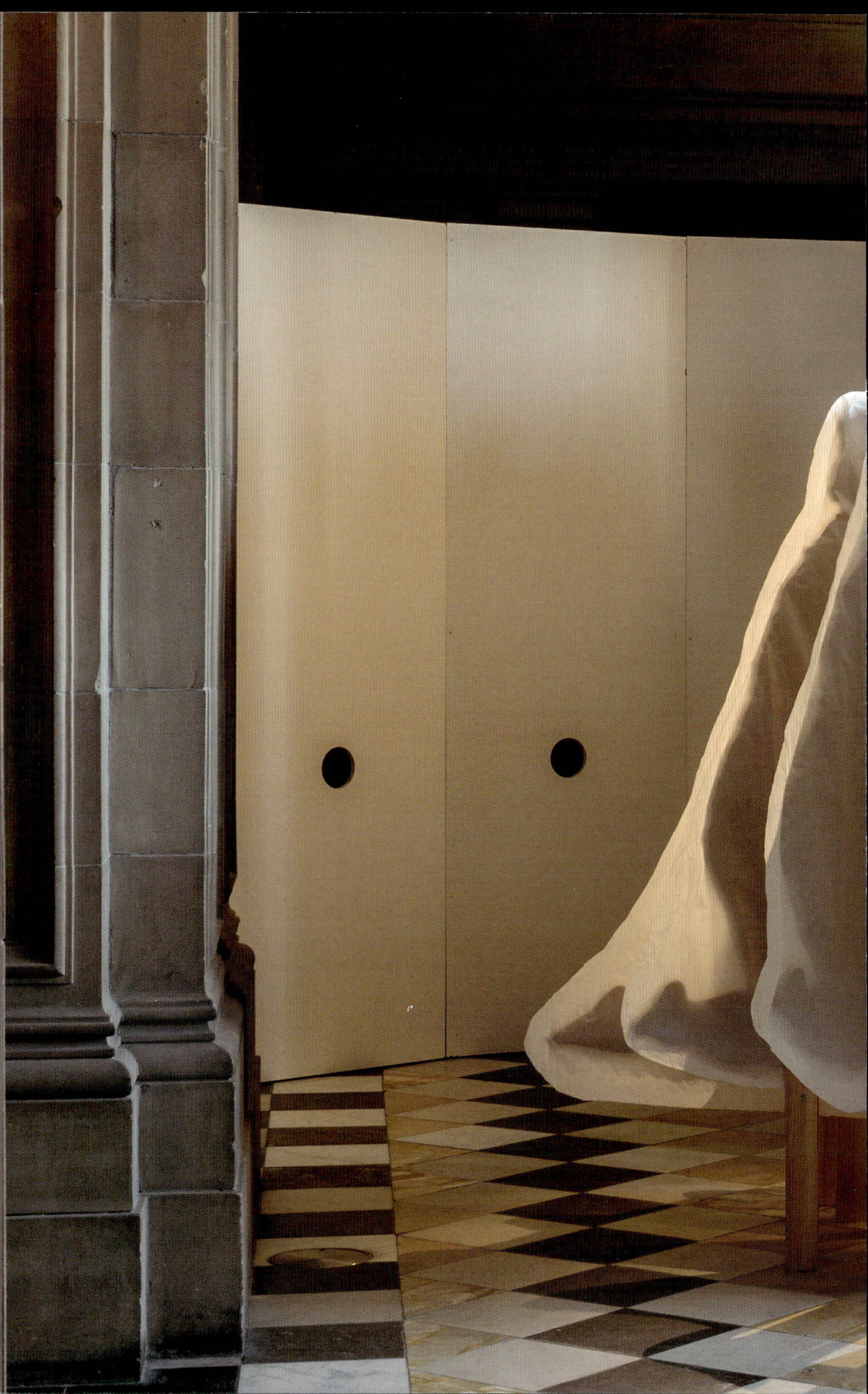

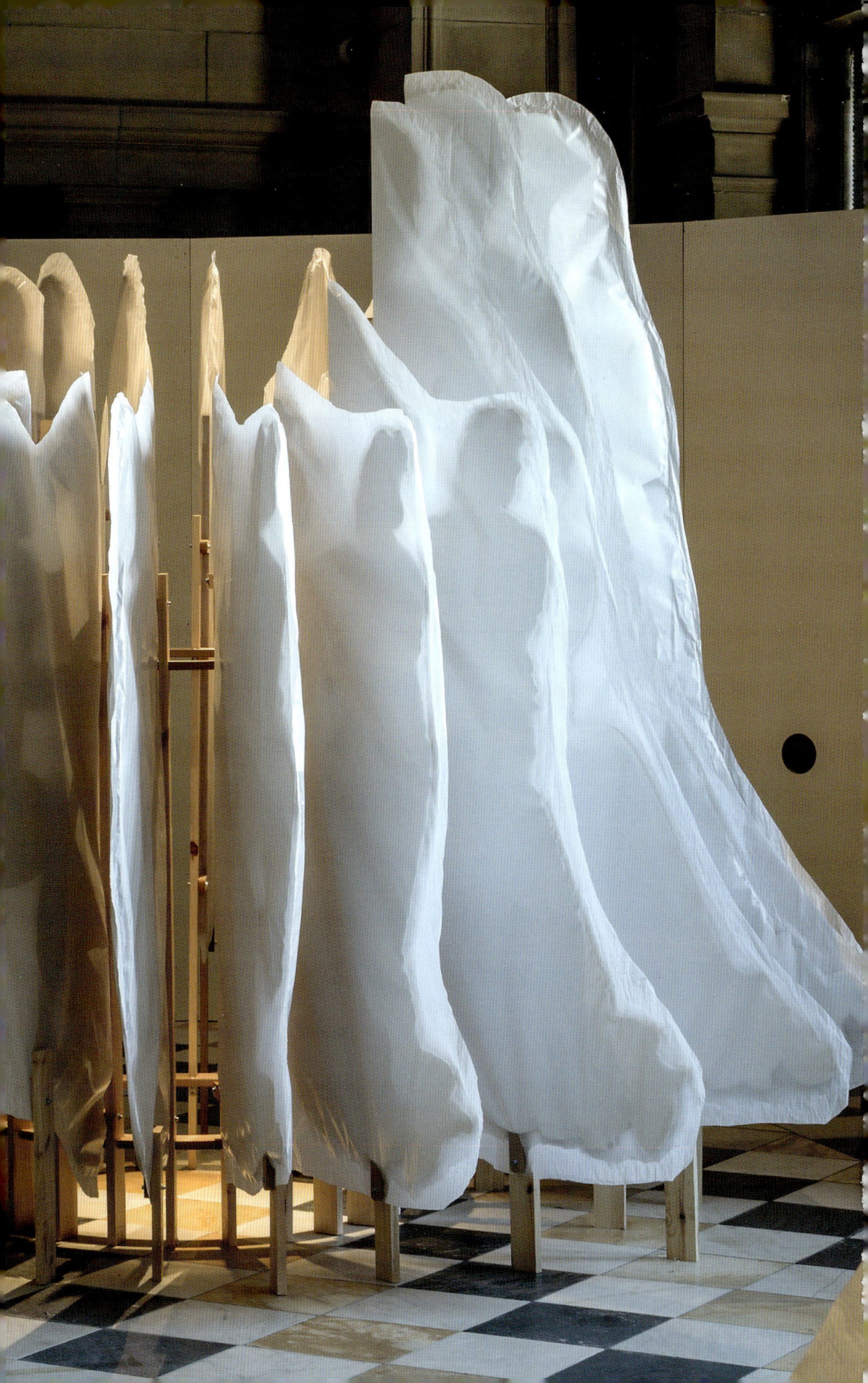

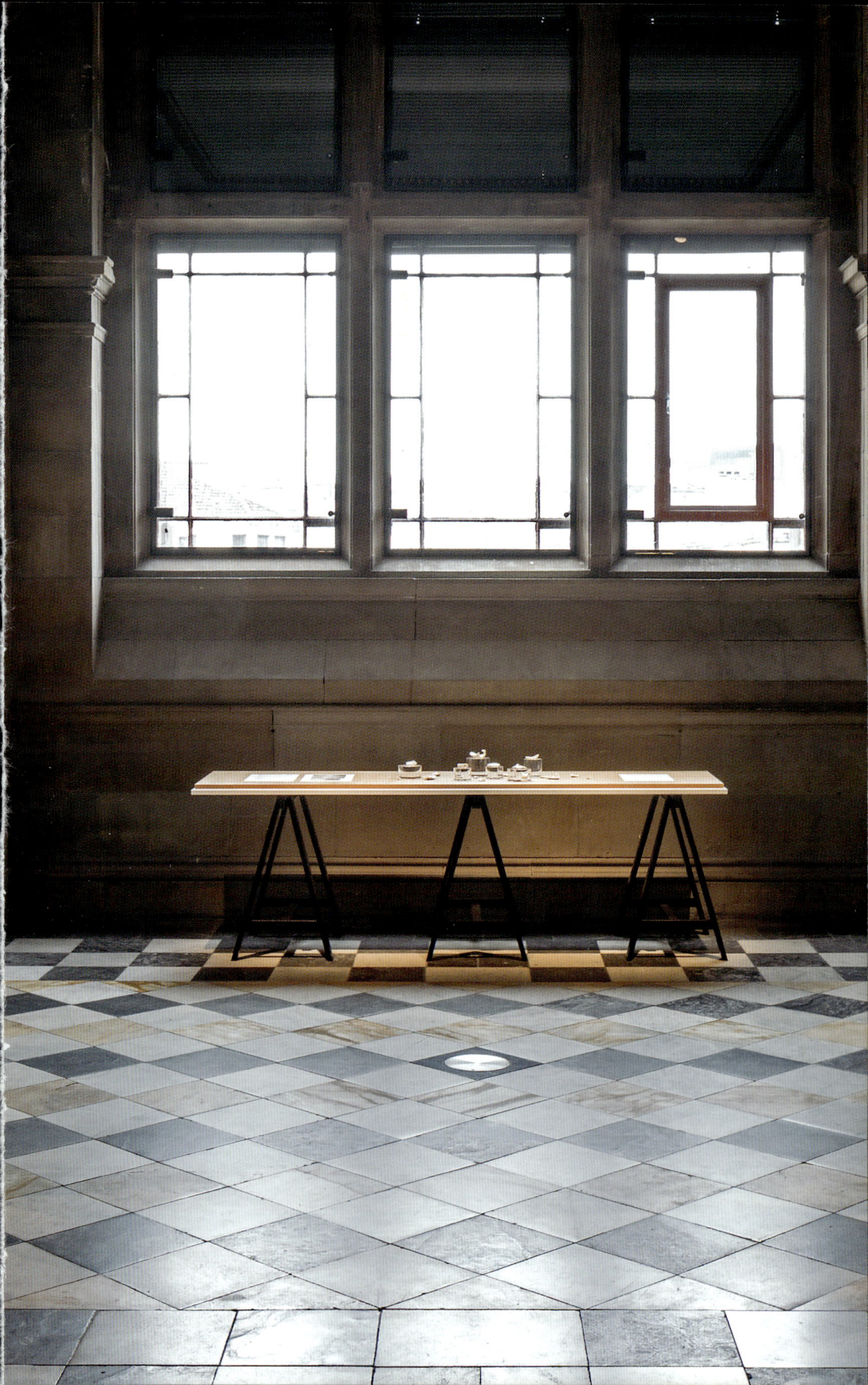

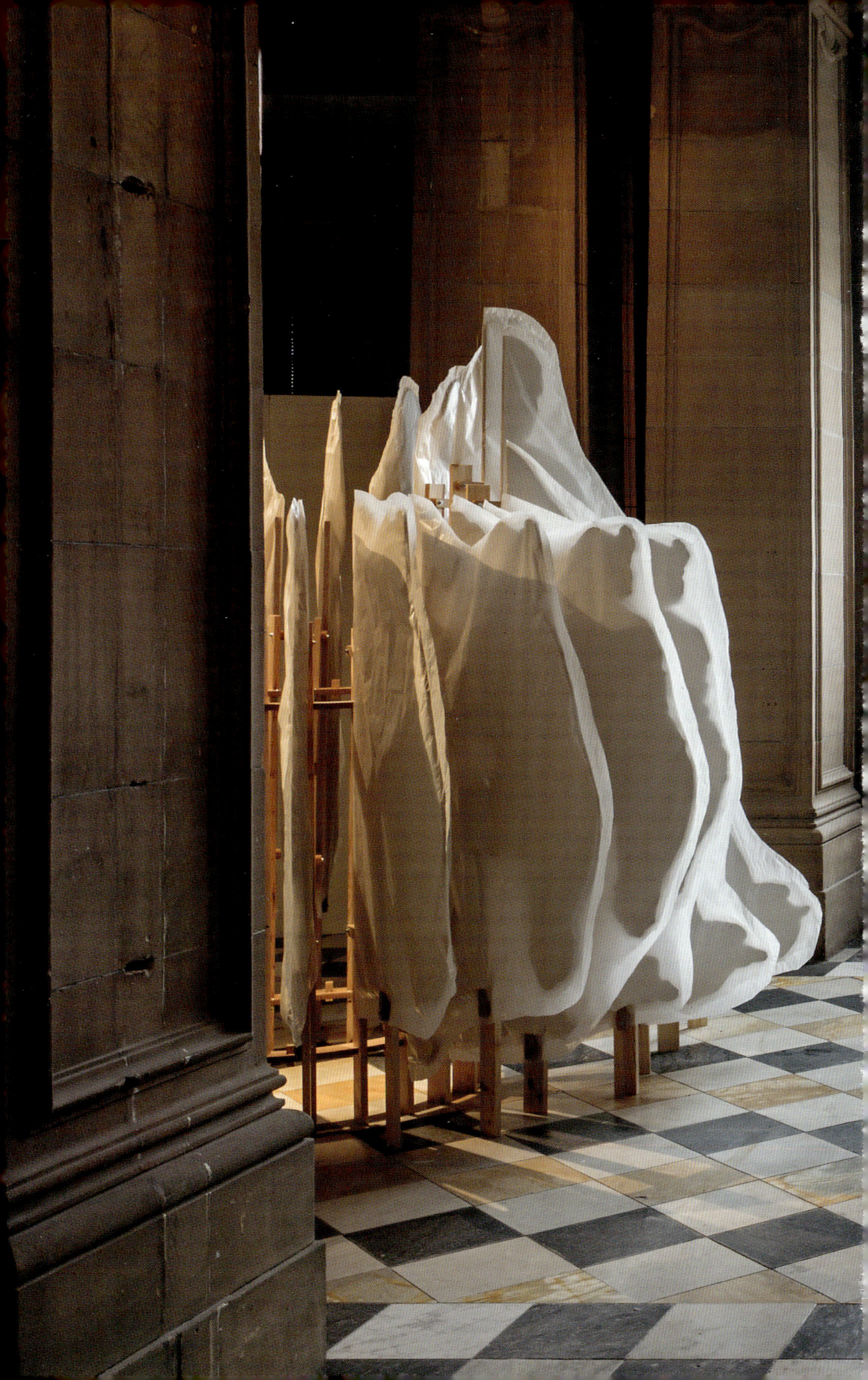

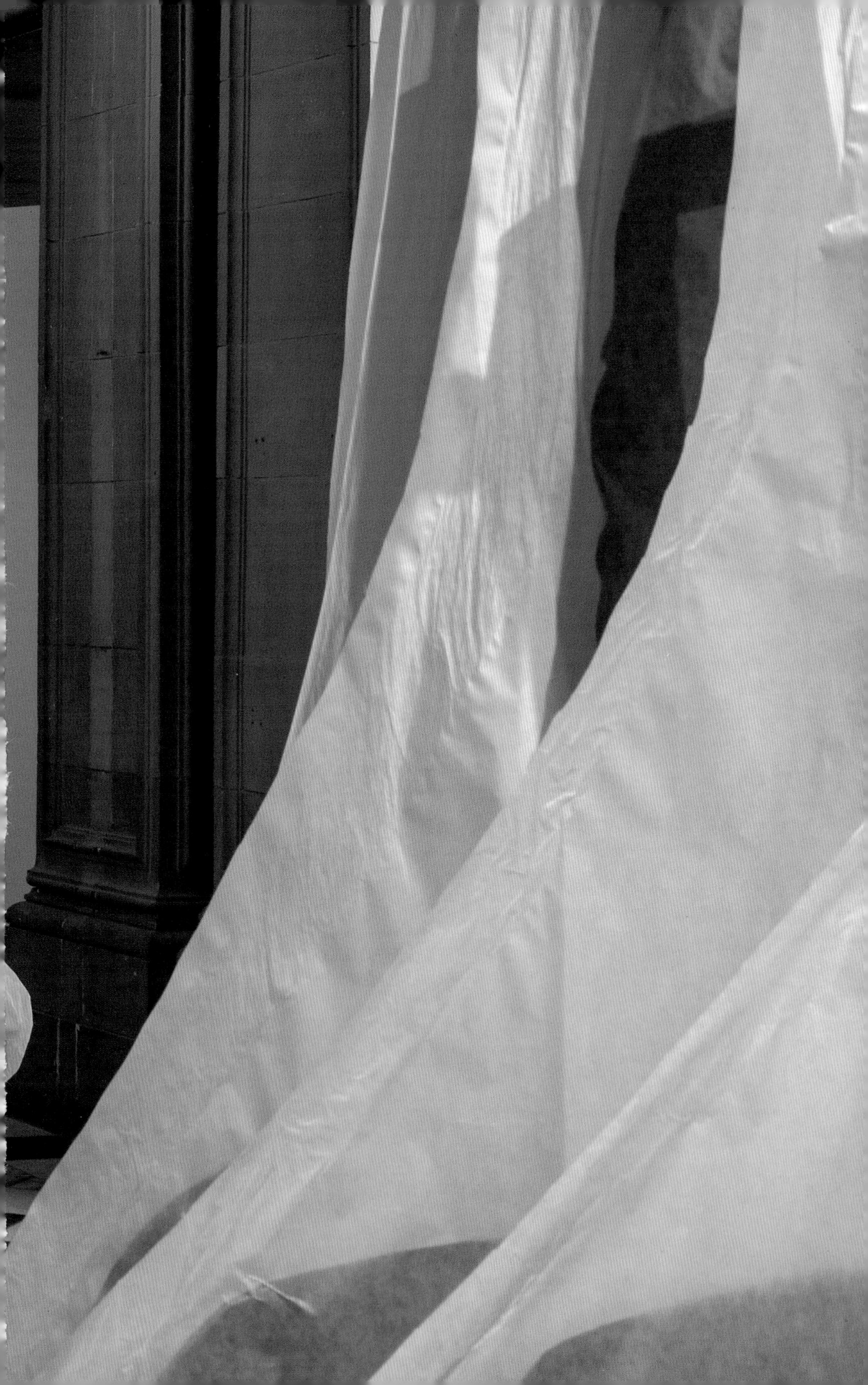

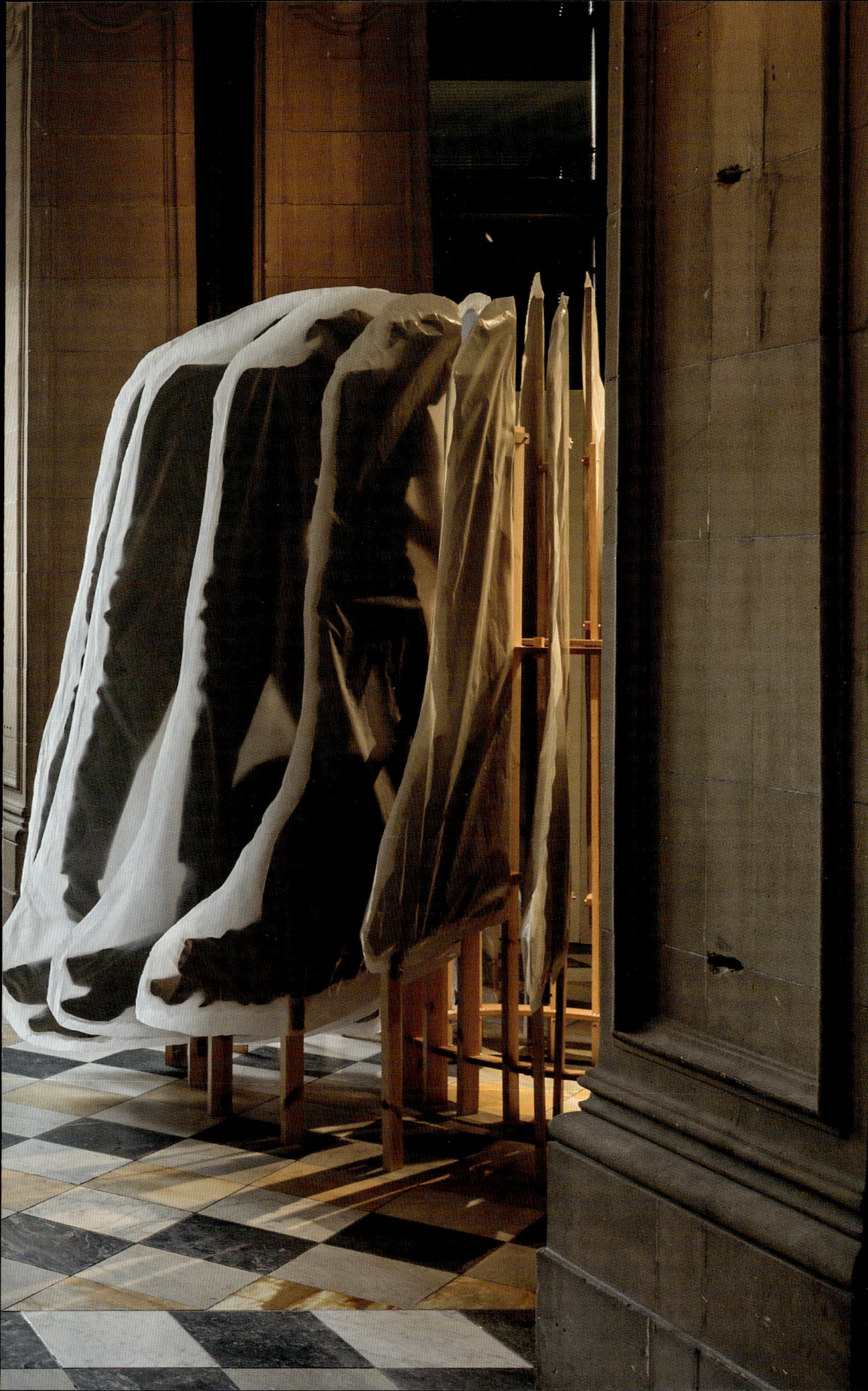

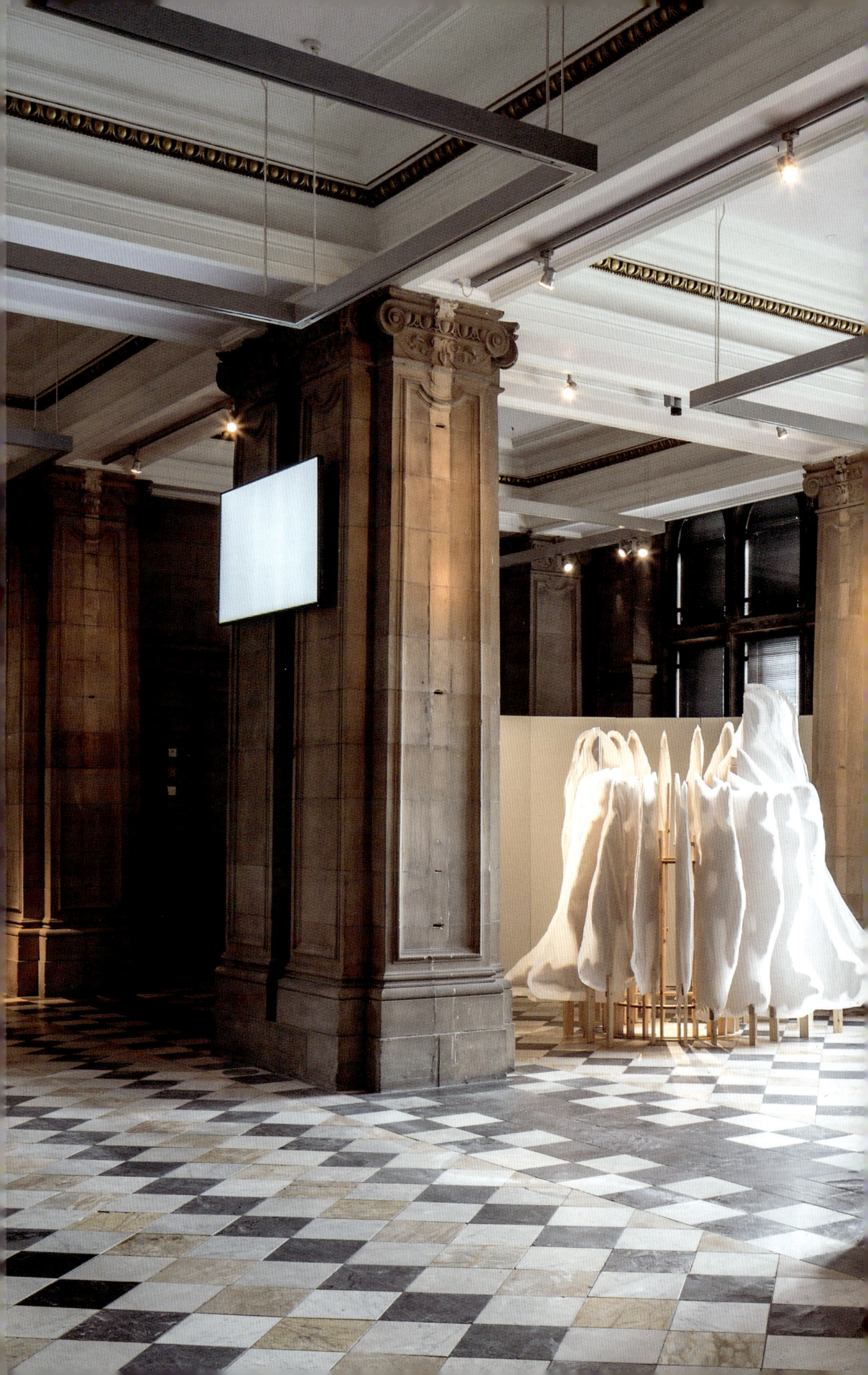

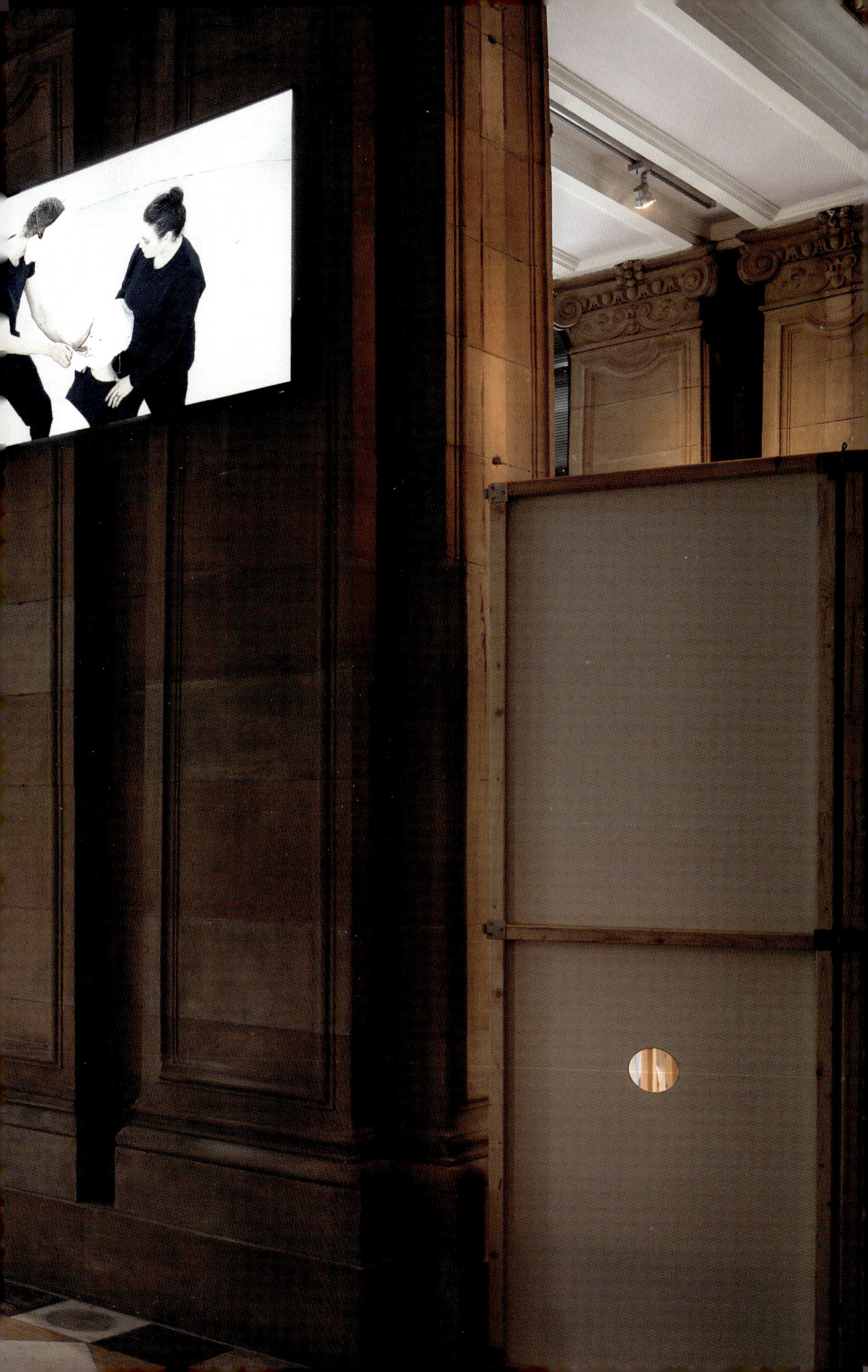

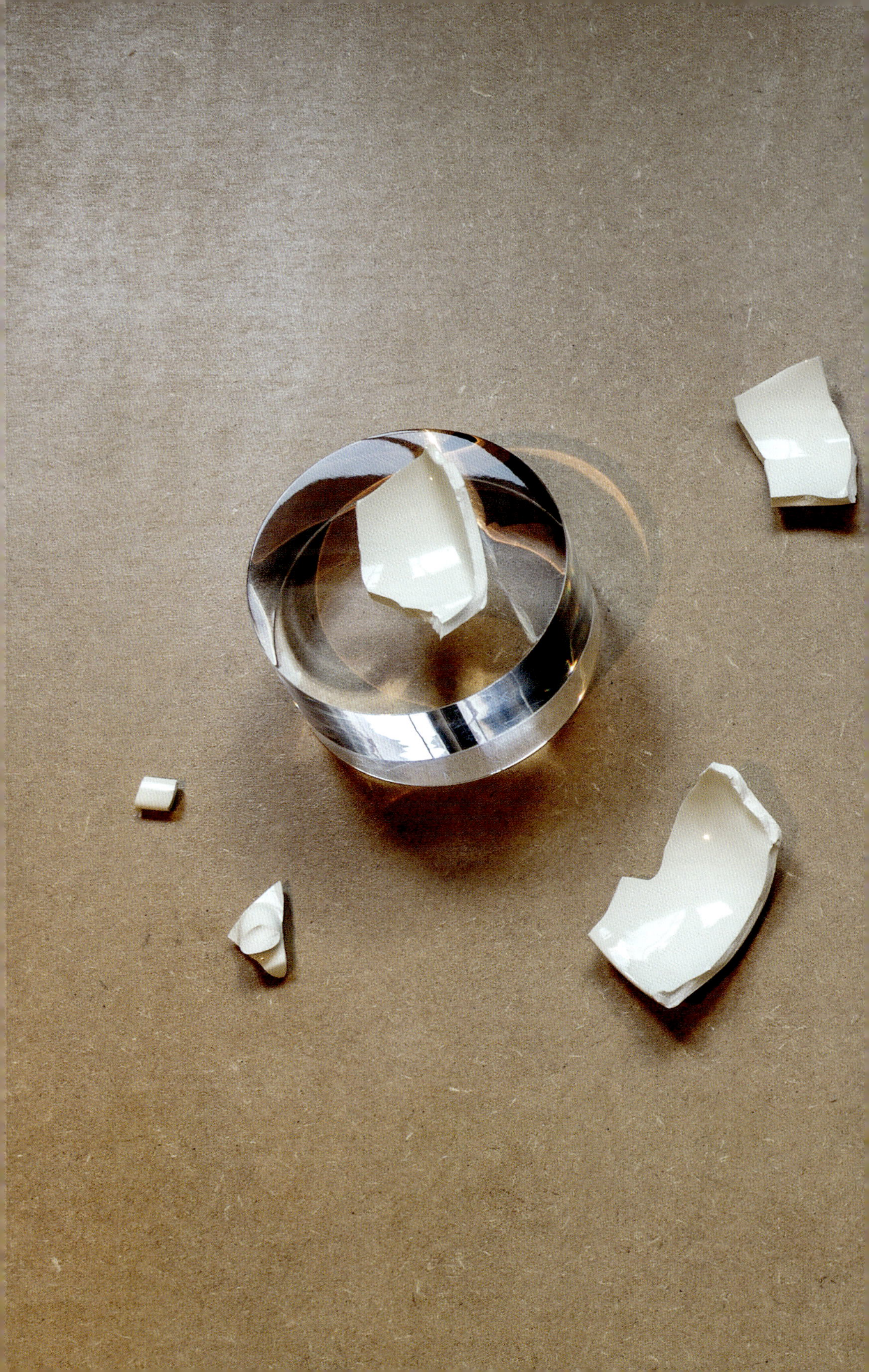

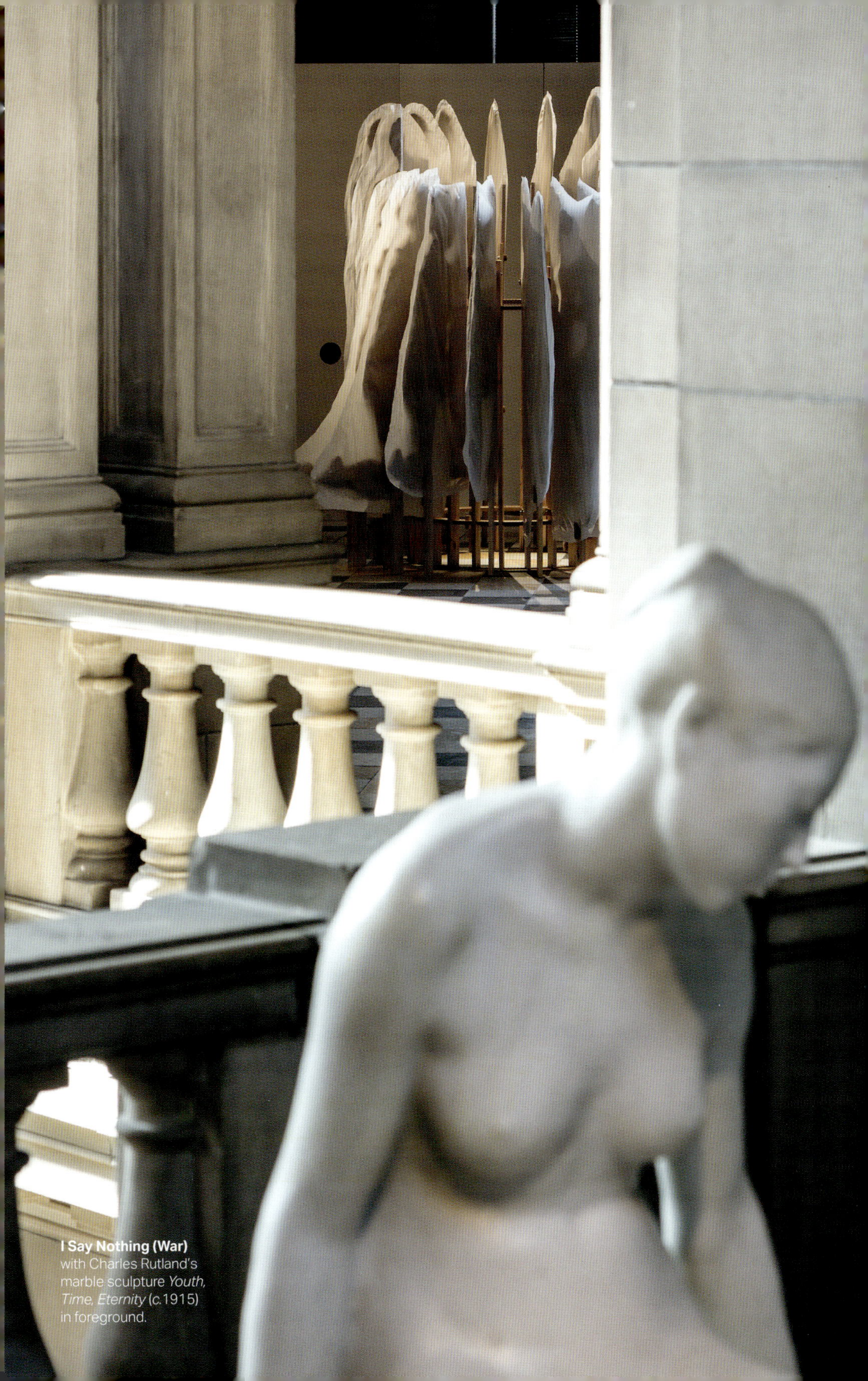

I Say Nothing (War) with Charles Rutland's marble sculpture *Youth, Time, Eternity* (c.1915) in foreground.

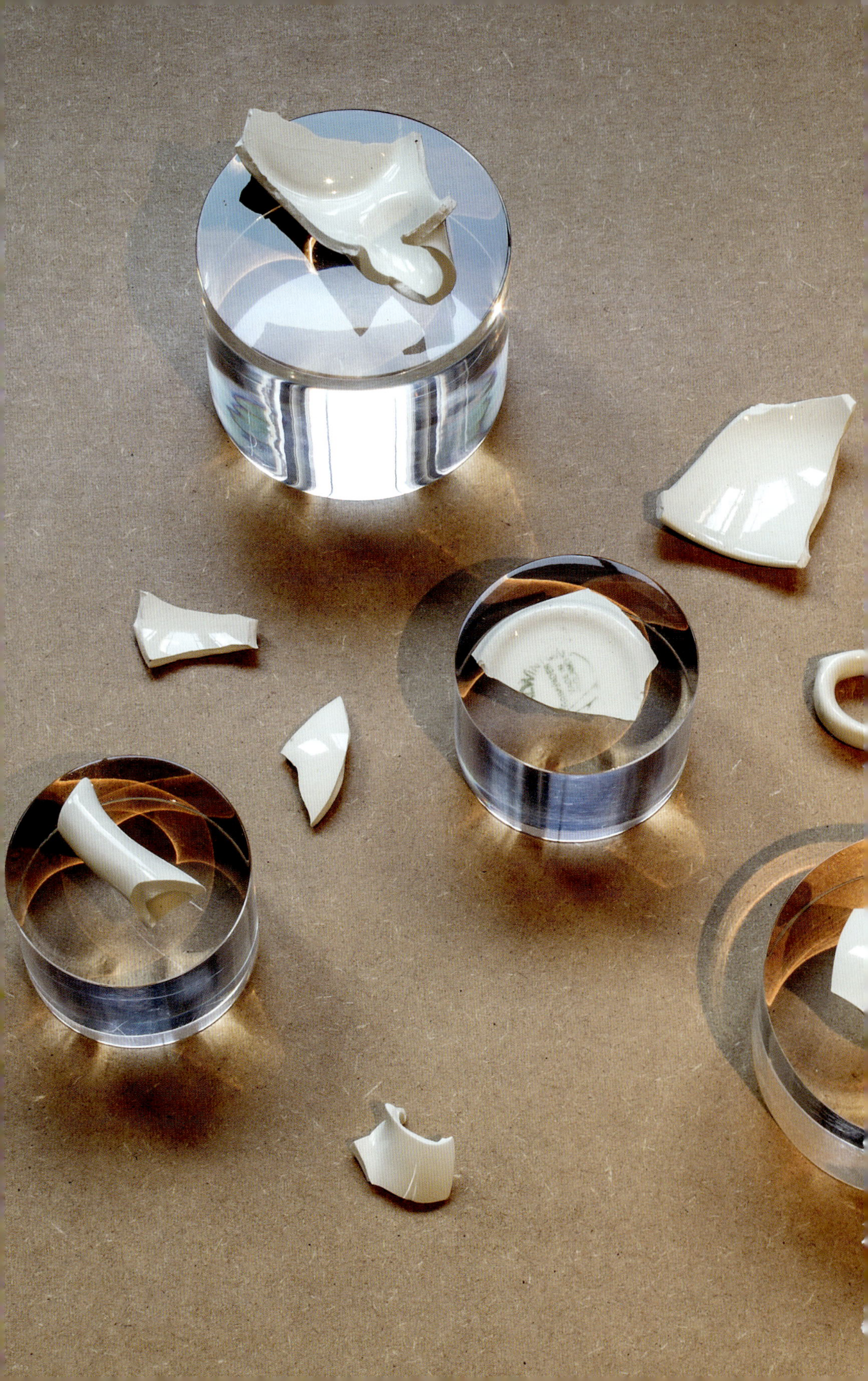

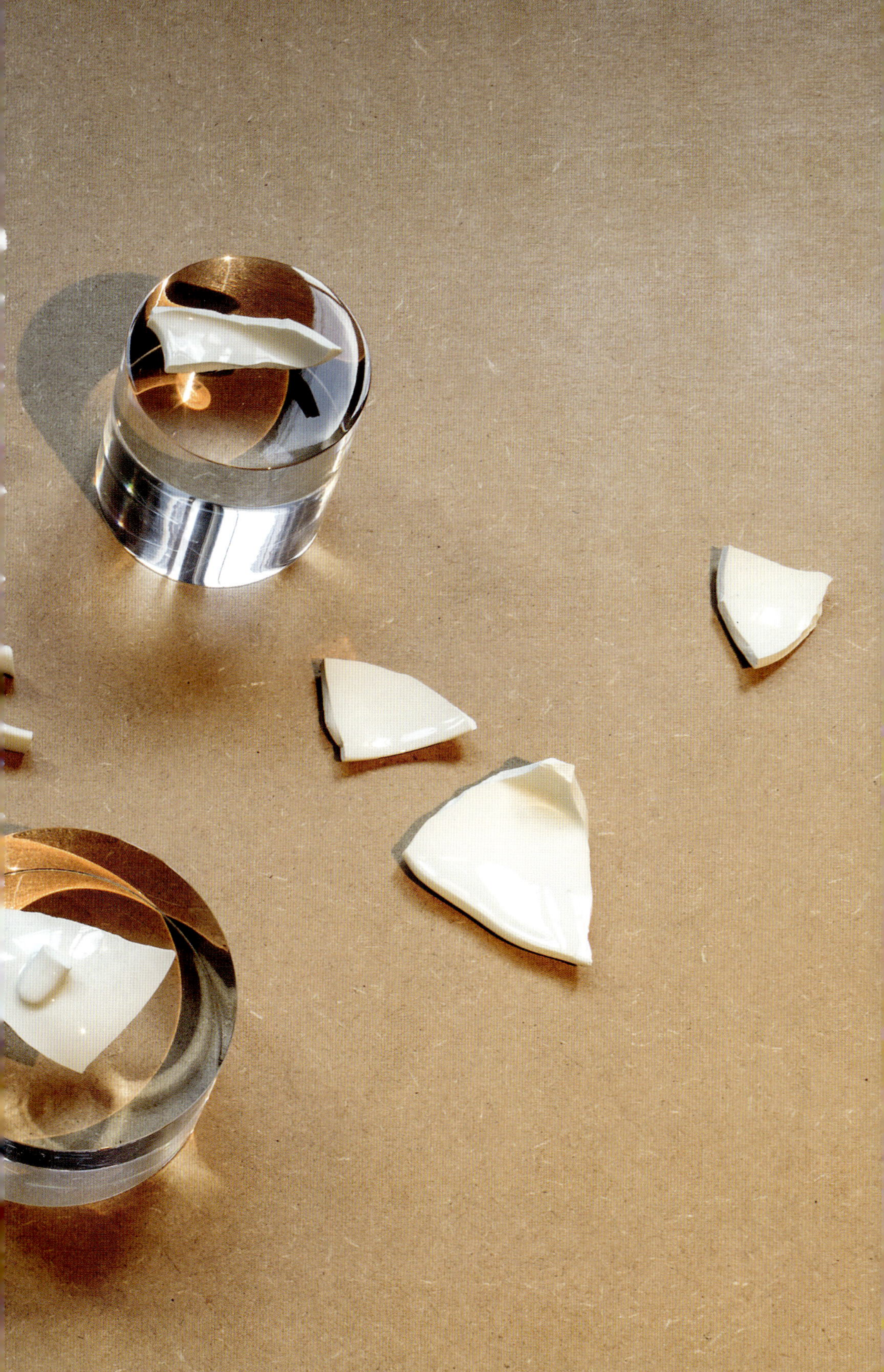

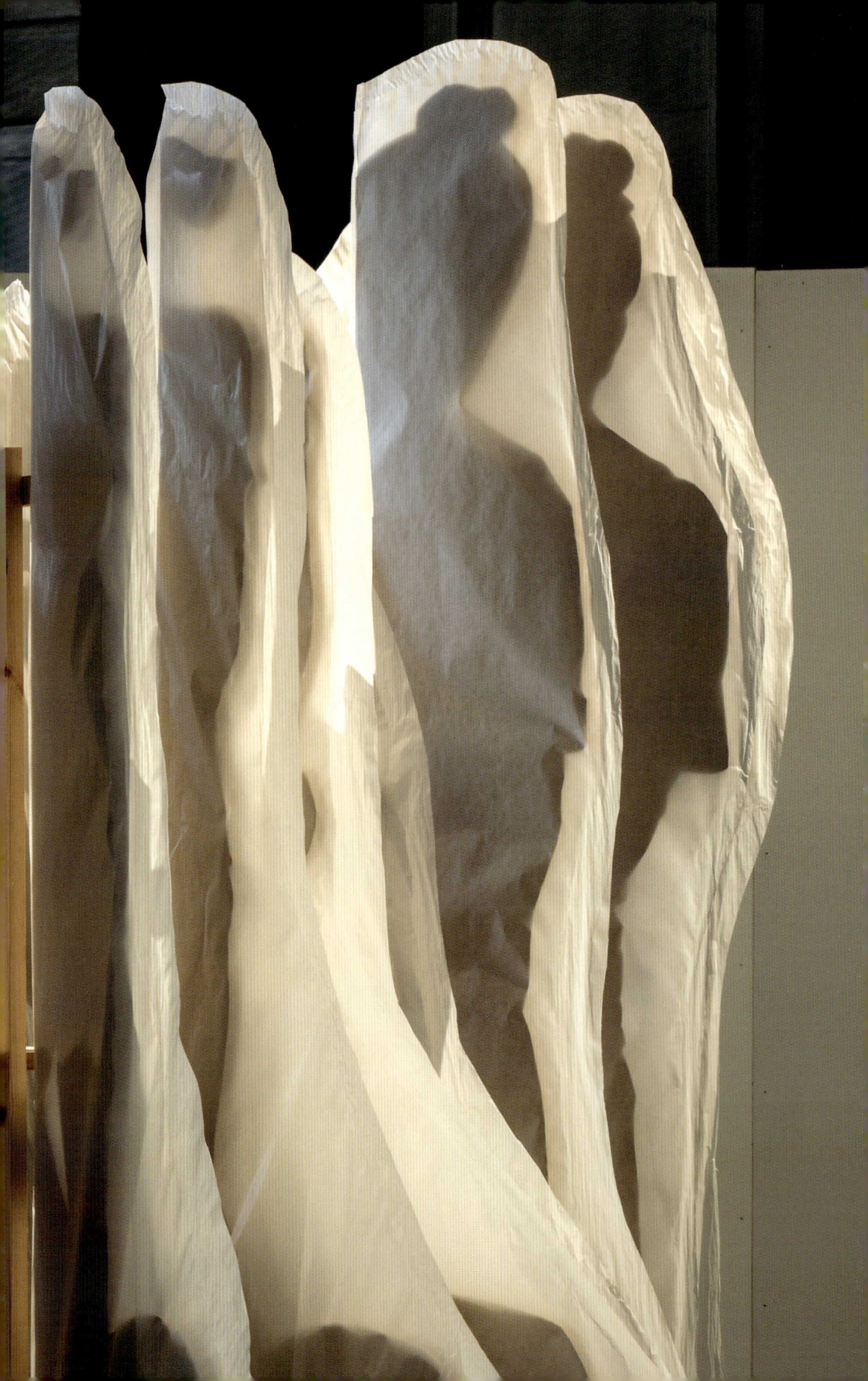

Christine Borland
in conversation with Jo Meacock

Jo: At Glasgow Museums we were thrilled by the opportunity to have an artist research the World War I objects in our collection and respond creatively to them, and ultimately encourage further dialogue and creative enquiry amongst our visitors. We had no idea what specific objects you might be drawn to and the direction your research would take. It was all incredibly exciting. Was it an equally stimulating venture for you? How did you begin to tackle the more than two thousand World War I-related objects in our collection?

Christine: It was unique from the beginning because Glasgow Museums invited me to tailor-make the structure of the whole commission to best fit my own way of working, both in researching the subject matter and in subsequently developing the work in the studio.

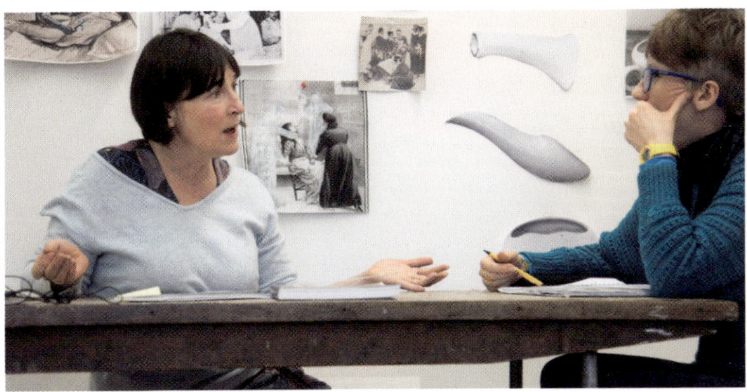

○ Christine Borland and Jo Meacock in the artist's studio.

The opportunity to begin the commission as a research project, without any fixed idea of its endpoint, was very special. It was so important to build in enough time to really look at and consider the World War I objects listed in Glasgow Museums' collection. I also wanted to ensure I could reflect on the concentrated periods I spent in the stores, hence the decision to develop a timetable with staff at Glasgow Museums Resource Centre (GMRC) that ran for a year – selecting and looking at objects intensively, then a pause and returning several weeks later with a new selection or a request to look again.

At first I wasn't too rigorous with myself about why certain objects suggested themselves more than others; some things intrigued me

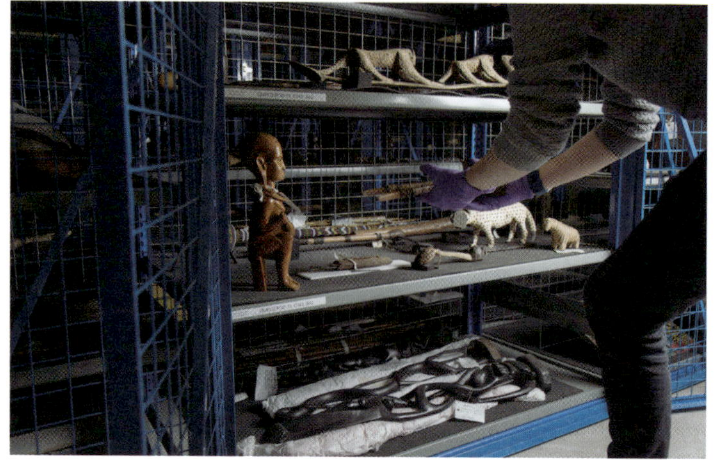

because they were made from strange, unlikely materials or they suggested hidden narratives, around personal stories. Because it was the beginning of a two-year period, I tried to allow myself these indulgences – to just revel in not knowing and be led through my selection of objects quite intuitively.

J: Would you say that your approach to research as an artist differs from that of a 'traditional' or non-artist researcher?

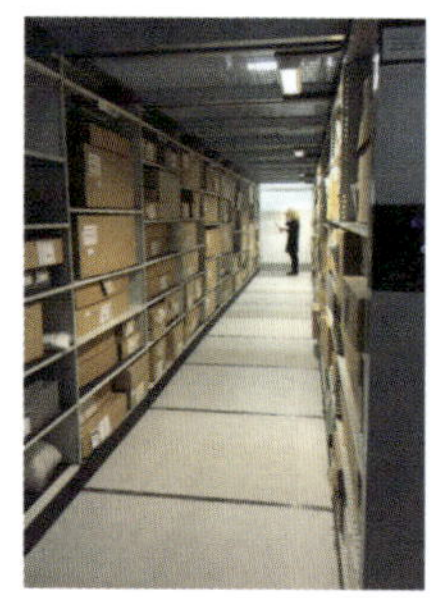

C: I think artistic research does differ from other kinds of research because it's rooted in the practice of being an artist, which is so individual and ultimately led by making and doing. Over the course of my career, through trial and error, I've worked out methods which suit me, many of which might be in common with other researchers: archival and web research, background reading and interviewing experts – but, of course, working in parallel in the studio. Ultimately, there's got to be room for experimental thinking and making, for unexpected or chance associations between things … and then for me, I make some sense of it by digging back into the research again. You've got to build in these freedoms to come up with work which embodies some kind of new way of looking at a subject.

J: GMRC is quite an extraordinary place where curators, conservators, technicians and many other staff all work together, and in which diverse objects – including machinery and vehicles, arms and armour, natural history specimens, archaeological finds, social history artefacts and fine and decorative art – are stored, with

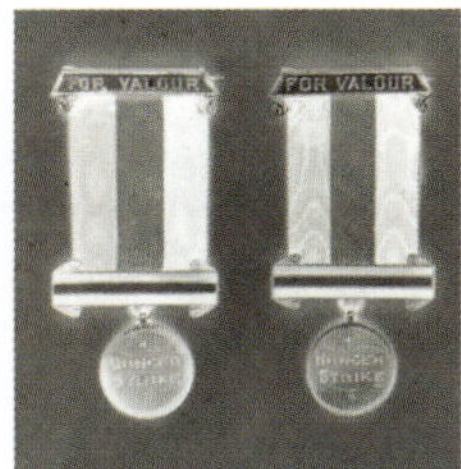

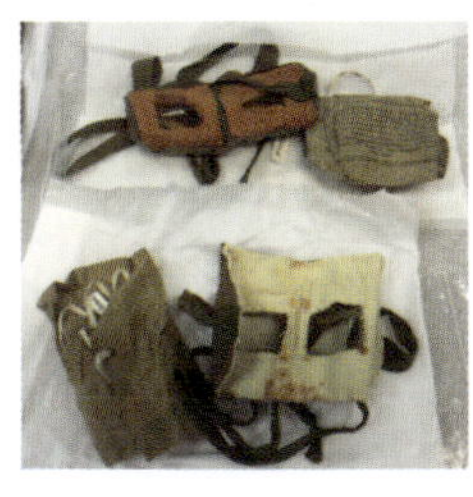

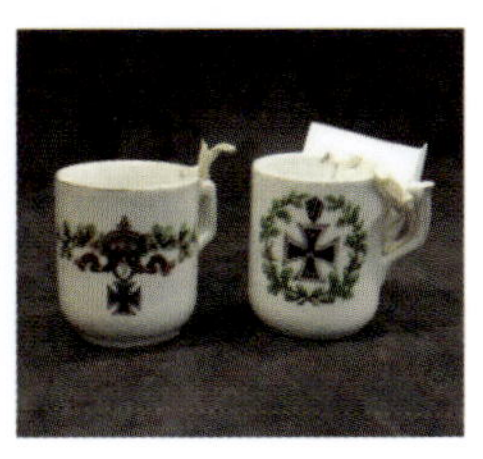

○ top: Detail from a black-and-white photographic negative in the Glasgow Museums Photo Library, which shows one of the Women's Social and Political Union (WSPU) hunger-strike medals presented to Margaret and Frances McPhun for hunger strike, HM Prison Holloway, 4 March 1912.

middle: Royal Artillery safety goggles, part of Glasgow Museums' World War I collection.

bottom: Porcelain mugs made in Germany in the early 20th century, part of Glasgow Museums' World War I collection.

unprecedented access for external researchers and visitors. At *Doubtful Occasion*, your creative symposium held at GMRC on 5 October 2017, colleagues from museums, universities and the arts came together to share in your research, contribute ideas and reflect creatively; the building should certainly be used for this kind of event and we hope that it will be the start of future creative conversations and collaborations. Looking back, what are your reflections on your year being a part of life at GMRC?

C: In terms of a place to work, GMRC has been incredibly inspiring. Although I was focusing on World War I objects, so many different areas of the collection are housed within the stores that as I was making my way to an object (or an object was making its way to me), the thousands of other objects sitting between it caught my eye and often sparked unexpected connections. The duration of the commission has allowed me to savour these details and follow their lead deeper into the collection; I have followed up record books and seen handwriting from acquisitions made during the World War I period, thought about the resonance of notes made by various curators across a hundred years.

These many small things have accumulated along the way to have a big influence; one of my main goals in *Doubtful Occasion* was to work together with curators and conservators to accentuate the performative potential of the usually static objects in the stores, which involved unboxing, unwrapping and re-presenting. To allow the objects to occupy a central place, witnessing the presentations and conversations of *Doubtful Occasion*, was satisfying.

J: I'm intrigued by the objects that you have been drawn to in your research, many of which have never been on display before and have had very little research attention. Most are unassuming in size and material, without significant provenance information and seem to fall between traditional disciplines. What is it that interested you about them? Has your research brought up anything unexpected?

C: The unexpected things that have come up during the research process have been the connections between objects, narratives around objects and unusual materials and processes. For example, a moss pillow and a little cracked glass box which contains samples of moss: these are unassuming objects made from or containing a humble natural material which had no significant monetary value, but it was a joy to discover that during World War I moss was prized for its antiseptic and absorbent properties, and that it was home-front work for women, children and conscientious objectors to gather it for use in stuffing bandages and pillows which were sent to the front lines. Another modest object made from an atypical material, which popped up in the collection, is a towel, labelled as being made of paper and being commonly used by the German army; when I went to Germany to look at collections there, I found that paper was developed as one of many 'ersatz' (substitute) materials used instead of those which had become scarce, in this case imported cotton.

The Berlin iron jewellery which intrigued me is related to substitution, too; 'symbolic' jewellery like this was given in exchange for gold or silver donated by the public for the war effort. Exchanges of objects and alchemical, slightly magical associations have been connected with many of the objects that I have been interested in … they've led me from one to the other – little themes developing within the objects themselves and in relation to each other.

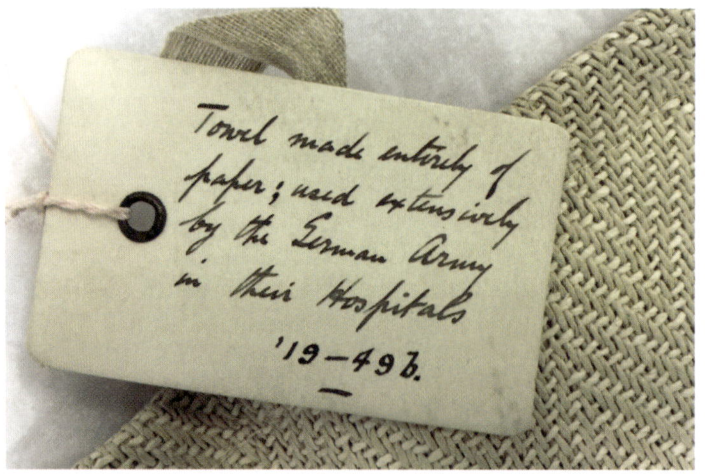

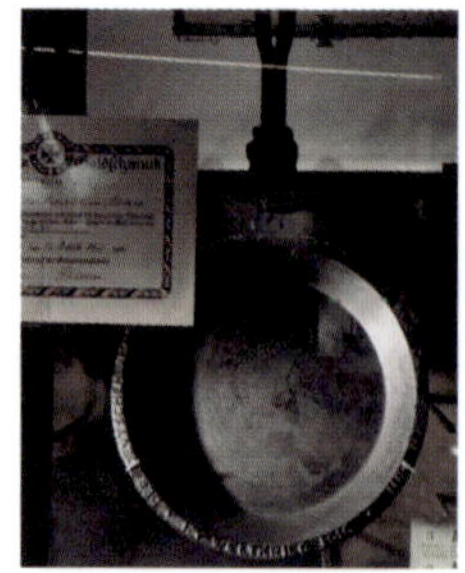

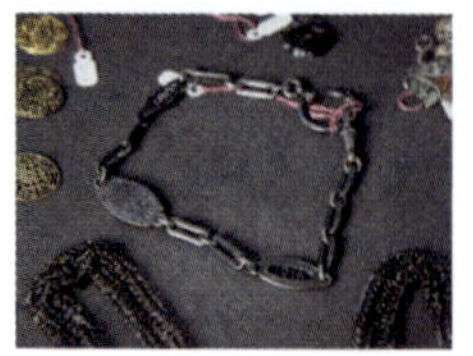

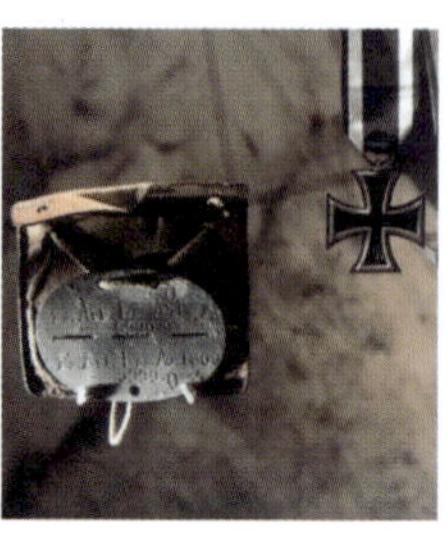

⬥ **top:** Copper pot exchanged for iron, 1916. Artist's research image from Stadtmuseum Kassel, Germany.

middle: Berlin iron jewellery, Glasgow Museums Resource Centre.

bottom: World War I identification disc and Iron Cross medal. Artist's research image from Stadtmuseum Kassel, Germany.

⬥ **main image, above left:** World War I towel made from paper in Glasgow Museums' collection, GMRC.

I've been really drawn to a collection of charms and amulets that are recorded as having been taken into battle or used by soldiers as lucky charms. I've had to look at a broader folklore context to try to make sense of the objects and their role and relevance at the time. That research led me to Edward Lovett; he was a folklorist from London and collecting these particular objects associated with soldiers was one very small aspect of his voracious wider collecting. I was amazed to find that Glasgow Museums' charms and amulets were purchased directly from Lovett in 1918 and 1919, and to conclude that it's most likely Lovett's own copperplate handwriting on the boxes.

It was especially touching that twelve of these charm boxes were empty and didn't contain the objects described on the front. Emptiness, stasis and absence have been recurrent in the objects I have encountered throughout my research of the collection; I hope the final work will reference and build on these themes. The lack of a very explicit narrative or provenance for some objects provides a space for myself, and subsequently for audiences, to insert our own thoughts and imaginative interpretations, making otherwise inaccessible objects personally relevant.

J: After a year of research, when you not only worked at GMRC, but also made research visits to Germany and Flanders, was it a difficult transition to make to go back to the studio? How do you go about translating all the research you have done into actual making? Do you have a strategy or is it a much more organic, intuitive process?

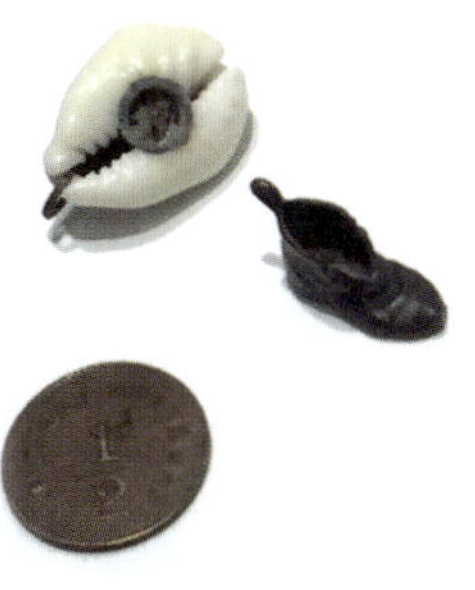

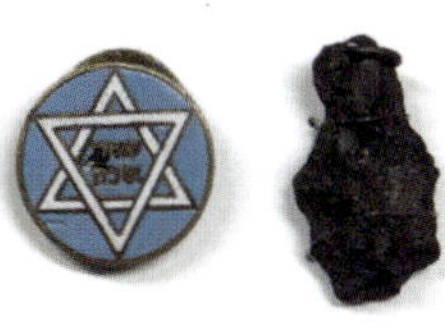

⬥ Some charms and amulets that are part of a Glasgow Museums' Open Museum handling kit.

⬦ Boxes for World War I charms and amulets, now empty, inscribed by the collector Edward Lovett in about 1914–18.

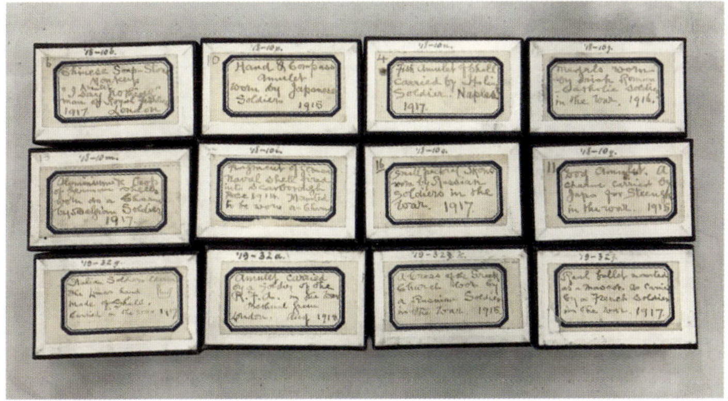

C: It feels great to go back to spend time in the studio. It's rare to be able to carve out such a golden period of time when you've got a whole repository of new thoughts and ideas in the form of photos or notes in a sketchbook, ready to be reconsidered and developed. It's such a pleasure to be able to take the time to work through them in the studio and let them form relationships to the favoured materials I work with here.

This is the moment of exploring through materials and processes, led by the research material. It's quite a natural focusing down and acknowledgement that recurring ideas, materials and thoughts are happening for a reason and are a foundation from which to build the work.

J: One of the objects you were particularly attracted to at GMRC was the invalid feeder cup in an Open Museum World War I handling kit. This mass-produced item was purchased specifically as a handling

object to go out into the community, rather than be accessioned into the collection, either to go into storage or on display in one of Glasgow Museums' venues. It had no known story or provenance attached to it. However, it was an object full of meaning. Can you talk a little bit about the significance of this object, and why you were drawn to it?

C: Ceramic invalid feeder cups were widely used in nursing during World War I. The use of invalid feeder cups is intrinsically linked with the use of the term 'invalid' to describe people with chronic illness or disability and their treatment, largely centred around bed rest; the Collins English Dictionary tells us the use of the word peaked in 1935. (Interestingly, the feeder cup from the handling kit was made around this date, in the same form as feeder cups used during World War I.) The cups themselves are now invalid (adjective) – 'not valid; having no force; null or void'.[1]

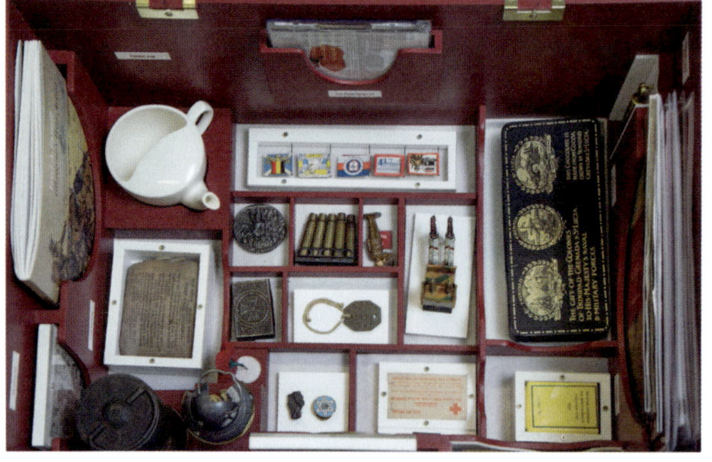

It feels appropriate that the cup was actually part of a World War I handling kit that was curated to go out into the community with the Open Museum team. It did, therefore, have a more active existence than museum objects: it was not exhibited under glass or kept in the special storage required for accessioned items. The form of the object itself was intriguing too, caught halfway between the utilitarian and luxury individualized china teapot.

Ceramic is a material that I've often been drawn to because, when discarded, it remains in the earth without degrading. Pottery and ceramics are very prominent in the archaeological record and when excavated and pieced together the fragments build vivid pictures of previous civilizations. Yet it is literally of the earth, clay, the same material as we plant and grow

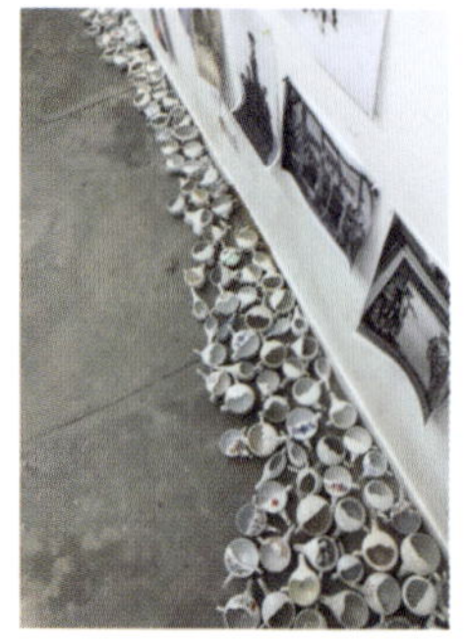

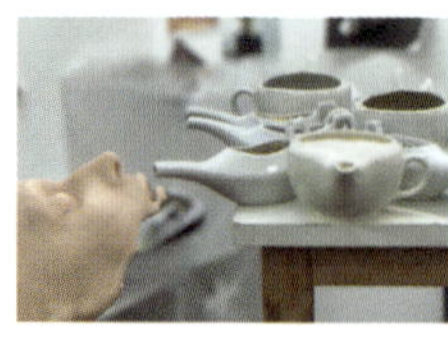

⬆ **top:** Some of the invalid feeder cups in Christine Borland's collection, artist's studio.

above: Work in progress in the artist's studio.

◀ The invalid feeder cup within Glasgow Museums' Open Museum World War I handing kit which the artist incorporated into *I Say Nothing*.

1. www.collinsdictionary.com/dictionary/english/invalid (accessed 21 May 2018)

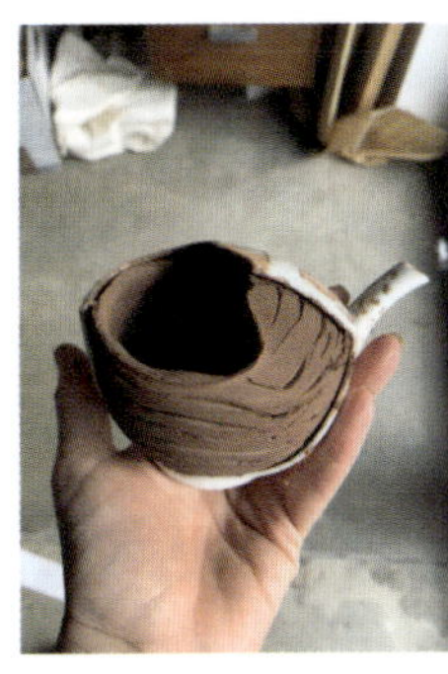

Work in progress in the artist's studio.

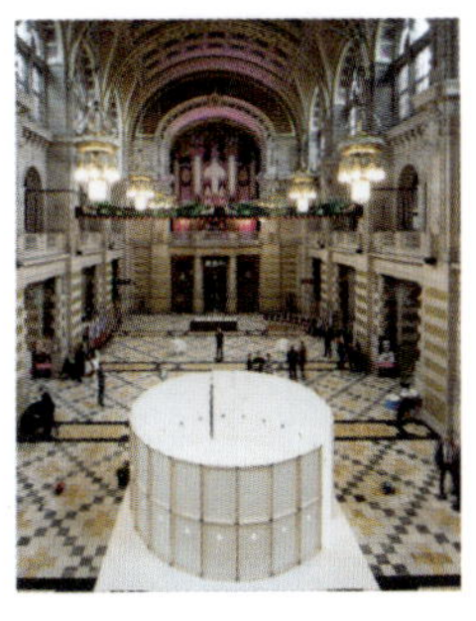

Constructing the *PhotoSculpture* structure in the Centre Hall at Kelvingrove Art Gallery and Museum.

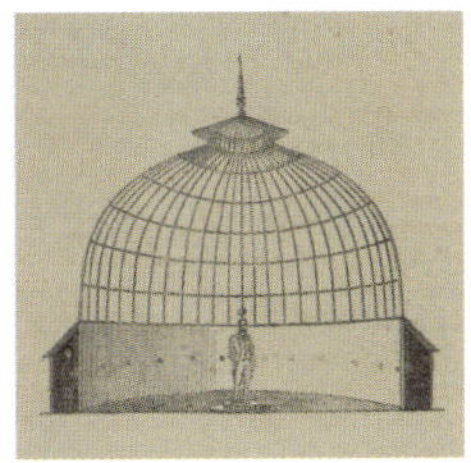

François Willème's glass dome, housing a perimeter ring of cameras directed inward at a central subject. Courtesy of the George Eastman Collection.

our food in. Visiting battlefields and World War I sites, as I did recently, the physicality of mud and earth as a material, in relation to life and death, is particularly relevant.

Most of all, though, my attraction to this object was largely based on a series of inherent contradictions associated with its use. As well as the nursing associations, I've also come across the feeder cup in relation to imprisoned, hunger-striking suffragettes in the years just before World War I. The feeder cup was mentioned as a method of force-feeding. So we have photographic images of it used in a nursing capacity and we have this duality of it being used as an instrument of torture. Unsurprisingly, there appear to be no photographic records of any kind of force-feeding in prison, though there are a number of artist impressions and photographic reconstructions. For one small non-accessioned object to embody all these associations and contradictions was an incredible starting point to develop the work.

J: On 23 April 2018 Kelvingrove Art Gallery and Museum became the venue for *PhotoSculpture*, a unique participatory event that was an intrinsic part of the development of the commission. Fellow artists, photographers and colleagues in the museum and art history world were invited to contribute, with the results feeding directly into the final artwork. Intriguingly, the event was based on historical precedent and yet used the most up-to-date technology. Meaningfully, it all took place in the Centre Hall, below the South Balcony where the final piece is situated. Can you tell us a bit more about the thinking behind this remarkable event and what you hoped to achieve?

C: The *PhotoSculpture* event centred on an adapted reconstruction of the photo-sculpture studio of François Willème that operated in Sedan, France, during the mid nineteenth century. The photo-sculpture process combined experimental photographic and sculptural methods to reproduce three-dimensional replicas of live models. When I came across the process it was of immediate interest as a non-traditional means of representation with links back to neoclassical sculpture as well as forward to 3D scanning, a period of time which spans from the First to the Fourth Industrial Revolution, taking a timeline from the First Industrial Revolution until today, with World War I somewhere in the middle.

Mindful of the inherent theatricality of the space, I selected two poses that I wanted to see reproduced using the photo-sculpture method: one representing 'invalid care', based on a World War I image of nurses feeding

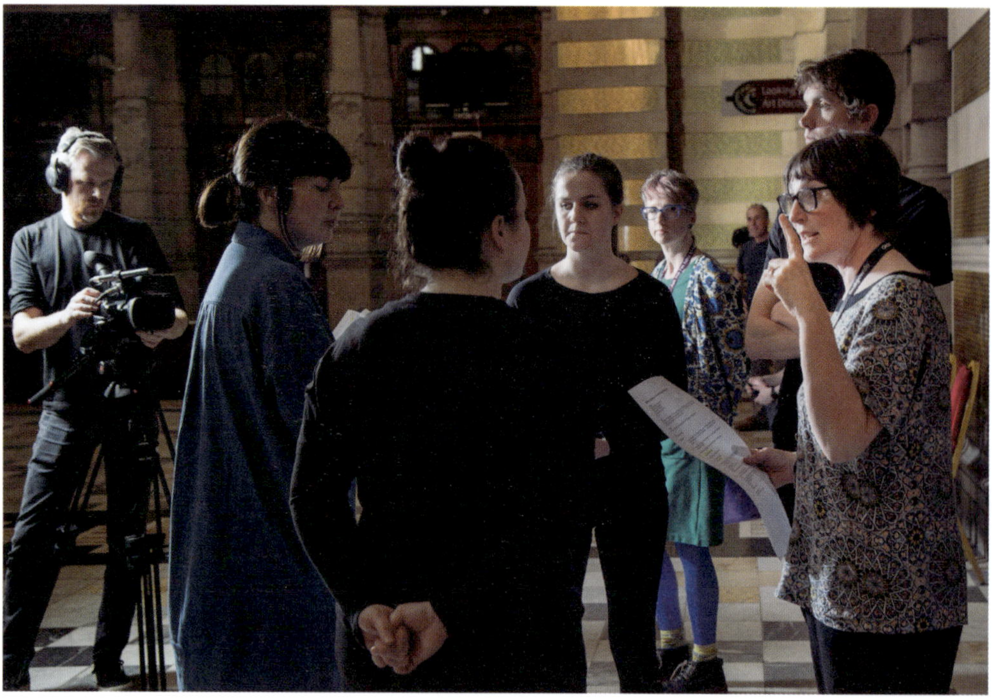

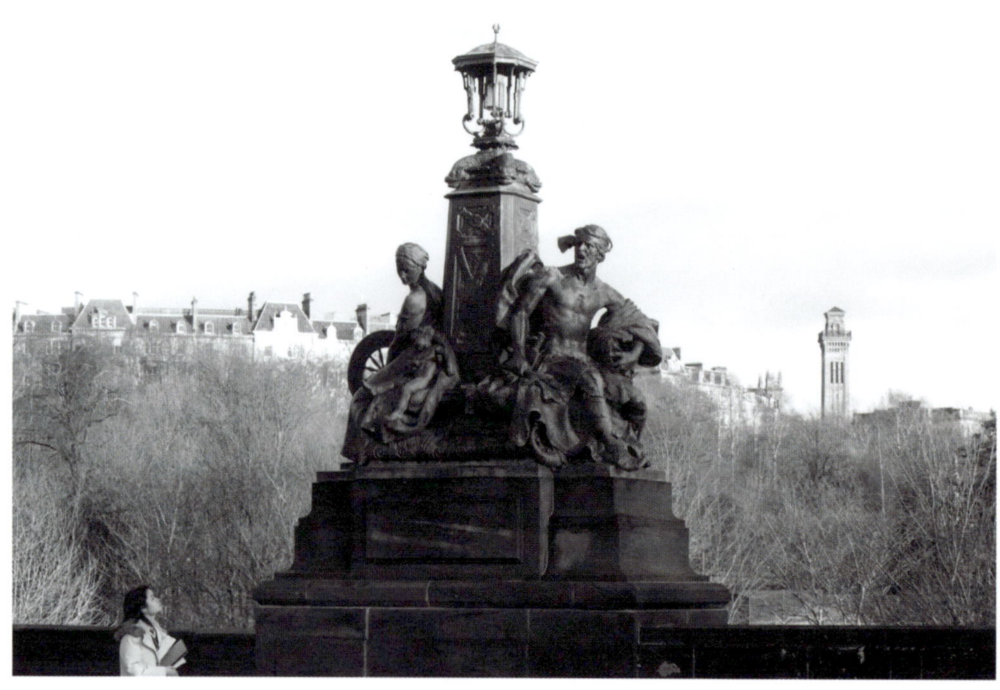

a wounded German soldier with an invalid feeder cup, and one based on a description of the cup being used in the force-feeding of suffragettes. Male and female models participated in a series of rehearsals and photo-shoots where the poses were tested and documented and developed further in the studio.

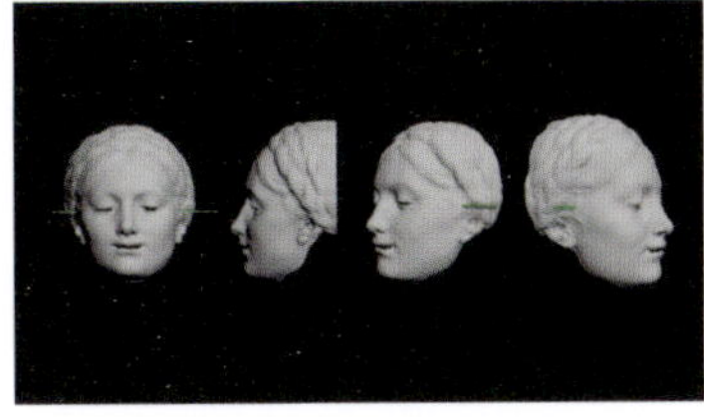

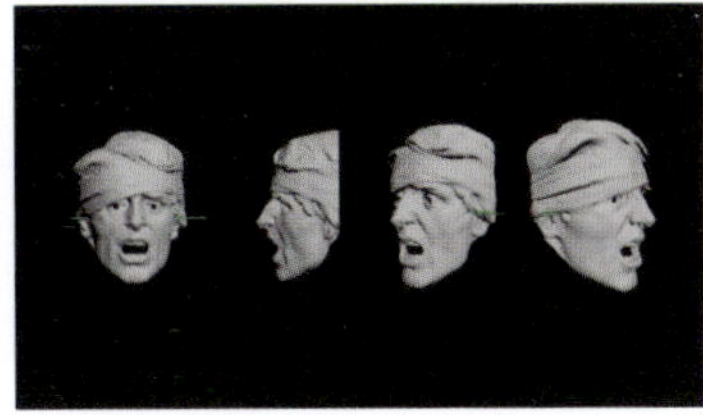

From these tests I determined that the faces of the models should be altered by masking. The male and female subjects were given the faces of figures from existing sculptures sited on Kelvin Way Bridge, the bridge over the River Kelvin near to the entrance to Kelvingrove Art Gallery and Museum that faces the river and Kelvingrove Park. *Peace* and *War* form one of four pairs of sculptures adorning the bridge; despite their title, they are not associated with war memorials. The faces of the sculptures were replicated by laser-scanning the originals on the bridge and then 3D printing them in ABS plastic in order to make the masks.

It was wonderful to create a photo-sculpture structure in Kelvingrove based on the studio of François Willème, and invite museum staff and those who had already participated in the *Doubtful Occasion* symposium as well as other artists and friends to be the 24 camera operators required to take all the images. Now they have played a lasting part not just in the research process but in the production of the finished work.

J: It was significant that you used the Open Museum feeder cup as part of the posed tableaux within the *PhotoSculpture* event, particularly in the light of what was planned for it afterwards. Can you explain why you sought permission from Glasgow Museums to explode the cup in a controlled explosion in Flanders (replacing it with two virtually identical feeder cups from your own personal collection, one designated for Glasgow Museums' community handling kit and one to become part of its accessioned collection)?

C: When I visited the former Western Front in Flanders, I was interested to see whole and fragmented invalid feeder cups displayed in museums as part of exhibits of objects that are regularly unearthed from the land – especially around harvest time and in the process of construction

Caption (left column, top):

Caption:
Laser scanning of the *Peace* and *War* sculptures, Kelvin Way Bridge, by the School of Simulation and Visualisation, The Glasgow School of Art, 6 April 2018

◐ *Peace* and *War* by Paul Raphael Montford, sculptures on Kelvin Way Bridge.

◑ Christine Borland exchanging the feeder cup from Glasgow Museums' World War I Open Museum handling kit with one from her own collection.

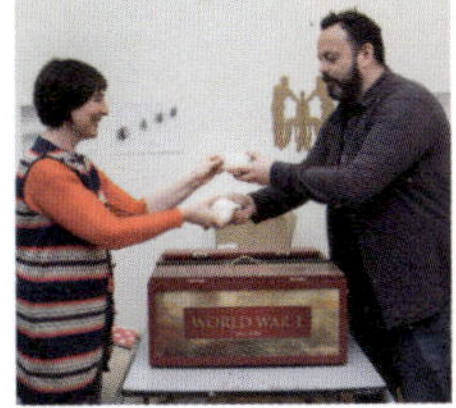

projects. World War I is still very much part of the day-to-day lives of the people who live in the area, where an 'iron harvest' of unexploded bombs is reaped every year; in 2017, 222 tons of ammunition from in and around the Ypres Salient alone was deactivated in controlled explosions by the Belgian bomb disposal unit DOVO-SEDEE.

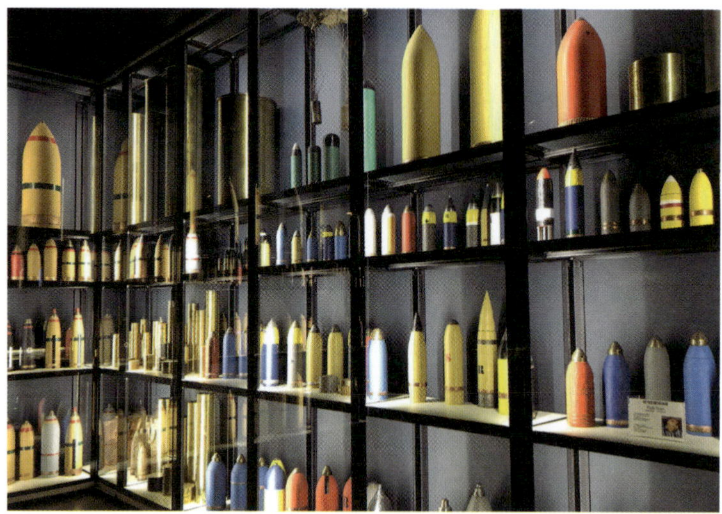

◐ Munitions recovered at Passendale, Flanders. Artist's research image from Memorial Museum Passchendaele 1917.

The idea to involve the Open Museum feeder cup in a controlled explosion came about gradually as a fitting way to deal with the dual legacy of the cups – which were used both as an aid to nourishing patients and to brutally coerce; exploding the cup meant it could no longer function but had actively been translated into a different form. This act suggests an altered power relationship between the 'feeder' and the 'fed'. While the method could be considered brutal, it is important that, unlike war-time explosions, this one was *controlled* in a context where munitions are being exploded in order to *save* lives.

I very much enjoy the circular nature of the whole process and the changes in value that occurred when I was given permission to take the non-accessioned, Open Museum handling kit feeder cup (which was replaced by one from my own collection) – which after it had been exploded entered the collection not only as an accessioned object, but with its status elevated to part of an artwork.

J: As an artist you often choose to work collaboratively, and this is no less the case in this commission, where you specifically designed participatory events that would feed into the commission. You engaged an artist and poet to document the creative symposium

◖ **top:** Comparing feeder cups in the artist's studio.

bottom: Conservator Stephanie de Roemer writing a condition report for the feeder cup from Glasgow Museums' Open Museum World War I handling kit, artist's studio.

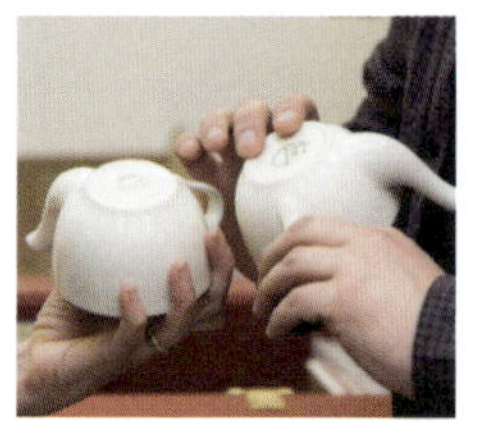

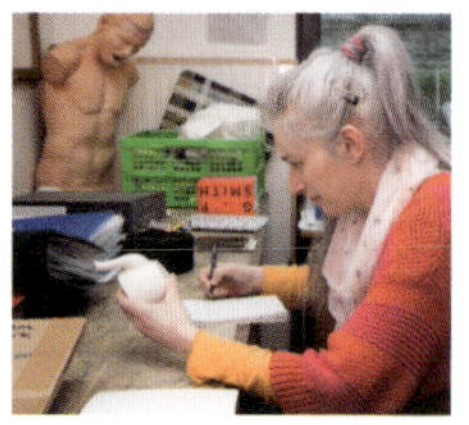

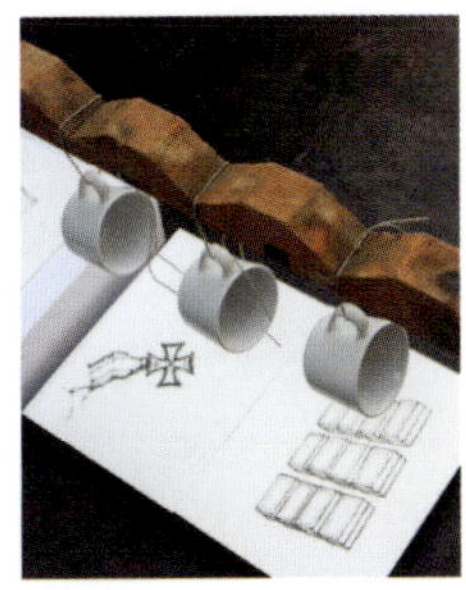

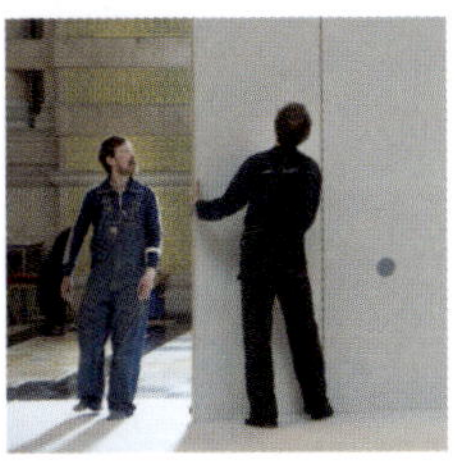

⬥ **top:** Trial explosion of ordinary household cups from the artist's collection by DOVO-SEDEE, with witness boards, March 2018.

bottom: Assembly of the *PhotoSculpture* structure in the Centre Hall at Kelvingrove.

Doubtful Occasion, **to which you also invited your artistic and academic peers to contribute; you developed relationships with the School of Simulation and Visualisation at The Glasgow School of Art, with local art fabricators Sculpture and Design and with the film-maker Andy McGregor for an event which relied on external participants taking simultaneous photographs; and you worked with the bomb disposal unit DOVO-SEDEE in planning the explosion of the feeder cup. How important is this collaborative practice intellectually and practically for the final artwork?**

C: I think there are several different things going on here, all related to the fact that, for me, the process of working as an artist is fundamentally in relation to other people – their stories, experiences and knowledge. In this commission it has been built into the whole process. At the end of the research phase of the commission, *Doubtful Occasion* was devised as a public forum to share the objects which had become meaningful to me and receive feedback and input which made an active contribution to my research (and maybe to that of the researchers, artists, museum staff and others who attended). It's such an energizing moment, when ideas are still uncertain, before a future artwork becomes fixed in concept or form and everything still seems possible.

Extending that energy to the production of the work itself was made possible through the participation of the many people who enabled the *PhotoSculpture* experiment to happen in Kelvingrove – both museum staff, models and those 24 people who operated the cameras. I do enjoy that the event created general excitement among the participants, and extends the life of the commissioned artwork just a little more.

Building in public events, like the public tour of the storage pods at GMRC, is an important touchstone to test whether what's going on in my brain actually lands anywhere when I open my mouth and talk about ideas or about why I am interested in objects. It's really reassuring to air the work at all stages in its development rather than hide away the process for a big, nerve-wracking reveal at the end.

Working with agencies like the Belgian bomb disposal unit DOVO-SEDEE allows me to bring in an important different perspective, looking outwith our own national context at the lasting impact of World War I. The people I worked with there also deal with the destructive legacy of current and historical conflicts all over the world. In the first controlled explosion tests I included – with the artist's consent – prints which were made from the drawings Birthe Jorgensen made of selected objects from the collection.

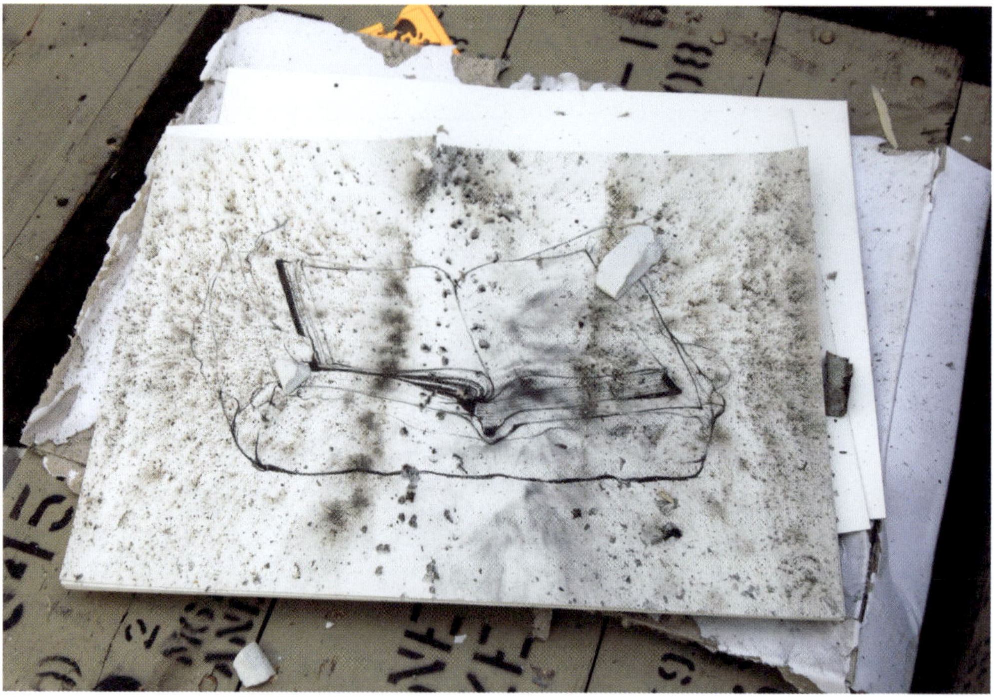

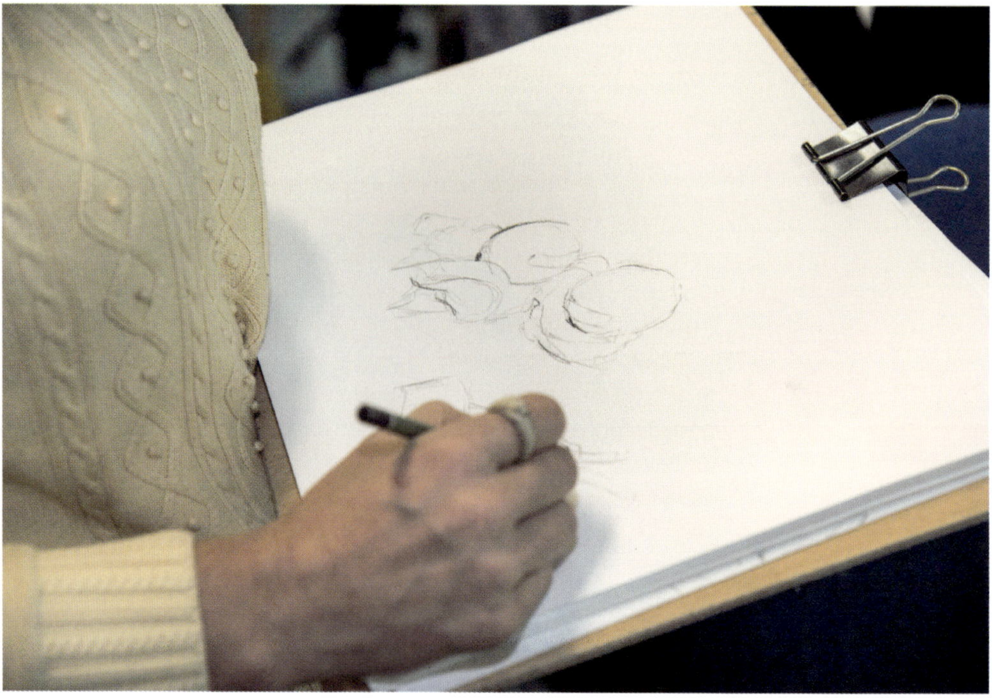

I used these as 'witness boards'. This term refers to materials specifically designed to bear the traces of explosions re-enacted by forensic or ballistic experts to gather evidence in relation to crimes or accidents.

As for working with expert fabricators and film-makers, well that is very pragmatic; it's important for me to have the freedom to follow ideas and work across a wide range of disciplines and materials. Although I work in the studio with many processes at an experimental level, it isn't possible to master all of them, so without the support of trusted producers and fabricators, I wouldn't be able to produce the final work at all.

J: The South Balcony of Kelvingrove Art Gallery and Museum, opposite the organ and above the Centre Hall, is a prime location for your artwork and was selected in conjunction with you early on in the commission. How important was the architecture and history of Kelvingrove for the subsequent development of the artwork? Did knowing the location change things at all?

C: From the very beginning, knowing the location of the final work and thinking site-specifically, throughout both the research and making period, has been key. Enacting the *PhotoSculpture* experiment in the Centre Hall, underneath the balcony, was a very literal way to embed the context of Kelvingrove into its production.

The building that is now Kelvingrove Art Gallery and Museum first opened as the Palace of Art at the 1901 Glasgow International Exhibition. The magnificent central space was a sculpture court full of figurative sculptures, mostly in plaster and marble. The explorations and adaptions of new and ancient technology, processes and materials that I've been using in the development of this artwork are associated with a period of great change linked to innovation in technology and industry. This period includes the planning and building of Kelvingrove from the profits of the International Exhibition of 1888. The modern era, sometimes referred to as the Fourth Industrial Revolution, is marked by technological breakthroughs like 3D printing and their application to our lives through, for example, individualized prosthesis and implants made in titanium using the process of scanning and selective laser-sintering. The First and Second Industrial Revolutions, with their frenetic pace of scientific and industrial developments, is what made it possible for World War I to be the first war to incorporate technology to such devastating effect: a reminder of all the possibilities around technological innovation, both creative and destructive, is built into the work.

◖ Witness board, test print of a drawing of the book *Grammaire Française* within Glasgow Museums' collection, by Birthe Jorgensen, after it had been exposed to an explosion at the DOVO-SEDEE explosives range, Flanders.

◖ Birthe Jorgensen drawing museum objects at GMRC.

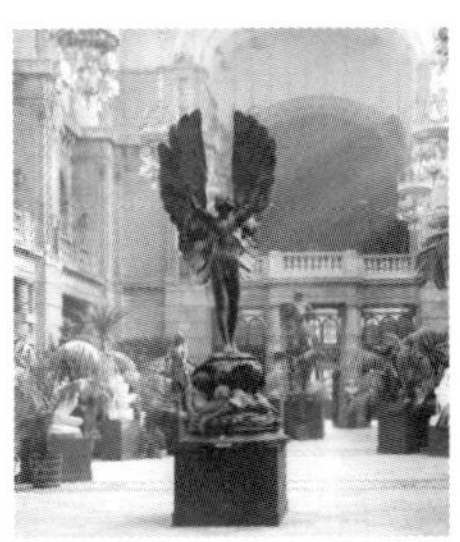

◓ Sculptures exhibited in the Centre Hall of Kelvingrove Art Gallery and Museum as it was when the building first opened as the Palace of Art at the 1901 Glasgow International Exhibition.

 J: Your ideas around the commission were constantly evolving as you responded to new ideas, materials, techniques and technologies. Were there specific changes of direction in this commission prompted by your experience during actual production?

C: The production period of a big sculptural work is nearly always a fast-moving time; it's both exciting and a little disconcerting when materials don't necessarily do what you expect, or want them to. It can produce a sort-of time lag, then a frantic period of catch-up. After seeing the maquettes at Sculpture & Design, produced from the *PhotoSculpture* event, I expected that I would move the silhouettes into another material for the final sculptures. I experimented with different processes and substances, from papier mâché (an idea suggested by the decoy soldiers made by women on the Front, which were used to draw sniper fire and then determine the shooter's position) to plaster, for its close associations to the sculpture court of Kelvingrove Art Gallery and Museum at the beginning of the twentieth century. None of these test materials were satisfying enough, either because of how they looked or how they conveyed the *PhotoSculpture* idea. Eventually I came full circle back to a more direct relationship with the information gathered by the cameras at the event; rather than 'transform' the figures into a completely new material, I have used glassine to cover the MDF forms which were CNC (computer numerical control) cut directly from the silhouettes of photographs taken of the posed model groups. The use of glassine is something I couldn't have predicted: it relates to my time spent researching in GMRC, as, historically, objects in museum stores were wrapped in protective layers of this material. It is still used today for interleaving photographs and negatives.

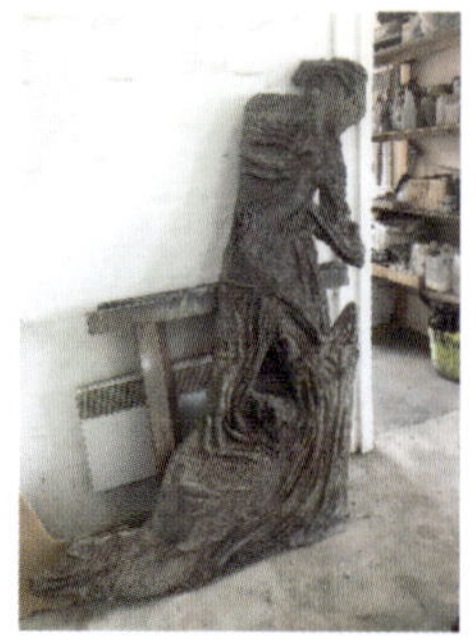

⬥ Test figure in cement fondue, Sculpture and Design workshop, Glasgow.

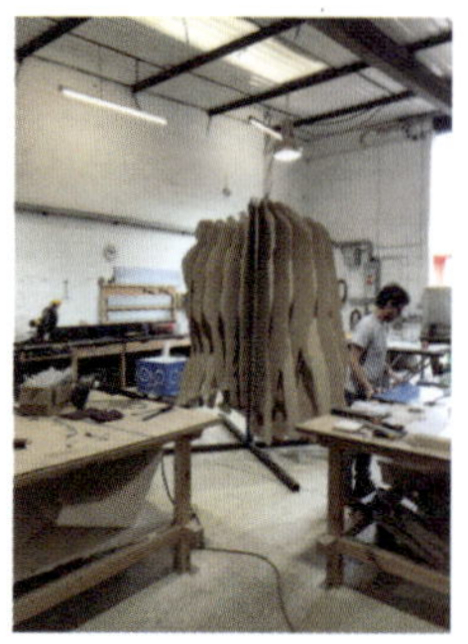

⬥ Maquettes of *I Say Nothing*, Sculpture and Design workshop, Glasgow.

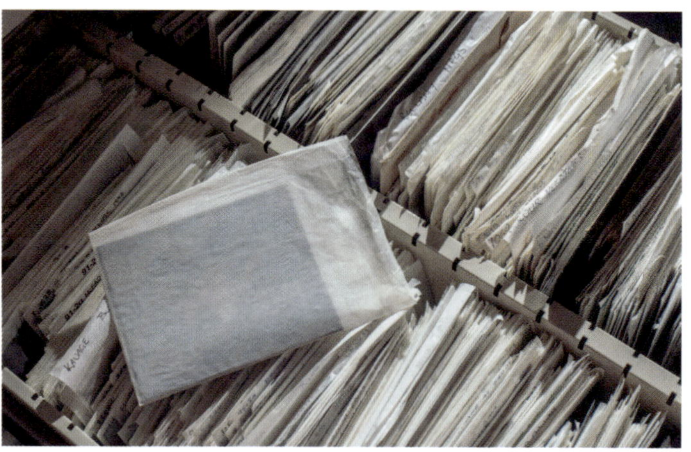

◀ Photographic negatives in glassine envelopes, Glasgow Museums Photo Library.

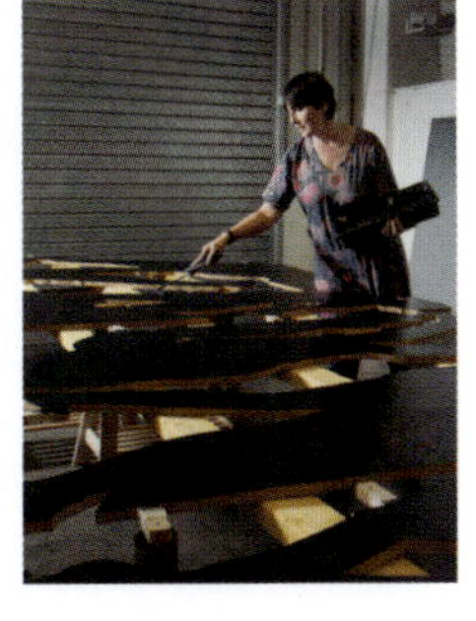

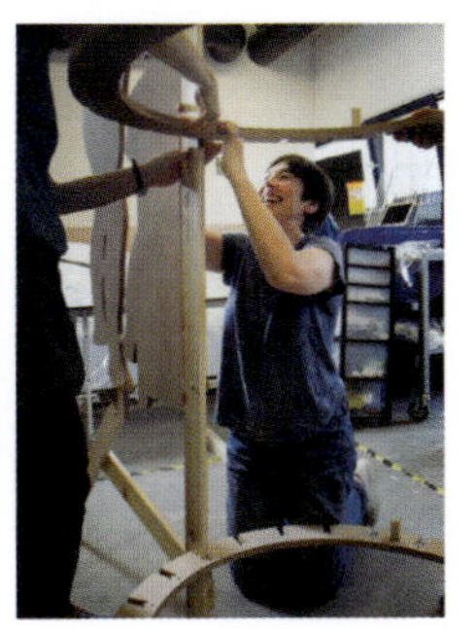

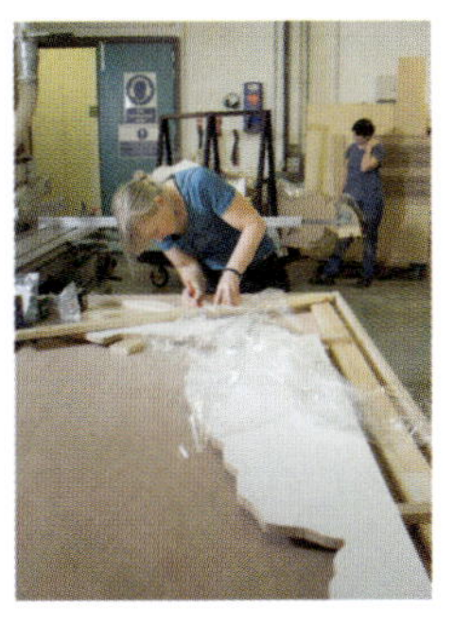

○ Christine Borland
bringing *I Say Nothing*
to completion at GMRC
with the help of Glasgow
Museums staff.

J: It has been a privilege to work with you throughout the commission and have an insight into your thinking and artistic practice and to watch everything gradually coalesce, with objects that you encountered at GMRC being subtly referenced and responded to in the final creation. Can you say something about the themes the artwork addresses and the form the final artwork takes?

C: The positioning and placement of all the elements which go to make up the work have all been decided in direct relationship to the architecture of Kelvingrove and the way the public use the space. Working with the dominant symmetry and considering supports and apertures was my starting point, but practicalities like access and public safety became a real consideration once I came to install the work and have definitely had a big impact on final decisions; considering viewpoints – what's concealed or inaccessible and why – is fundamental to my thinking.

The final artwork plays with a series of holes and circles and forms in positive and negative; the silhouettes of the two groups are pulled apart to make a circular void in the middle of each group, meaning the relationship of feeder cup to mouth is largely removed. To reflect the monochrome nature of the models' clothes and the *PhotoSculpture* set, one group of 24 figures is painted black, one is white, although that is made more subtle by the shadows and tricks of the light as a result of the glassine layers. The structure from the *PhotoSculpture* event, which is also included, simultaneously blocks off and protects the sculptures, providing literal different points of view through the holes, which were cut to accommodate the participants' cameras. The feeder cup is included in a central position too, returning to Glasgow Museums and now, as part of the artwork, entering its collection in its new, fragmented form. Although it has experienced the energy of being taken to Flanders and exploded, it is now protected under cover as a precious museum object – its life as an Open Museum handling object has ended.

All the elements of the installation have perhaps experienced a 'controlled explosion' of some sort. They have been on a journey, which marked and changed them into this final form, in which they are now fixed. The complex and arguably irrational series of processes leading to this end point underline the impossibility of definitively capturing, representing and remembering significant moments.

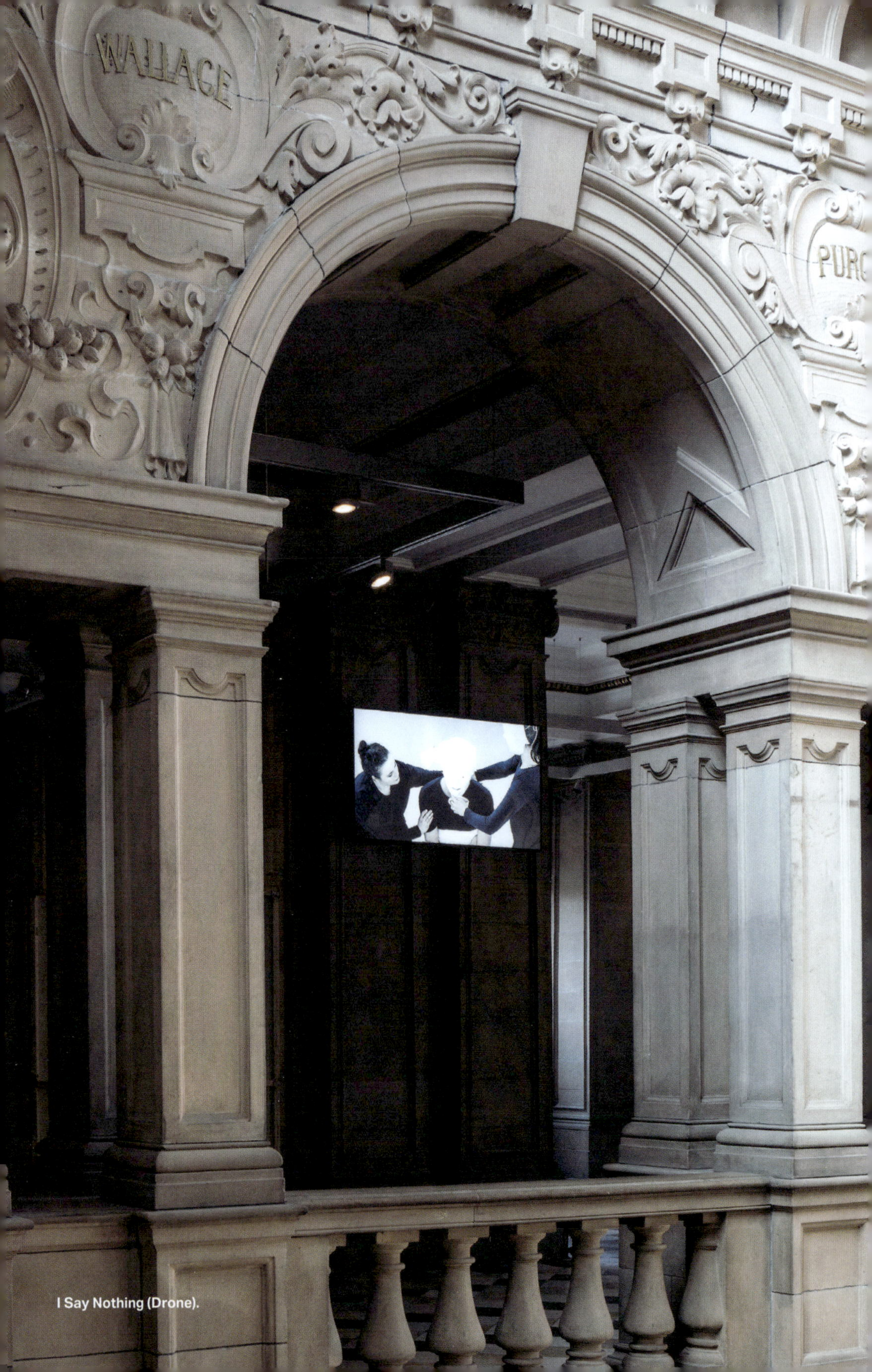

I Say Nothing (Drone).

Christine Borland: Biography

Born	Darvel, Ayrshire, Scotland
Lives and works	Kilcreggan, Argyll, Scotland

1983–7	BA (Hons), The Glasgow School of Art
1987–8	MA, Fine Art, Ulster University, Belfast
2016	D Litt., University of Glasgow

Academic

1993–2000	Part-Time Lecturer, The Glasgow School of Art
2000–11	Academic Researcher, The Glasgow School of Art
2006–9	NESTA Creative Fellow
2011–	Medical Humanities Research Fellow, School of Medicine, University of Glasgow
2010–13	Honorary Professor, Peninsula College of Medicine and Dentistry (PCMD), University of Exeter, University of Plymouth and the NHS in Devon and Cornwall
2011–16	BALTIC Professor of Contemporary Art, BALTIC and Northumbria University, Newcastle
2016–	Professor of Fine Art, Northumbria University, Newcastle

Selected Solo Exhibitions, Projects and Commissions

* Denotes that there is an associated publication

2018

I Say Nothing: A World War I Centenary Art Commission Kelvingrove Art Gallery and Museum, Glasgow*
The Power of Twelve, Mount Stuart, Isle of Bute, Argyll*
Wrong Right Hand, Patricia Fleming Projects, Glasgow

2017

Common Groin, Timespan, Helmsdale, Sutherland

2016

Positive Pattern, Pittenweem Arts Festival, Pittenweem, Fife
Circles of Focus: The Fall Experiment (with Brody Condon), Stroom Den Haag, The Hague

2015

Circles of Focus (with Brody Condon), Centre for Contemporary Art (CCA), Glasgow

2014

Support Structure (permanent public sculpture commission), Whitworth Gallery, Manchester

2013

Daughters of Decayed Tradesmen (with Brody Condon), Edinburgh Art Festival Commission*

2012

Divine Imperfect, Pier Arts Centre, Orkney

2011

Cast From Nature, Camden Arts Centre, London*

2010

Cast From Nature, Glasgow Sculpture Studios
SimBodies & NoBodies, Galeria Toni Tàpies, Barcelona
SimBaby, Loop Video Fair, Hotel Barcelona, Barcelona

2009

SimBodies & NoBodies, Ormeau Baths Gallery, Belfast
The Unknown Girl (commission for permanent work), St Olaf Collage, Northfield, Minnesota
Air Heads (commission for permanent work), Norwich Castle Museum (and touring)

2007

Preserves, The Collection, Lincoln*
With Practice, Newlyn Art Gallery, Cornwall*
SimMan, Public Project, Künstlerhaus Bregenz, Bregenz

2006

Selected Preserves, Galeria Toni Tàpies, Barcelona
Preserves, The Fruitmarket Gallery, Edinburgh*

2005

Repeat Pattern, Dick Institute Museum, Kilmarnock

2004

Conservatory, Centre for Contemporary Art of South Australia, Adelaide; Anna Schwarz Gallery, Melbourne
Simulated Patient, Lisson Gallery, London

2003

An Hospital, Mount Stuart, Isle of Bute, Argyll
Take All the Time you Need, Dunkers Kulturhus, Helsingborg

2002

Christine Borland, Contemporary Art Museum, Houston*
To be Set and Sown in The Garden (permanent sculpture commission), University of Glasgow
Christine Borland Survey (presentation of projects throughout 2002), Kunstverein München, Munich
Significant Notes, Aarhus Kunstforening af 1847, Aarhus*
Dragon Doll, Glasgow Print Studio

2001

Nephila-Mania, Fabric Workshop and Museum, Philadelphia
Christine Borland, Art Gallery of York University, Toronto; Contemporary Arts Museum, Houston*
Hoxa Sound, part of *The Constant Moment: Site Specific Millenium Projects*, Orkney
Christine Borland, Lisson Gallery, London
Fallen Spirits, Anna Schwartz Gallery, Melbourne

2000

Spirit Collection, Sean Kelly Gallery, New York
Treasury of Human Inheritance, Galeria Toni Tàpies, Barcelona
New Commissions, Royal Armouries, Leeds*
Christine Borland, Galerie cent 8, Paris

1999

Christine Borland, Museum für Gegenwartskunst, Zürich*; Fundação Serralves, Porto
What makes for the fullness and perfection of life, for beauty and happiness, is good. What makes for death, disease, imperfection, suffering is bad, Dundee Contemporary Arts*
Christine Borland, Galerie Eigen + Art, Berlin

1998

Christine Borland, De Appel, Amsterdam; Fundação Serralves, Lisbon; Museum für Gegenwartskunst, Zürich*
Conservatory, Galerie cent 8, Paris
L'homme double, Århus Kunstmuseum, Aarhus*

1997

Turner Prize Exhibition, Tate Gallery, London*
Christine Borland, Galerie d'Eole, Frac Languedoc-Roussillon, Montpellier*
Christine Borland, Lisson Gallery, London
The Dead Teach the Living, Skulpturen Projekte III, Münster*

1996

Second Class Male, Second Class Female, Sean Kelly Gallery, New York
From Life, Kunst-Werke, Berlin*
Christine Borland, Galerie Eigen + Art, Leipzig
To Dust We Will Return (Part of *Sawn-Off*), Gallery Enkehuset, Stockholm*

1995

Inside Pocket, British Council Gallery, Prague

1994

From Life, Tramway, Glasgow*

Selected Group Exhibitions

2018

Strange Foreign Bodies, Hunterian Art Gallery, Glasgow
NOW 3 Scottish National Gallery of Modern Art (Modern 1), Edinburgh

2017

Transparency, Walker Art Gallery, Liverpool Museums

2016

Devil's in the Making, Gallery of Modern Art (GOMA), Glasgow
Nightfall. Gothic imagination since Frankenstein, Musée d'art et d'histoire, Geneva
The Scottish Endarkenment: Art and Unreason 1945 to the Present, Dovecot Studios, Edinburgh
Transparency, Yorkshire Sculpture Park
That Which Remains, Mount Stuart, Isle of Bute, Argyll

2015
Forensics: The Anatomy of Crime, The Wellcome Collection, London

2014
Below Another Sky, Aberdeen City Art Gallery; Inverness Art Gallery; Glasgow Print Studio (followed by a British Council exhibition touring to Commonwealth countries, 2016)*
Biometric, Media Gallery, Vancouver
Generation: 25 Years of Contemporary Art in Scotland, Dick Institute, Kilmarnock; Maclaurin Art Gallery, Ayr; Mayfield House, Dumfries; Scottish National Galleries, Edinburgh; City Art Centre, Edinburgh
Urban Suburban, City Art Centre, Edinburgh

2013
Extraordinary Renditions, BALTIC Centre for Contemporary Art, Gateshead*

2011
RSA Exhibition, Royal Scottish Academy, Edinburgh

2010
Pivot Points IV, MOCA, Miami
Death to Delawab, Space Delawab, Belfast
Reflecting Glenfiddich, A Selection of Works from the Glenfiddich Artists in Residence, The Fleming Collection, London
Doppler Effect, Kunsthalle zu Kiel, Switzerland*
SimWoman, The Knowledge Spa, Truro, Cornwall

2009
An Entangled Bank, Talbot Rice Gallery, Edinburgh
Genipulation, Centre Pasquart Biel Bienne, Switzerland*
Not for Sale, Galeria Toni Tàpies, Barcelona
The Green Room, CCS Bard Hessel Museum, Annandale-on-Hudson, New York

2008
Darwin's Canopy, Natural History Museum, London
Imagining Science, Art Gallery of Alberta*
Centre for Health Science, Inverness
What is Life? Royal Botanic Garden, Edinburgh
Communication Suite, University of Glasgow
Maternity: Images of Motherhood, Scottish National Gallery of Modern Art, Edinburgh
Genesis – The Art of Creation, Zentrum Paul Klee, Bern*

2007
Kunsthaus Bregenz Billboards, Kunsthaus Bregenz, Bregenz
A North Light – Cynosure, The Pier Arts Centre, Stromness, Orkney
Sculpture in the Close, Jesus College, Cambridge*
Anatomy Acts, Collins Gallery, Glasgow*

2006
Collezionami, 2nd Biennial of Southern Italy, El Macelli Generali, Bari
Gregor Mendel: Planting the Seeds of Genetics, The Field Museum, Chicago*
How To Improve the World, 60 Years of British Art, Arts Council Collection, The Hayward Gallery, London*
If it didn't exist you'd have to invent it: a partial Showroom history, The Showroom Gallery, London
Uncanny Nature, Australian Centre for Contemporary Art, Victoria*
Corps étranger, Le Quartier, Centre d'Art Contemporain, Quimper
Christine Borland, Peter McCaughy, Thomas Joshua Cooper, Mackintosh Gallery, The Glasgow School of Art
Anatomy Acts, City Arts Centre, Edinburgh*

2005
Home Testing, The Knowledge Spa, Royal Hospital, Truro
New Acquisitions, Gallery of Modern Art, Glasgow

2004
Designer Bodies: Towards the Posthuman Condition, Stills Gallery, Edinburgh
Won-Der-Ful. Visions of the Near Future, Arnolfini Gallery, Bristol; Bristol Industrial Museum; Magna, South Yorkshire*
Paradise now. Picturing the Genetic Revolution, Newcomb Art Gallery, Tulane University, New Orleans; The Center for Art and Visual Culture, UMBC, Baltimore*

2003
Fresh: Contemporary British Artists in Print, Edinburgh Printmakers
Arrangement, Rhodes+Mann, London
Liquid Sea, Museum of Contemporary Art, Sydney*
Love Over Gold, Gallery of Modern Art, Glasgow
Paradise Now: Picturing the Genetic Revolution, Newcomb Art Gallery, Tulane University, New Orleáns*
From Dust to Dusk, Charlottenborg Udstillingsbygning, Copenhagen*

Upon reflection… ,Sean Kelly Gallery, New York
Beinal Da Maia 3, Forum da Maia
Bloom–mutation, toxicity and the sublime, Govett-Brewster Art Gallery New Plymouth*

2002

Apparition: the Action of Appearing, Arnolfini Gallery, Bristol*
Dragon Doll, Glasgow Print Studio Gallery
Remarks On Color, Sean Kelly Gallery, New York
Happy Outsiders, Zacheta Gallery, Warsaw; Gallery of Contemporary Art BWA, Katowice; Peter & Paul Fortress, St Petersburg*
Mendel, The Genius of Genetics, Mendel's Monastery, Brno*
Mirroring Evil, the Jewish Museum, New York*
The Gap Show, Young Critical Art from Great Britain, Museum Ostwall, Dortmund*
Leopold and Rudolf Blaschka: The Glass Aquarium, TwoTen Gallery, The Welcome Trust, London
Hygiene The Art of Public Health, London School of Hygiene & Tropical Medicine, London
Iconoclash: Beyond the image wars in science, religion and art, Zentrum für Kunst und Medientechnologie, Karlsruhe*
Recent Acquisitions of Contemporary British Art, Scottish National Gallery of Modern Art, Edinburgh

2001

Breaking the Mold: Conceptual Glass works, Cleveland Contemporary Arts Center
Gene(sis): Contemporary Art Explores Human Genomics, Henry Art Gallery, University of Washington, Seattle; Berkeley Art Museum; Frederick Weisman Museum of Art, Minneapolis; The Contemporary Museum, Honolulu, and University of Hawaii, Honolulu*
Paradise Now: Picturing the Genetic Revolution, Exit Art, New York; University of Michigan Museum of Art; the Tang Teaching Museum and Art Gallery, Skidmore College, Saratoga Springs, New York*
Paradise (lost), École Supérieure des Beaux Arts, Perpignan
Working Drafts. Envisioning the Human Genome, TwoTen Gallery, the Wellcome Trust, London
Space, Glasgow Print Studio
Devoler, Institut d'Art Contemporain, Villeurbanne
La Gam Costruisce Il Suo Futuro, Galleria Art Moderna, Torino
Spectacular Bodies – The Art and Science of the Human

Body from Leonardo to Now, Hayward Gallery, London*
Humid, Spike Island, Bristol; Melbourne Festival at the Australian Centre for Contemporary Art, Melbourne*
G3 NY, Cassey Kaplan, New York
Open Country – Scotland, Musée cantonal des Beaux-Arts de Lausanne*
Circles'4: One for one, ZKM, Karlsruhe*
Here+Now: Scottish Art 1990-2001, Dundee Contemporary Art*
From Beuys To Hirst: Art Works at Deutsche Bank, Dean Gallery, Edinburgh
At the Threshold of Evil, The Jewish Museum, New York*

2000

Know Thyself, Hayward Gallery, London*
Konfrontace, Czech Centre, London
Warning Shots!, Royal Armouries Museum, Leeds*; Galeria Toni Tàpies, Barcelona; Bleibe, Akademie der Künste, Berlin.
The British Art Show 4, Manchester: Upper Campfield Market, Castlefield Gallery, Chinese Arts Centre, City Art Galleries, Cornerhouse, Metropolitan Galleries, Whitworth Gallery. Edinburgh: City Art Centre, Collective Gallery, Fruitmarket Gallery, Royal Botanic Garden, Scottish National Gallery of Modern Art, Stills Gallery, Talbot Gallery. Cardiff: Chapter Arts Centre, Ffotogallery, National Museum of Wales, Oriel Gallery*
A Shot in the Head, Lisson Gallery, London
Paradise Now, Exit Art, New York*
Biennale de Lyon, Halle Tony Garnier, Lyon*

1999

High Red Center, Centre for Contemporary Arts (CCA), Glasgow
Sampled: The Use of Fabric in Sculpture, Henry Moore Institute, Leeds
Rewind the Future, Chac Mool Contemporary Art, West Hollywood

1998

In Your Face, The Andy Warhol Museum, Pittsburg*
artranspennine98, Tate Liverpool*
Nettverk Glasgow, Museet for Samtidskunst, Oslo*
To Be Real, Yerba Buena Center for the Arts, San Francisco*
Groupshow, Sadie Coles HQ, London
Close Echoes, City Gallery, Prague; Kunsthalle Krems, Krems-Stein*
Artists' Editions, The Modern Institute, Glasgow

New Art from Britain, Kunstraum Innsbruck*
Artranspennine' 98, Tate Liverpool*
*Manifesta 2: European Biennale of
Contemporary Art*, Luxembourg*
Commission for Royal Armoury, Leeds

1997
Turner Prize 1997, Tate Gallery, London*
Flexible, Museum für Gegenwartskunst, Zürich*
Contemporary British Art, Museum of Contemporary Art,
Sydney; Art Gallery of South Australia, Adelaide;
City Gallery, Wellington*
Absence/Presence, Kopavogur Art Museum, Reykiavik*
Connections Implicites, École Nationale Supérieure
des Beaux-Arts, Paris*
Wish you were here too, 83 Hill Street, Glasgow
Material Culture, Hayward Gallery, London*
*Sculptur Projekte Munster 3**
Letter and Event, Apex Art CP, New York*
Hebben Wij Het Geweten?, Galerie van Laetham, Hasselt
Building Site, Architectural Association, London

1996
*Material Culture, The Object in British Art of the 1980s
and 90s*, Hayward Gallery, London*
The Cauldron, Henry Moore Sculpture Studio, Halifax*
21 Days of Darkness, Transmission Gallery, Glasgow
More Time/Less History, Fundação de Serralves, Porto*
Live/Life, ARC Musee d'Art Moderne de la Ville de Paris;
Centro Cultural de Belem, Lisboa*
*Christine Borland, Roddy Buchanan, Jaqueline Donachie,
Douglas Gordon*, Galerie Eigen + Art, Berlin
Were we Conscious?, Provinciaal Museum voor Aktuele
Kunst, Hasselt
Are You Talking to Me?, Specta Gallery, Copenhagen
Nach Weimar, Museum for Contemporary Art, Weimar*
Strange Days, The Agency, London
Girls High, The Fruitmarket, Glasgow*
Full House, Kunstmuseum Wolfsburg*

1995
Eigen + Art at IAS, Independent Art Space, London
In Search of the Miraculous (In Honour of Bas Jan Ader),
Starkmann Library Services Ltd, London
External Links, Mackintosh Museum,
The Glasgow School of Art
Wild Roses Grow by the Roadside, 52c Brick Lane,
London
SWARM, The Scottish Arts Council, Traveling Gallery*

New Art in Britain, Museum Sztuki, Lodtz*
Pulp Fact, The Photographers Gallery, London
Maikäfer Flieg, The Bunker, Köln-Ehrenfeld, Köln*
The British Art Show 4, Uppercampfield Market,
Manchester; Edinburgh; Cardiff*
You Show, Galerie Hans Knoll, Budapest
Breakfast in Budapest, Uljak Exhibition Hall, Budapest

1994
The Spine, De Appel Foundation, Ámsterdam*
Watt, Witte de With Centre for Contemporary Art,
Rotterdam*
Ik & De Ander, Dignity for All: Reflections on Humanity,
Beurs van Berlage, Amsterdam*
Institute of Cultural Anxiety, ICA (Institute of
Contemporary Arts), London*
Riviera, Oriel Mostyn, Llandudno*
Little House on the Prairie, Marc Jancou Gallery, London
Heart of Darkness, Kröller Müller Museum, Otterlo*
The Institute of Cultural Anxiety, ICA (Institute of
Contemporary Arts), London
Multiples of the 60's & 90's, South Bank Centre Touring
Exhibition*
*East of Eden: Site Specific Works for Castle and
Grounds*, Schloss Mosigkau, Mosigkau*

1993
Christine Borland and Craig Richardson, Chisenhale
Gallery, London*
Aperto, Venezia Biennale, Venezia*
Fontanelle, Kunstspeicher, Potsdam*
Wonderful Life, Lisson Gallery, London
Walter Benjamin's Briefcase, Porto*
2nd Tyne International, Newcastle*

1992
Contact, Transmission Gallery, Glasgow
Guilt by Association, Irish Museum of Modern Art, Dublín*
In and Out/Back and Forth, 578 Broadway, New York*
Artists Show Artists, Galerie Vier, Berlin

1991
Kunst Europa, Kunstverein Karlsruhe*
Speed, Transmission Gallery, Glasgow

1990
Self Conscious State, Third Eye Centre, Glasgow*
Once Supported But Now Removed, Collective
Gallery, Edinburgh
Human Being part of *Sites/Positions*, Glasgow

Contributor Biographies

Professor Bettina Bildhauer

Professor of Modern Languages,
University of St Andrews

Bettina Bildhauer is a specialist in medieval German literature. She has written *Medieval Blood* (2006) and *Filming the Middle Ages* (2011), and co-edited the collections *The Monstrous Middle Ages* (2003), *Medieval Film* (2009) and *The Middle Ages in the Modern World* (2017). Underlying much of her research is an interest in the limits of the human, both of individual human bodies and of what counts as human. She is currently working on a monograph project concerned with the agency of things in medieval German narratives. Bettina is also interested in the role of the Middle Ages in modernity, in particular how the Middle Ages are represented in cinema and politics.

Professor Chris Dorsett

Artist and Professor of Fine Art,
Northumbria University

Chris Dorsett is an artist whose career has been built on curatorial partnerships with collection-holding institutions. In the UK he is best known for a sequence of exhibitions held at Oxford's Pitt Rivers Museum between 1985 and 1994. Projects overseas include museum 'interventions' across the Nordic region and fieldwork residencies in the Amazon and at the walled village of Kat Hing Wai in the Hong Kong New Territories. He has written extensively about the interface between experimental art practices and the museum/heritage sector. His publications include: 'Exhibitions and their prerequisites', in *Issues in Curating: Contemporary art and performance* (2007); 'Making meaning beyond display', in *Museum Materialities: Objects, engagements, interpretations* (2009); 'Things and theories: The unstable presence of exhibited objects', in *The Thing about Museums: Objects and experience, representation and contestation* (2011); 'The pleasure of the holder: Media art, museum collections and paper money', in *International Journal of Arts and Technology* and 'Studio ruins: Describing unfinishedness', in *Studies in Material Thinking* (both 2018).

Birthe Jorgensen

Artist, educator and cross-disciplinary researcher

Birthe Jorgensen is a visual artist, educator and cross-disciplinary researcher. Between 2005 and 2011 she developed a role as 'Live Visual Artist' within the interdisciplinary company Apocryphal Theatre in London, through which insights were gained that continue to inform her practice. In 2018 she was awarded the British Council's Scotland–Argentina Residency Exchange Programme, and she has exhibited, performed and spoken about her work in Scotland, Europe and the USA. Fusing traditional media with more fast and fluid technologies, Birthe is currently exploring the power and potential of poly-vocal forms of expression in complex, multicultural times, in collaboration with artist Sogol Mabadi, Taseralik (Sisimuit, Greenland), VA Space (Isfahan, Iran) and Glasgow Women's Library and Platform, Glasgow. Between 2013 and 2017 she lectured at The Glasgow School of Art, and she has guest lectured at the Royal Conservatoire Scotland and Iceland Academy of the Arts.

Daisy Lafarge

Writer, editor and artist

Daisy Lafarge works across poetry, fiction, criticism, theory and visual art. In 2017 she received an Eric Gregory Award from the Society of Authors, and her poetry pamphlet, *understudies for air*, was published by Sad Press. She is an editor at MAP (a commissioning and publishing project for artist-led production) and a PhD researcher at the University of Glasgow, working alongside a team of vets and social scientists studying zoonoses in rural farming communities in northern Tanzania. Daisy was recently runner-up in the 2018 Edwin Morgan Poetry Award.

Dr Francis McKee

Director of the Centre for Contemporary Arts, Glasgow, and Research Fellow, The Glasgow School of Art

Francis McKee has worked at the CCA, the Centre for Contemporary Arts, in Glasgow since 2006. Prior to that, from 2005 to 2008, he was the director of the biennial visual arts festival Glasgow International. He is also a researcher and teaches on the Master of Fine Arts course at The Glasgow School of Art. He has recently published two books, *How to Know What's Really Happening* (2016) and *Even the Dead Rise Up* (2017). Currently he is collaborating with curators, Zuzana Blochova and Edith Jerabkova, and students at UMPRUM, the Academy of Arts, Architecture and Design in Prague, who are establishing an archive of materials belonging to the Czech filmmaker Ester Krumbachova.

Dr Jo Meacock

Curator of British Art,
Glasgow Museums

Jo Meacock is responsible for painting, sculpture and works on paper (1600–1960) in Glasgow Museums' collection. Her specialism lies in nineteenth-century and early twentieth-century British art, with a particular interest in Scottish art, the Aesthetic Movement, religious iconography, women artists and war art. Jo was the Scottish Regional Research Manager for the Public Catalogue Foundation, Data Editing Manager for the National Inventory Research Project, Research Associate for *James McNeill Whistler: The Etchings: A Catalogue Raisonné* and Editor for *Mapping the Practice and Profession of Sculpture in Britain and Ireland 1851–1951*. She is a Trustee of the Wilhelmina Barns-Graham Trust. Her publications include *Fred A Farrell: Glasgow's War Artist* (co-authored, 2014) and a new book about the Holocaust artworks of Marianne Grant in Glasgow Museums' collection (co-authored, forthcoming 2019).

Professor Andrew Patrizio

Professor of Scottish Visual Culture, Edinburgh College of Art, University of Edinburgh

Andrew Patrizio has worked at Edinburgh College of Art since 1997. He has held curatorial posts at the Hayward Gallery, London, the Laing Art Gallery, Newcastle, and at Glasgow Museums. His publications include *Contemporary Scottish Sculpture* (1999), *Stefan Gec* (2002), *Anatomy Acts* (2006) and a forthcoming monograph *The Ecological Eye: assembling an ecocritical art history* (Manchester University Press, 2019). In 2016 he co-curated *The Scottish Endarkenment. Art and Unreason. 1945 to the Present*, shown at the Dovecot Studios, Edinburgh, and he is currently a member of the Little Sparta Trust. He has written about Christine Borland many times and commissioned work by her on seven occasions since 1990.

Stephanie de Roemer

Conservator (3-D Art) Sculpture / Installation Art, Glasgow Museums

Stephanie de Roemer studied Art History (Sculpture and Architecture) and Classical Archaeology and Anthropology at the University of Trier, Germany, prior to completing a BSc in Conservation and Restoration of Surface Decoration and Interiors at the London Guildhall University and an MA in the Conservation of Historic Objects (Archaeology) at the University of Durham. Before being employed as the conservator for sculpture and installation art at Glasgow Museums, she worked on the conservation of waterlogged archaeological artefacts and structures, such as the *Mary Rose*, and, for National Museums of Scotland, Edinburgh, organic remnants of early Iron Age settlements.

A member of the International Council of Museums Committee for Conservation (ICOM-CC) since 2004, Stephanie is currently serving for a second triennial (2017–2020) as the group coordinator for the ICOM-CC working group Sculpture, Polychromy and Architectural decorations.

Acknowledgements

The artist and Glasgow Museums are grateful to the following for their contribution to *I Say Nothing*:

All the participants at the *Doubtful Occasion* symposium, and especially the speakers and recorders at the event who have contributed to this publication.

Ian Dawson, Lecturer in Fine Art and Sculpture, Winchester School of Art, University of Southampton, and Louisa Minkin, MA Fine Art course leader at Central Saint Martins, University of the Arts London, for advice on replicating François Willème's photo-sculpture studio.

PhotoSculpture models Stephanie Black-Daniels, Connie Liebschner and Louie Pegna.

Participating photographers at the *PhotoSculpture* event: Penny Anderson, Cat Auburn, Claire Barclay, Katherine Baxter, Bettina Bildhauer, Fiona Crisp, Ian Dawson, Alan Dimmick, Jacqueline Donachie, Marion Eele, Patricia Fleming, Adam Fowler, Morven Gregor, Birthe Jorgensen, Daisy Lafarge, Francis McKee, Ray McKenzie, Charlotte McLean, Ali Mills, Louisa Minkin, Kate V Robertson, Stephanie de Roemer, Ross Sinclair, Karen Vaughan.

Katie Cunningham and Cara Simpson, Museum Studies students at the University of Glasgow, who assisted at *Doubtful Occasion* and *PhotoSculpture* and with research. Lola O'Donnell, who helped with research and assisted at *Doubtful Occasion*, and Jennifer Hopkins and Jessica Simmonds, Glasgow School of Art, who also assisted at *PhotoSculpture*.

Sculpture and Design, especially Graeme Raeburn, for design and fabrication support and advice.

Andy McGregor, Daniel Warren and team for filming at the *PhotoSculpture* event. Andy McGregor for creating the film in the final artwork; and for his tireless work designing this book.

Michelle Emery-Barker, Artist's Production Manager.

Patricia Fleming and all at Patricia Fleming Projects, who represent Christine Borland.

Comfort Tamanda Mtotha for advice relative to South and East African headrests.

The Belgian bomb disposal unit DOVO-SEDEE.

Ray MacKenzie for invaluable advice regarding the sculpture of *Peace* and *War*, Kelvin Way Bridge.

Jared Benjamin, Frank Calikes and Adam Frost, Glasgow School of Art's School of Simulation and Visualisation, for photographic direction at the *PhotoSculpture* event and 3D scanning of *Peace* and *War*.

Kate V Robertson for help with final production.

Keith Hunter for photography of *I Say Nothing* at Kelvingrove Art Gallery and Museum.

Gillian Hayes, Dapple Photography.

Alan Dimmick, photography.

Cat Auburn for photography, filming and assistance Flanders.

Sophie Crichton Stuart and Morven Gregor and all at Mount Stuart Trust.

All in the Glasgow Museums project team.

The artist extends special thanks to Ross Sinclair and the Borland Sinclair family.

Most important thanks are due to 14–18 NOW and Art Fund for making the commission and this publication possible. The additional Art Fund support for the publication is greatly appreciated.

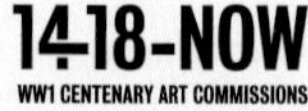
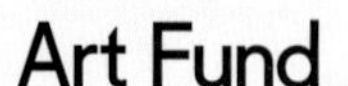
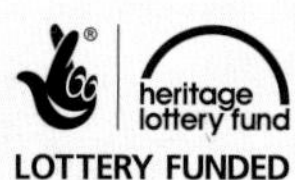
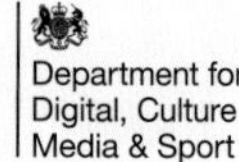
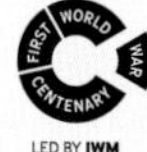